D1145310

NURTURING A

Living
Faith

CWR, Waverley Abbey House, Waverley Lane, Farnham, Surrey GU9 8EP

Scripture quotations are taken from NIV, unless otherwise indicated. Other versions include:
NKJ, New King James Version, © 1979, 1980, 1982, Thomas Nelson, Inc., Publishers.
RSV, Revised Standard Version, © 1972, Thomas Nelson, Inc., Publishers.
AMPLIFIED, The Amplified Bible, © 1965, Zondervan Publishing House.
TLB, The Living Bible, © 1971, Tyndale House Publishers.
J.B. PHILLIPS, The New Testament in Modern English, revised edition, © 1958, 1960, J.B. Phillips.
KJV, King James Version, © 1977, 1984 ,Thomas Nelson, Inc.
MOFFATT, The Bible, A New Translation, © 1950, 1952, 1953, 1954, James A.R. Moffatt.
THE MESSAGE, © 2002, Christian Art Publishers.

NURTURING A LIVING FAITH
A compilation of excerpts from *Every Day with Jesus* by Selwyn Hughes 1985, 1988, 1990, 1993, 1998
edited by Jenny Crickmore-Thompson
© CWR 2003

Concept development, editing, design and production by
Struik Christian Books Ltd
A division of New Holland Publishing (South Africa) (Pty) Ltd
(New Holland Publishing is a member of the Johnnic Publishing Group)
Cornelis Struik House
80 McKenzie Street
Cape Town 8001

Reg. No. 1971/00972/07

DTP by Bridgitte Chemaly
Cover design by Joleen Coetzee
Cover photograph by Photo Access
Cover reproduction by Hirt & Carter Cape (Pty) Ltd
Reproduced, printed and bound by Kyodo Printing Co. Pte. Ltd.,
112 Neythal Road, Jurong Town, Singapore 628599

ISBN 1 85345 279 3

SELWYN HUGHES

NURTURING A

Living Faith

What awe,
what wonder,
for tiny man on
frail earth
to realise that
size
is no measure of
worth
in God's enormous eyes.

SUSAN L. LENZKES
EDWJ 1987
Used with permission of
Zondervan Publishing House

January / February
Living faith

March / April
The divine anchorage

May / June
The redeeming fire

July / August
The armour of God

September / October
A bride for his Son

November / December
The all-sufficient Christ

A New Year's resolution

FOR READING AND MEDITATION – LUKE 17:1–10

'The apostles said to the Lord, "Increase our faith!"' (v.5: NIV)

Today we begin one of the most crucial themes ever considered – Living faith. The urge to write on this came when the Spirit whispered to me, 'My people are being destroyed.' When I asked why, the Spirit seemed to say, 'Because of their lack of faith.'

These words crystallised a conviction growing within me, that one of the most urgent needs in the life of the Christian church is for God's people to possess and demonstrate a stronger and more vibrant faith. Many believers are living their lives on a level far below what God intends.

They lack faith – and therefore lack power. The age in which we live is increasing in evil. If we Christians are to meet the challenge, there must be a corresponding increase in our faith.

How vigorous and vibrant is your faith? Is it just something you hold – or is it something that holds you?

I read recently about a church situated next door to a beauty salon. The beauty salon put up a sign saying, 'Come inside and have your face lifted.' The church went one better and put up a sign that read, 'Come inside and have your faith lifted.'

Our faith needs not merely lifting, but enlarging. On this first day of a new year, make this prayer of Jesus' disciples your very own. Personalise it.

Father, with all my heart I cry, 'Increase my faith.' Make this a year in which I shall experience, not only the deepening, but also the enlarging of my faith. In Jesus' Name. Amen.

The greatest word ever

' "... the just shall live by his faith." ' (v.4: AV)

Having aligned ourselves with the disciples' prayer, 'Increase our faith!' we now face the question: how vital is this matter of faith? Is it something merely desirable – or something indispensable?

This verse shows clearly that in relation to the life lived before God, faith is not something optional, but something obligatory. Not a matter of personal preference; it is a definite priority.

Dr G. Campbell Morgan describes this statement as 'the mightiest sentence in the Book of God'. Another commentator says it is 'the hinge on which the doors of Scripture are opened'. Yet another says, 'Apart from John 3:16, it is the greatest word ever.'

Why should this statement be regarded so highly by Bible expositors? Because it condenses into a single phrase a truth found everywhere from Genesis to Revelation – that the life which pleases God is the life of faith.

Many Christians regard faith as a special quality reserved to deal with difficult situations. While to some extent this might be true, faith is the underlying principle governing all Christian living – from start to finish. Faith is far more than a channel to receive special favours; it is a calling, a daily walk.

It is not just a force in Christian living – it is the focus of it. Not just an optional extra, but an everyday necessity. We live by faith, or we do not live at all.

✒ O God, I see that faith is not some extraneous thing introduced from without. Help me never to lose sight of this. In Jesus' Name. Amen.

A prophet in confusion

FOR READING AND MEDITATION – HABAKKUK 1:1–17, 2:4

'How long, O Lord, must I call for help, but you do not listen?' (v.2: NIV)

Habakkuk the prophet was in utter confusion at the continuance of evil in the nations around him. He could not understand why God did not intervene and was frustrated by God's apparent slowness in dealing with this issue.

Then Habakkuk gave up trying to reason things out, and instead took a leap of faith. He said, 'I will go up to my watchtower, and wait for God.' Those who are willing to wait for God to speak are never disappointed. Notice his words: 'Then the Lord replied . . .' (v.2).

When? After he had indicated his willingness to wait. The vision came in the form of words: 'The just shall live by his faith,' which Habakkuk inscribed on tablets.

Not so that he who reads may run, but that he who runs may read. Those who tear through life, never pausing for prayerful thought and consideration, must get hold of this.

Are you rushing through life trying to resolve the world's problems? Then stop, and meditate on this: the just shall live by faith. God knows what he is doing – so trust him. Hold on to this, and never again will your feet slip and slide on the rocky slopes of life.

You will have, as Habakkuk, hinds' feet in high places (3:19).

O Father, what a fool I am trying to hold the world together, when all the time things are safely in your care. Write these words prominently in my heart so I never again race past them: 'The just shall live by faith.' For Jesus' sake. Amen.

Two philosophies of life

FOR READING AND MEDITATION – HABAKKUK 3:1–19, 2:4

'"Behold, his soul which is lifted up is not upright in him:
but the just shall live by his faith."' (2:4: AV)

The vision which sustained Habakkuk was in these simple but powerful words: 'The just shall live by his faith.' Look at the statement immediately preceding: '"Behold, as for the proud one, his soul is not right within him"' (Hab. 2:4, NASB).

Unfortunately these words tend to be overshadowed and are seldom quoted – but they are extremely important. In this verse God is showing us that there are only two possible attitudes to life – faith or unbelief. Either belief in him, or denial of him.

These two philosophies are diametrically opposed. The first is that of the proud. Some translations use *swollen* or *puffed up*, a graphic picture of pride and self-sufficiency. That is one philosophy of life – proud, puffed up, swollen, self-sufficient.

The other is that of the just – those who have a sense of certainty despite adversity, who walk through life with confidence and poise.

Dr Martyn Lloyd Jones described this as 'the great watershed of life – and all of us are on one side of it or the other'. Life, when stripped to its minimum, consists of one of two attitudes: we live by what God says, or we do not.

Habakkuk learned this lesson as he sat in his watchtower. It is one that we too must learn.

✎ *O my God, I begin to see the challenge: either I take what you say and live by it, or I do not. Help me to turn from the way of pride and self-sufficiency to the way of trust. For Jesus' sake. Amen.*

Standing in God's smile

FOR READING AND MEDITATION – ROMANS 1:1–17

'. . . as it is written, "The just shall live by faith."' (v.17: AV)

Either we live by faith, or we do not live at all. This statement is found not only in Habakkuk, but on three separate occasions in the New Testament – each one having deep significance. God plucks this jewel out of the Old Testament and holds it up in the New Testament, slowly turning it facet by facet, to reveal even more of its truth and beauty.

The first time it appears is in the book of Romans. In Romans Paul deals with the great truths of salvation, showing how God has accomplished the task of justifying sinners: making them appear as if they had never sinned.

The emphasis in Romans is on the word *just*. How wonderful to be 'justified by faith'. It means, quite simply, that those who believe and accept the fact of Christ's substitutionary death on Calvary stand in God's presence just as if they had never sinned.

A little boy was standing by his father's desk. Where he stood, a shaft of sunlight was shining directly on him. 'Daddy,' he said, 'I'm standing in the smile of God.'

The good news of the Gospel is that when we stand in Christ, we stand in God's smile. If you feel you are standing in God's frown, move over into God's smile. That's justification.

✎ *Lord Jesus Christ, what a delight it is to know that you are the smile of God – and when I stand in you, I stand in God's smile. It is just as if I had never sinned. Glory!*

What a way to live!

FOR READING AND MEDITATION – GALATIANS 3:1–14
'. . . no man is justified by the law in the sight of God . . .
for, "The just shall live by faith."' (v.11: AV)

The second time 'The just shall live by faith' appears in the New Testament is in the book of Galatians. Galatians is supremely the letter of freedom. Here Paul proclaims the truth that in Christ, the Christian is set free from every yoke of bondage which can be placed upon the human soul.

There were those in the Galatian church who felt that Christ was not enough. They wanted 'Christ and' – in this case, Christ and circumcision. Without the 'and' – their salvation was not complete.

How sad that we still do the same: Christ and becoming a member of our church; Christ and our interpretation of him; Christ and our doctrinal slogans; Christ and our forms of worship. Endlessly 'Christ and'.

Paul refused this. The freedom he portrayed in Christ was a freedom from endless 'ands'. Christ, and Christ alone, is necessary to salvation. Judaism contained 3 600 laws to be obeyed. What a relief to learn that in Christ they are reduced to two – love God, and love your neighbour as yourself. Keep these, then all the others are kept – automatically. What a way to live!

We are freed from complexity to simplicity, from the marginal to the central, from the trivial to the great. 'The just shall live by faith.'

O Father, how can I thank you enough for loosing me from a thousand inner and outer bondages. I'm free to love you, and through you to love others. Hallelujah!

Faith – a principle of living

FOR READING AND MEDITATION – HEBREWS 10:19–39

'"... the just shall live by faith ..."' (v.38: AV)

We come now to the third and last occasion where 'The just shall live by faith' is found in the New Testament – the letter to the Hebrews. This is the epistle of faith, and it reveals how living by this principle enables us to triumph over all kinds of difficulties and problems. Unquestionably the purpose was to strengthen the early Hebrew Christians, who felt they had lost so much in turning from the grand ritual and ceremony of the Hebrew religion to the simpler but more effective things of Christ.

If Romans places the emphasis on *just*, and Galatians on *live*, then Hebrews places it on *faith*. Romans emphasises the fact that faith enables us to stand in the sight of God just as if we had never sinned. Galatians draws our attention to the truth that, in Christ, we are freed from endless bondages, that in him we live.

Hebrews makes the point that faith is the underlying principle governing all Christian living – from start to finish. The life that the just person shall live is a life of faith.

A missionary put it like this, 'Every moment of the day – not just on certain specific occasions – a Christian has to exercise faith. We live by it. Indeed the Christian life would be paralysed without it.'

⊲ *O God, can my lungs do without air, my eyes without light, my stomach without food? No more can I do without faith. Teach me, not simply to get by, but to live by faith – really live. In Jesus' Name I ask it. Amen.*

What faith is not

FOR READING AND MEDITATION – ROMANS 10:1–13

'... if you confess with your mouth, "Jesus is Lord,"
and believe in your heart ... you will be saved.' (v.9: NIV)

Having looked at the importance and significance of faith, we now face the question: what precisely is faith, its nature and its constituent parts? In my experience, the subject of faith causes more misunderstanding than any other in the Bible.

Great confusion exists even over the meaning of the word. One woman said that she joined the church on 'confusion of faith'. She meant, of course, 'confession of faith'.

Some see faith as a magic lamp which they rub, and hey presto! – all their wishes come true. Others see it as something that functions only on certain occasions. Perhaps, before arriving at a definition of what faith is, we should consider what it is not.

Firstly, faith is not mere intellectual acceptance. A person can have an intellectual belief in everything the church and the Bible affirm, and not have faith.

One of the great tragedies of today is that people sit in church, Sunday after Sunday, reciting creeds and yet having no real contact with the Creator. I am not against creeds – indeed, whenever we formulate a statement of faith, we subscribe to a creed.

Faith is not merely the acceptance of certain truths about God; faith goes beyond those truths to touch God himself.

Father, thank you for showing me that faith is not merely head-acceptance, but heart-acceptance: not just the assent of my mind but the commitment of my life. Help me to act on this understanding – now and always. Amen.

Faith rests on God's character

FOR READING AND MEDITATION – ROMANS 2:1–16
'Now we know that God's judgment . . . is based on truth.' (v.2: NIV)

Faith is not mere intellectual assent, or the acceptance of truths about God. It is not a discussion – it is a decision.

Faith is also not blind credulity. A boy, asked to define faith, said, 'Faith is believing something you know isn't true.' That is not faith; that is foolishness.

Some Christians are so desirous of possessing faith that they believe, not in the impossible, but in the ridiculous.

A man in Wales once said to me, 'I am praying for God to give me £10 000 for a certain project for him.' 'How do you expect God to answer?' I asked. 'I believe he will create 10 000 new banknotes and make them appear in my desk drawer,' he said. I would be the last person in the world to dampen or destroy anyone's faith, but I thought his request was ridiculous – and I told him so.

God is able and willing to do the impossible, but he is not willing to do the unreasonable. John Stott says that faith is a reasoning trust. Notice that: not just trust, but a reasoning trust. And why? Because faith rests on the character of God, and since God is reasonable – then faith must be reasonable also.

✎ *Father, thank you for showing me that although faith may be above reason, it is never against it. Help me to experience an ever-growing consciousness of this reasoning trust. For Jesus' sake. Amen.*

Faith – unafraid of reality

FOR READING AND MEDITATION – 2 CORINTHIANS 4:1–18

'...we know that the one who raised the Lord Jesus from
the dead will also raise us with Jesus ...' (v.14: NIV)

It is undoubtably true that optimism, in its purest form, is an ingredient of faith. The right kind of optimism can be a very desirable
quality. There are many Christians, however, whose use of optimism
is incredibly naive.

I once saw a church poster that said, 'Cheer up – it may never
happen!' Imagine someone who had suffered a tragic loss reading
that! The best illustration I know of naive optimism is the story of
a man who, falling from the top floor of a twenty-storey building
shouted as he passed the eleventh floor: 'So far, so good!'

A teaching quietly spreading in some Christian communities
says it is the nature of faith to ignore reality and focus only on the
end in view. Not true. Faith does not ignore reality. Naive optimism
may do that, but faith – never!

It is not a healthy thing to look at difficulties and refuse to admit
they are there – either mentally or spiritually. That does not mean
we should go to the other extreme, and focus solely upon our problems – if we look too long at them, they will adversely affect us. We
must look at them, but not focus on them. We glance at them, but
we gaze at God.

✎ *O Father, I do not ask for a faith that has to put on blinkers when confronted by problems, but for a faith that looks issues full in the face, and then
rises to surmount them. In Jesus' Name. Amen.*

Try-ing Christians

FOR READING AND MEDITATION – HEBREWS 4:1–16

'... anyone who enters God's rest also rests from his own work ...' (v.10: NIV)

Trying hard to believe is not faith. That is anxiety dressed up. Harold Horton says of faith that, 'Faith is not rasping tight and clenching fists and furrowing rows and gritting teeth and shouting in a kind of hopeless hope, "I do believe; I will believe." Faith is absolute rest in God – absolutely knowing and absolutely trusting according to his gracious promises and commands.'

I meet many Christians who are almost on the point of exhaustion due to struggling hard to believe. They are trying, not trusting. Faith is the easy, restful, fearless attitude of an infant reposing on its mother's breast – with no thought of fear, effort or uncertainty.

A young minister I know, whose ministry was failing because of trying too hard, was told by his church that they thought he should give up the ministry and return to secular employment. For three days he struggled over this, then God spoke to him and said, 'Stop struggling – and let me hold you.' He did just that – he surrendered his ministry to God and, within weeks, became a new man with a new ministry. He passed from fighting to faith, from trying to trusting – and then accomplished much in the Lord.

Father, help me to grasp the fact that passing from trying to trusting means changing the basis of my life from myself to you. May that transition take place right now. In Jesus' Name. Amen.

The awesome power of thought

FOR READING AND MEDITATION – ISAIAH 55:1–13

'"As the heavens are higher than the earth, so are my ways higher than your ways and my thoughts than your thoughts."' (v.9: NIV)

Faith is not positive thinking. The concept of positive thinking is based on the famous statement of Emerson, who said, 'A man is what he thinks about all the day long.' When we think positively, we tend to act positively. Our thought processes are extremely powerful, and by determined and positive thinking we can overcome failure and conquer disabilities.

The difference between positive thinking and faith can be seen when we ask the question: is our positive thinking in line with God's thinking? Our thoughts may be positive, but are they the thoughts on which God wants us to focus? The tragedy is that we can think ourselves into situations where God may not wish us to go.

Many years ago, I talked to a millionaire in Georgia, USA, who told me that by the power of positive thinking, he had amassed a huge fortune. Then, with tears in his eyes, he said, 'But I realise now that this was not the path that God wanted me to pursue.'

I am afraid that much of what passes as 'faith' in Christian circles is nothing more than positive thinking, and positive thinking that is not in harmony with Biblical thinking turns out to be nothing more than wishful thinking.

✎ 0 Father, when I consider the tremendous power that is locked up in the mind, I tremble lest my thoughts become self-centred rather than God-centred. I ask today not only that you will live in me and love in me, but that you will also think in me. For Jesus' sake. Amen.

Knowing the difference

FOR READING AND MEDITATION – PSALM 19:1–14

'Keep back thy servant also from presumptuous sins;
let them not have dominion over me ...' (v.13: RSV)

This may be the most important statement we have made so far – faith is not presumption.

The line between presumption and faith is finely drawn and is often difficult to discern. Some of the greatest tragedies in the church happen because people act on what they believe is faith, which subsequent events show is nothing more than presumption.

A diabetic woman I knew, read these words, 'I am the Lord who heals you' (Ex. 15:26). She took it as a direct word from the Lord, and in 'faith' gave up her insulin injections. Within three days she had died. Sadly, she acted in presumption and not faith.

What then is presumption? Basically it is a failure to differentiate between the general and the specific. The words, 'I am the Lord who heals you,' is a general statement showing God to be the healer of his people.

How that statement is applied must be approached with care. As a general principle, it is perfectly true that God delights to heal. In some specific instances he may have good reasons for withholding healing. Those who fail to apply general principles prayerfully and carefully in specific situations, are in danger of acting, not in faith, but in presumption.

Gracious Father, I want to be rid of all that corrodes my soul. I begin to see the deep significance of David's prayer: 'Keep back your servant from presumptuous sins.' I ask that you will do the same for me. Amen.

The rhema and the logos

Presumption, we said, is an inability to differentiate between the general and the specific.

Bible scholars point out that two different Greek terms are used in the New Testament for 'word': *logos*, meaning the Word, and *rhema*, meaning a directed word from God – a special word for a special situation.

Faith comes as the result of a *rhema*, a specific word from the Lord, flowing into the *logos* – the general persuasion that 'God has said'. *Rhema* will not go beyond *logos*, but it stakes its all on it.

Naaman was the only person healed by dipping seven times in the Jordan; only Peter walked on the lake of Galilee. These miracles came as a result of God's direct word to specific individuals on specific occasions.

Today, we see Israel moving presumptuously into battle. The result? A bitter defeat for the Israelites. The word *presumed* used here is the same Hebrew word used to describe those who act in unbelief: *aphal* (Hab. 2:4). It means, as we saw, 'proud, self-centred, conceited'.

The presumptuous person speaks whether God has spoken or not. He seeks to get God to do what he wants, irrespective of whether it is what God wants. When presumption prevails, then death, not life, is the result.

Father, now that I see that faith to deal with issues comes from the rhema *– your specific word for my situation – I turn eagerly to learn how the* rhema *of God becomes a faith-producing word. For Jesus' sake. Amen.*

Where faith begins

FOR READING AND MEDITATION – HEBREWS 11:1–6
'Now faith is the assurance of things hoped for,
the conviction of things not seen.' (v.1: RSV)

Now let's focus on what faith really is. Over the years, I have come across many interesting and intriguing definitions of faith. Not one, however, matches the definition given in the opening verse of Hebrews 11, the only definition of faith to be found in the Bible.

So then, faith begins with hope. In this context, a confident expectation. Hope for what? Things not yet attained, things not yet in our possession. What sort of things are we hoping for? Ask yourself this question: what is the greatest longing of my life, my greatest hope? Consider your answer carefully – for by it you will stand revealed. If you say it is for a bigger house, a new car, a better job, or greater financial security, then sadly, I have to tell you that you are a million miles off the mark. As the poet put it:

*The earth of a dusty today,
is the dust of an earthy tomorrow.*

Faith begins, not with the hope of realising our self-centred interests, but of realising the highest interests of the universe – with the realisation of Christian ideals, the compensation for the things to be endured, and the ultimate victory of good over evil.

Father, I see that this is the crunch point: my faith has not thrived because it has been too parochial and has failed to take the 'long look'. Now I know the secret – unfold it to me further. For Jesus' sake. Amen.

Sharpening faith's focus

FOR READING AND MEDITATION – HEBREWS 11:1, 7–12
'Now faith is the assurance of things hoped for ...' (v.1: RSV)

Faith begins, not with the hope of the realisation of self-interests, but of the highest interests of the universe. If we don't start there, we don't start.

Many Christians think that faith begins with the hope of a new house, greater financial security or perhaps a physical healing – but not so.

It has something to do with those things, of course, but it doesn't begin there. Faith begins with the hope that there will come a time in human affairs when an even balance will be struck.

In fact, the whole thrust of Hebrews 11 is that, when we live by faith, we have the solid hope that, through all adversities, we shall arrive safe and secure in our Father's presence. What a hope!

Why is it necessary to focus on this ingredient of hope as being so vital to faith? Because it is only as we understand faith on its highest level that we can implement it on the lower levels. Faith to know that God's long-range purpose is to right all wrongs and usher in his triumphant kingdom has to be cultivated.

The more that hope prevails in our hearts, the more certain will be our hope in God's ability to meet our personal and individual needs. If we are not assured of the highest, then how can we be assured of the lowest?

Father, I think I see what you are asking of me: if my faith has an eternal focus, then it will not fade when it meets the problems of time. Teach me more, dear Lord. Amen.

The long look

FOR READING AND MEDITATION – HEBREWS 11:1, 13–16
'Now faith is the assurance of things hoped for …' (v.1: RSV)

Faith does not begin with the hope that our material and physical needs will be met, but with the hope that God will bring all things to a triumphant conclusion.

What was the single truth that served and nourished the heroes of faith listed in Hebrews 11? This: 'These all died in faith, not having received what was promised, but having seen it and greeted it from afar …' (v.13, RSV).

They took the 'long look'. They saw that no matter what happened in the present, the future was certain. Christians, above all others, ought to be people of the long view. We ought not suffer from spiritual short-sightedness – seeing no further than today with its pressing personal needs.

If we don't absorb the thrilling truth that God will one day conclude all things gloriously, we become the prisoners of today, rather than the pioneers of tomorrow. When, however, we practise faith on the highest level, we are assured of the fact that we shall see all this: the realisation of our ideals, the ultimate victory of good and compensation for every wrong.

Then we have a focus for our faith that will equip us for handling anything that comes our way – a basis of faith for dealing with day-to-day demands.

O God, you have taken the 'long view' over the years of history, and quietly work out your long-range purposes. Help me to catch the sweep of your mind, your eternal confidence and hope. For your own dear Name's sake. Amen.

The sure and certain hope

FOR READING AND MEDITATION – HEBREWS 11:1, 17–22

'Now faith means that we are confident of what we hope for,
convinced of what we do not see.' (v.1: MOFFATT)

To have faith, we must first be focused on the certain hope that, one day, God is going to bring all things to a good and glorious conclusion. If we can't trust God to work out his long-range purposes, how can we trust him to work them out in the short-term? It's all a matter of perspective. I have seen many Christians trip up at this point.

An artist said of his nature paintings, 'I can get the picture right if I can get the sky right.' Well, it's the same in this matter of faith – you have to get the Sky right. Catch the sweep of God's mind and the glory of his eternal purposes, become a part of them, then your faith finds a powerful focus. Your Sky is right – and the rest of the picture will be right.

Many Christians, however, start with the temporal and lose sight of the eternal. If we lose our perspective on eternity, we shall most certainly lose it on time – but when we are sure of heaven, we shall be sure of earth. It's as simple as that. Recognise this – once you have won the battle in the eternal realm, you will not lose it in the earthly realm.

Father, I see that if my Sky – the eternal picture – is right, then the whole of life becomes meaningful. Make that focus so clear that never again will I doubt it. For Jesus' sake. Amen.

Seeing the invisible

FOR READING AND MEDITATION – HEBREWS 11:1, 23–28

'. . . faith is . . . the conviction of things not seen.' (v.1: RSV)

It's easy to believe in things we can see, but not so easy to believe in the things we cannot see. Yet this is exactly where faith operates. Doubtless we have all heard the phrase, 'seeing is believing,' but when we stop and examine it we find that, really, it is not true. Believing is being sure without seeing.

Faith operates in the realm of things the physical eye cannot see, and is able, as the writer to the Hebrews puts it, to 'see the invisible'.

This is not a contradiction, but a paradox. A paradox is something that may seem contrary to reason, but is nevertheless true. The law of the road, for example, is a paradox. Did you ever learn this verse at school?

> *The law of the road is a paradox quite*
> *and that you may tell by my song*
> *if you go to the left, you are sure to go right*
> *and if you go right, you go wrong!*

The law of the road is a perfect paradox; apparently wrong, contrary to reason, but nevertheless true. So is faith a paradox.

Faith sees the invisible, knows the unknowable, hears the inaudible, touches the intangible – fights in chains, and rests in conflict. Contradictory? No – paradoxical. And therefore true.

Father, when I see the dazzling potential that there is in faith I feel myself being stretched. Stretch me more, dear Lord, stretch me more. Amen.

'Lord, open his eyes'

FOR READING AND MEDITATION – HEBREWS 11:1, 29–34

'... faith is ... the evidence of things not seen.' (v.1: AV)

Faith is a paradox. By faith a Christian 'sees' the unseen. He is as conscious of the reality of the spiritual world around him as he is of the material objects which he handles day by day. Speaking for myself, I am often more aware of the spiritual world around me than I am of the computer on which I write these lines. Faith has put me in touch with the ultimate reality – the kingdom of God.

These realities, these unseen forces, which cannot be measured, analysed or touched are my life. To be without them now would not be life, but mere existence. How aware are you of the reality of the 'unseen'? Can you become so conscious of the spiritual world around you that all your fears are dispelled?

If not, I pray what happened to Elisha's servant (2 Kings 6: 15–17) will happen to you today. The prophet prayed: 'O Lord, open his eyes,' and instantly he looked and 'saw the hills full of horses and chariots of fire' (v.17).

If you really knew what spiritual forces are available to you through faith, you would never be afraid again. Wesley said,

Lo to faith's enlightened sight,
all the mountains flamed with light
hell is nigh but God is nigher
circling us with hosts of fire.

❧ O Father, I long to have a deeper awareness of the unseen world that surrounds me. Open my eyes that I might really see. In Jesus' Name. Amen.

A working definition

FOR READING AND MEDITATION – HEBREWS 11:1, 35–40

'...faith is the assurance of things hoped for,
the conviction of things not seen.' (v.1: RSV)

What, then, are the basic principles of faith? There are two – the first being hope. The word *hope* in Scripture is not something speculative, but something that is sure and certain. It is an unshakable confidence that the promises of God – 'things hoped for' – whether they be for the distant future, or for the hours and days that lie immediately ahead, will be realised.

The second ingredient of faith is awareness – the sentient knowledge that within this physical universe there is something else present. And what is that 'something else'?

It is a spiritual world that is as real as the world to which we relate with our physical senses.

Faith always operates in the world of the unseen, for when we cease to believe in unseen things, hope dies. Putting these two basic ingredients together we come up with this as a working conclusion: faith is an inner conviction that banks on the *bona fide* promises of God.

It reaches out to the unseen, focuses upon it, grasps its reality and then acts upon it in the confidence that what God has said will inevitably come to pass.

༁ *Father, in the presence of such a challenging definition of faith as you give me in Hebrews 11, I can only echo the words of a man who once said, 'Lord, I believe; help thou my unbelief.' In Jesus' Name. Amen.*

A distant drumbeat

FOR READING AND MEDITATION – HEBREWS 11:2; 1 JOHN 5:1–12
'Anyone who believes in the Son of God has
this testimony in his heart.' (v.10: NIV)

'For by it [faith] the elders obtained a good testomony' (Heb. 11:2, NKJ). The usual interpretation is this: just as we brought home a good school report at the end of term, so did the spiritual leaders of the Old-Testament era. Because they lived and acted by faith, they received the highest possible marks.

I do not believe this to be the correct interpretation. It is best seen in the *Amplified Bible*, which reads: 'For by faith ... the men of old had divine testimony borne to them and obtained a good report.'

Borne *to* them, not borne *about* them. The thought in the text is that these men were listening to a Voice that came to them with increasing power and conviction. This Voice, speaking with great authority, delineated no doubt the majestic truth that 'the just shall live by faith'. Henry David Thoreau is famous for some words which help to illuminate this. He said, 'If a man is unable to keep step with his companions, perhaps it's because he hears the beat of a distant drummer.'

That is an excellent description of faith: people walking through the world as though they are listening to another drumbeat. It was this that made the Old-Testament saints so different from those around them. Does it make a difference in you?

❧ *Father you know how a thousand voices clamour for my attention. Help me to walk through this world conscious of that distant drumbeat of faith. For Jesus' sake. Amen.*

Yes – we can know

FOR READING AND MEDITATION –
HEBREWS 11:3; COLOSSIANS 1:15–23

'For by him all things were created: things in heaven and on earth,
visible and invisible . . .' (v.16: NIV)

'By faith we understand'. What do we understand? The *Amplified Bible* puts it thus: 'By faith we understand that the worlds [during the successive ages] were framed – fashioned, put in order and equipped for their intended purpose – by the word of God . . .'

Notice carefully what this statement says. It does not say 'by faith we accept', or even 'by faith we affirm', but 'by faith we understand that the worlds were framed . . . by the word of God.' I wonder whether you recollect a line in one of Tennyson's poems, 'We have but faith; we cannot know.'

I believe Tennyson to be entirely wrong in relation to this matter of faith. The truth is, *when we have faith, we can know.* Men who shut out God from their thinking, and then exercise their minds to try to discover the origin of the universe, almost reach mental exhaustion in their efforts to explain it.

I do not decry scientific study and research, but the man of faith does not depend upon scientific knowledge in order to understand the origins of the universe; he understands it by faith.

We understand the simple but basic truth that it was all put together by our great and wonderful God.

⊲ *Father, I am so grateful that faith introduces me, not to a world of speculation, but to a world of reality. It pierces all illusions and brings me to the heart of every issue. I am so grateful. Amen.*

The God of order

FOR READING AND MEDITATION – HEBREWS 11:3; ISAIAH 40:10–31

'Do you not know? Have you not heard? The Lord is the everlasting God,
the Creator of the ends of the earth.' (v.28: NIV)

Some scientists claim that the universe happened by chance. Quite frankly, even in my unconverted days I found that more difficult to believe and understand than the account given to us in Genesis.

Formed by chance into a cosmic orderliness extending from a single atom to the farthest star, and controlling everything in between? Maintained by chance throughout the long years of history? That would be an astounding miracle – universal chaos, by chance, giving birth to universal order!

The genius of faith is that through it we can leap over the tortuous windings of reason, avoiding the need to grope by trial and error.

We can lay hold of the basic facts of the universe in a single moment. Faith pierces the illusions that tend to distract us, and brings us right to the point where we see things as they really are.

Science, that is science apart from God, cannot tell me how the universe began – or, for that matter, how it will end. But by faith I understand and know. To trust God's word may not be an easy path in this scientific age, but it is an absolutely sure one.

Gracious and loving heavenly Father, help me to have a simple childlike faith, so that I might ever trust your love and believe your word. This I ask in Jesus' Name. Amen.

Popping with excitement

FOR READING AND MEDITATION –
GENESIS 1:1–31; HEBREWS 11:3

'And God said, "Let there be light," and there was light.' (Gen 1:3, NIV)

'... so what is seen was not made out of what was visible.' (Heb 11:3, NIV)

We can never explain the things which are seen until we come to understand the things that are unseen. Many scientists and philosophers struggle over the mysteries of the universe. They fail to recognise the existence of unseen things, and are therefore unable fully to understand the things that are visible.

A scientist in Swansea, South Wales, told me that prior to his conversion, he was greatly perplexed about the nature of creation. He said, 'I felt as if I was looking at creation through a dark glass. I tried as hard as I could to make the glass come clear, but it just wouldn't. Now, however, I can read creation like an open book. Almost every day a new secret unfolds itself. The universe is popping with excitement!'

Notice the contrast in the terms he used: before, 'through a dark glass'; now, 'popping with excitement'. What made the difference? Conversion!

This scientist discovered something greater than creation – he discovered the Creator. And the more he understood God and fellowshipped with him in the world of the unseen, the more clearly he came to understand the secrets of the world around him.

Father, I see that when I know you, everything is light – and life pops with excitement. Outside of you, despite all my intellect and knowledge, it is darkness. I am so thankful I know you, dear Lord. Amen.

I knew ... all the time

FOR READING AND MEDITATION – HEBREWS 11:6; ROMANS 4:13–25

'...anyone who comes to him must believe that he exists and
that he rewards those who earnestly seek him.' (Heb. 11:6, NIV)

Have you noticed how the Bible never argues for the existence of
God – it assumes it? Even our Lord himself never argued for the
existence of his heavenly Father – he merely proceeded in all his
teachings and his mighty miracles to act on this assumption.

If we come to God we must believe that he is – that he exists.
Ah, says someone, but that is the hardest and most difficult thing
to do – to believe that God exists.

I disagree – in fact I would say that to believe in God is the
easiest thing in the world. It requires effort to disbelieve, but it
requires little effort to believe.

Everyone born into this world starts out by believing God exists.
It is only when they are trained not to believe, that they come to the
place of declaring God does not exist.

That is why children have very little difficulty with the concept
of God. You would think, bearing in mind that God is unseen, that
children would stumble over this – but they don't.

Helen Keller was deaf, dumb and blind. Miss Sullivan, her teacher, approached Bishop Brooks to help her explain the concept and
nature of God. As he did so – in sign language – Helen Keller's face
became radiant. She replied, 'I see what you mean, but I have
known that all the time.'

✎ *Father, I am so thankful that I do not have to prove you exist. All I have
to do is to let you prove yourself to me. For Jesus' sake. Amen.*

His Master's Voice

FOR READING AND MEDITATION – HEBREWS 11:6; JOHN 10:22–39

'"My sheep listen to my voice; I know them, and they follow me."' (v.27: NIV)

Tertullian, one of the church fathers, said on one occasion, 'The soul is naturally Christian.' What did he mean? Did he mean that conversion and regeneration are unnecessary? No, he meant that the soul is created in such a way that, left to itself and without the influences of secularism and atheism, it will come to the conclusion that the words 'created by him and for him' (Col. 1:16) are imprinted on it.

For many years now, a company has used as a trademark a picture of a dog listening at the horn of an old-fashioned phonograph. This famous picture appeared on every record they produced, under the name *His Master's Voice*.

Is this not a parable of humanity listening to their Master's Voice, which is inherent in the nature of things? If we would listen we would hear his voice everywhere – particularly in our inner beings.

We were made by him, designed by him and will never be at peace until we are indwelt by him.

Some time ago someone sent me a book entitled *Seven Reasons Why I Disbelieve in the Existence of God*. As I browsed through it, I was staggered at the effort the writer made to explain God away. And even those who deny the existence of God slip, as Khrushchev did, when he said, 'Thank God I'm an atheist!'

✑ *Father, something within me tells me that you are true. I listen to the whispers that are within my soul – and I hear my Master's Voice. I am so grateful, Father. Amen.*

The great Rewarder

FOR READING AND MEDITATION – HEBREWS 11:6; MATTHEW 7:7–14

'... anyone who comes to him must believe that ...
he rewards those who earnestly seek him.' (Heb. 11:6, NIV)

Faith begins when we believe in the existence of God. But it is possible to believe that he exists, and still not make contact with him. That is why this second statement is so vitally important: 'anyone who comes to him must believe that he rewards those who earnestly seek him.'

Here, by the way, is the answer to the question I am often asked: what about the heathen who have never heard the Gospel? Well, even they have the opportunity to exercise faith, for faith, at its simplest level, is believing that God exists, and that he rewards those who seek him.

Any man who believes this, and obeys that revelation, will be brought to a knowledge of the truth of Jesus Christ.

An African Christian tells how he looked up at the stars and said, 'God, I know you exist, but that is all – please help me to get to know you better.' The Holy Spirit guided him through the bush for six weeks until he heard a missionary tell the story of the Cross. He responded, and accepted Christ as his Lord and Saviour.

As Dr Sam Shoemaker used to say, 'When coming to God, use the little faith you have and God will give you more.'

I am so grateful, Father, that you delight in faith, and that without faith it is impossible to please you. Amen.

The Westminster Abbey of the Bible

FOR READING AND MEDITATION – GENESIS 4:1–15

'By faith Abel offered God a better sacrifice than Cain …' (Hebrews 11:4: NIV)

The writer to the Hebrews now goes on to show us how faith works.

The list of names recorded – beginning with Abel and ending with Jesus – has been called 'The Westminster Abbey of the Bible', because so many heroes of faith are enshrined here.

Did the writer to the Hebrews pull these names out at random, or was there some significant reason underlying his choice? He selects them I believe because each illustrates a particular aspect and characteristic of faith. How many of their distinguishing marks of faith are present in our own lives?

The first name we encounter is that of Abel. Why Abel? Because it is in Abel that the primary note of faith is struck: that in coming to God, one must be prepared to lay aside independent judgment and take God's way in all things.

Cain believed that 'one way is as good as another,' and brought fruit and vegetables as his offering. As a result, Cain was rejected.

Abel believed God, and brought the offering he knew God wanted – a blood sacrifice. Faith recognises that the only way into God's presence is by way of an atoning sacrifice.

☙ *Father, help me to lay hold of this important truth – that your way is always right, and nothing else is right. Help me to take your way even though the heavens seem to fall. Thank you, Father. Amen.*

Enoch and Noah

FOR READING AND MEDITATION – GENESIS 5:21–24, 6:1–13
'By faith Enoch was taken from this life ...
By faith Noah ... built an ark ...' (Hebrews 11:5, 7, NIV)

Enoch is one of the only two men in the Old Testament who went to heaven without dying – the other being Elijah. Enoch walked so closely with God that he found a fellowship which death could not interrupt.

As a little girl said, 'One day Enoch walked so far with God that God said, "Look, Enoch, it's too far for you to go back now: come on home with me." ' Enoch has become forever a picture of what death is to the Christian – not a termination, but a transition. Faith fears nothing – least of all death.

Noah was, without doubt, one of the greatest men in the Old Testament. Noah believed that God was in charge of history, and was prepared to bank everything on that belief. When God told him that he was about to judge the world by a flood, Noah set about informing the people about their imminent danger. The response he got was one of ridicule and scorn.

By faith, however, Noah continued his preaching for 120 years. He did so just because God had commanded it – thus giving God a vantage point for a strategic movement in history.

Faith acts on what God says, even though circumstances seem to say that it is all futile. This is what God calls you and I to do – to witness by faith when everything seems contradictory.

O blessed Master, how can I ever cease thanking you that amid the stumblings of life, my feet have found the Way that Enoch and Noah once trod. Amen

Abraham – the friend of God

FOR READING AND MEDITATION – GENESIS 12:1–9, 13:14–18, 22:1–18

'By faith Abraham, when called to go to a place he would later receive as
his inheritance, obeyed and went ...' (Hebrews 11:8, NIV)

Abel shows us how faith takes God's way in all things; Enoch that
faith fears nothing – not even death; and Noah that faith always acts
on what God says. Today we come to Abraham – the friend of God.

Abraham is held in high esteem, not only by Christianity but
also by Judaism and Islam. In this classic chapter on faith, the writer
implies that the patriarch stands head and shoulders above the rest.

Three great movements of faith are referred to in this passage:
(1) Abraham obeying God's call; (2) Abraham sojourning in the
land of promise; and (3) Abraham offering up his son Isaac: faith
obeying, faith onlooking and faith offering.

Each movement of faith is significant, but the overall message
that comes through Abraham's life is that of unswerving obedience:
he obeyed, no matter what. Here is a man who set out on a journey
with an unknown destination – simply because God asked him to.

No wonder he has been called 'the father of the faithful'. Abraham may not have known where he was going, but he knew with
whom he was going.

*O Father, help me to drop my anchor into the depths of this reassuring
and encouraging revelation – that although I may not know what the future
holds, I know who holds the future. For your own dear Name's sake. Amen.*

Isaac, Jacob and Joseph

FOR READING AND MEDITATION – GENESIS 27:22–40, 49:28–33, 50:22–26

'By faith Isaac blessed Jacob and Esau … By faith Jacob … worshipped …
By faith Joseph … spoke about the exodus …' (Heb. 11:20–22, NIV)

Today we focus on three heroes of faith – Isaac, Jacob and Joseph. In each case, the illustrations of faith given are drawn from the latter part of the patriarchs' lives. The writer makes no reference to their earlier lives, but shows how in their closing days, these three great men demonstrated their faith in remarkable ways.

Isaac and Jacob, knowing God intended to build nations from their descendants, prayed and blessed their children in anticipation of what God had promised.

When Joseph was dying, he saw hundreds of years ahead to the coming exodus from Egypt, and he made arrangements by faith for his bones to be buried in the Promised Land.

In the course of time, that was the way it happened. The children of Israel took Joseph's bones with them and after 40 years in the wilderness, finally buried them in Canaan. That was most certainly the longest funeral procession in history!

The characteristic of faith illustrated here is that *faith anticipates*. It moves toward a clearly expected event in the future. Kierkegaard said, 'Life can be understood backwards, but it can only be lived forwards. Faith not only believes what God has promised, but looks with delight and anticipation for that which is to come.'

✎ *O God, help me, I pray, to be a forward-looking person – someone who waits with an unshakable eagerness and confidence for the things you have promised to bring about. In Jesus' Name. Amen.*

Amram, Jochebed and Moses

FOR READING AND MEDITATION – EXODUS 2:1–10, 6:1–8
'By faith Moses' parents hid him ... By faith he left Egypt ...'
(Heb. 11:23, 27, NIV)

When we read the Exodus story, the impression we get is that of loving parents acting out of concern for their baby, but the writer here says there was another ingredient present in their action – faith.

When Amram and Jochebed cast that ark and baby upon the waters, it was an act of great faith in the most hopeless circumstances. They ventured their all on the conviction that the Almighty would somehow overrule the king's decision. Thus they illustrated another characteristic of faith – *faith ventures*.

Most Christians are familiar with the wonderful story of Moses' life – a life spanning 120 years. The significant characteristic of faith illustrated by Moses is undoubtedly this – *faith evaluates*.

In Moses we see the mental process which faith follows. First – 'he refused'. On what basis did he refuse? By 'choosing'. How did he come to choose? By considering, or *accounting*. See the mental process here. The word *accounting* means balancing things, weighing the evidence in order to come to a decision.

He weighed the wealth of Egypt and the prestige of royalty against the possibility of being an instrument in the hands of the living God. By faith 'he regarded disgrace for the sake of Christ as of greater value than the treasures of Egypt' (v.26).

Father, thank you for reminding me that faith is not just a feeling, but a mental process in which I have to make a choice. Help me to weigh everything and come down on your side in every issue. For Jesus' sake. Amen.

Rahab and the Israelites

FOR READING AND MEDITATION – EXODUS 14:21–3; JOSHUA 2:1–21
'By faith the people passed through the Red Sea ...
By faith the prostitute Rahab ... was not killed ...' (Heb. 11:29, 31, NIV)

Two incidents concerning the nation of Israel are selected – first, the crossing of the Red Sea, and second, the conquering of Jericho. Despite all the failures of Israel, these two occasions show them demonstrating a faith that produced an amazing deliverance. That's what faith does – it pays no attention to impossibilities and believes in miracles.

Next, and in startling contrast, comes the name of Rahab. Why, we ask ourselves, should a pagan prostitute be placed alongside such heroes of faith? The answer, of course, is because she demonstrated great faith. Rahab had heard much about the approaching army of Israel (Josh. 2:10), and as a result, a great conviction possessed her soul. She said, 'For we have heard how the Lord dried up the water of the Red Sea before you ... for the Lord your God is he who is God in heaven above and on earth beneath' (vv. 10–11, RSV). As a result, she forsook her pagan religion, risked her life on behalf of the spies and put her faith firmly in God. *Faith risks everything* when once it is sure of God.

✎ *My Father and my God, you are stretching me to the utmost. Give me a faith that is so sure of you that it will risk its all upon you. Amen.*

The faith of others

FOR READING AND MEDITATION – HEBREWS 11:32–40

'... Others were tortured ... still others were chained and
put in prison.' (vv.35, 36: NIV)

This great chapter on faith finishes with a burst of exploits vibrant
with power, poignant in sufferings, and challenging in their revelation of triumph. The writer wants to take every name and deal with
them one by one but, as he explains, 'time would fail me to tell'. One
word stands out: 'others'. Who are these 'others'? The people who,
down the ages, have lived their lives by the principle of faith.

This chapter has been called the 'unfinished chapter of the
Bible'. It is easy to see why. God is still calling men and women to
live by faith, and the list will go on being added to until the last
moment of recorded time. If we venture our all on the living God,
we too shall have our names added to this list of heroes, and be
counted among those who received 'a good report'.

The final sentences bring us face to face with the least spectac-
ular, but the most important aspect of faith: that *faith perseveres*.
'These all died in faith, not having received what was promised'
(Heb. 11:13, RSV).

They were looking for more than their own personal satisfaction – they were waiting to see God's purposes being fulfilled on
earth. This may not be the most spectacular exercise of faith, but it
is by far the most important.

*My Father, save me from sacrificing the spiritual to the spectacular. I long
for a faith that can perform miracles, but give me first the faith that persists in
believing you, despite all appearances to the contrary. For Jesus' sake. Amen.*

A great cloud of witnesses

FOR READING AND MEDITATION – HEBREWS 12:1

'Therefore, since we are surrounded by so great a cloud of witnesses …
let us run with perseverance …' (RSV)

We begin by asking ourselves: who are the 'cloud of witnesses' to whom the writer refers? Those who have died, and are now leaning over the battlements of heaven watching to see how we are doing?

But the text is quite clear – it refers not to watching, but to witnessing. The thought in the writer's mind is that the examples of faith he has given us in Hebrews 11 are saying something important to us – they are testifying to us, they are witnessing to us about the force and potency of faith.

In the light of this, he bids us to 'lay aside every weight'. What are these 'weights'? Well, clearly the things that hinder us from running freely. Shall I name some? No, for what might be a weight to me might not be a weight to you.

He encourages us also to get rid of 'sin which clings so closely'. What is that? It can be expressed in one word – unbelief. It is the sin of failing to take God's word seriously.

Unbelief kept a whole nation out of the Promised Land for 40 years. Don't, I beg you, let it keep you from knowing and experiencing God's mighty and unlimited power!

O my Father and my God, I face now any unbelief that may be in my life, and I renounce it in Jesus' Name. Here and now I pledge to be among those who go all the way with you. Amen.

Looking unto Jesus

FOR READING AND MEDITATION – HEBREWS 12:1–3

'... let us run with patience ... looking unto Jesus
the author and finisher of our faith ...' (vv. 1–2: AV)

Notice how yet again the writer to the Hebrews underlines that most
significant characteristic of faith – *persistence*.

'Let us run with patient endurance and steady and active persistence ... the race that is set before us' (AMPLIFIED). Keeping on no
matter what happens.

But how? By looking to Jesus, the Author and Finisher of our
faith. The phrase 'looking unto Jesus' does not contain the real meaning of the writer's words. The *Amplified Bible* says: 'Looking away
from all that will distract ... to Jesus.'

The point here is this – although the illustrations of faith given
in Hebrews 11 are powerful, they are illustrations, not examples. We
are not to fix our eyes upon the saints of the past, but we are to
look away from them and focus our gaze upon Jesus.

Not one of those named in Hebrews 11 could be described as a
perfect example of faith. Abel needed an atoning sacrifice in order
to come into God's presence. Enoch walked with the Lord, but for
the first 65 years of his life he lived on the mediocre spiritual level
of his times. Abraham more than once turned aside from the simple pathway of faith. But with Jesus it was different. He is the perfect example: our example *par excellence*.

✎ *O Father, I am so grateful that, at long last, I have something I cannot
have too much of. I cannot have too much faith, and I cannot have too much
of you. Amen.*

Jesus – the standard note

FOR READING AND MEDITATION – JOHN 1:1–14
'In him was life, and that life was the light of men.' (v.1: NIV)

We see that, while we may draw inspiration from the lives of the heroes of faith, we are not to consider them our examples. Only Jesus Christ himself is to be our example! We run the race set before us, by keeping our eyes on Jesus, not Abel, Enoch, Noah or Abraham. We see and listen to the witnesses, but we look only to Christ.

Dr Campbell Morgan used to say that there were times when he wished that the lives of the saints had never been written. 'Quit looking at the saints of the Christian era,' he said. 'Look off; there is just one point where your vision may be fully satisfied – "looking off unto Jesus."'

Under the microscope, the saints are shown to be shot through with failure and imperfection. When Jesus is put under the microscope, he is vindicated by all that he does.

In America many years ago, a note was struck over the radio each day from Washington by which the nation could tune its instruments. It was known as a 440 – the standard note. Everything not tuned to that note was discordant. In Jesus, the standard note for faith – and, for that matter, everything else – has been struck. Everything that is tuned to him is in harmony, and everything that is not is discordant.

Blessed Master, I am so grateful that you are the Standard Note for all areas of living. From now on my life will be perfectly tuned to you. Help me, dear Jesus. Amen.

The Head of the procession

FOR READING AND MEDITATION – HEBREWS 12:2; EPHESIANS 4:7–13

'. . . Jesus the author and finisher of our faith . . .' (Heb. 12:2: AV)

Significantly, the word 'our' is not present in the Greek, and therefore the text should read: 'Jesus the author and finisher of faith.' The writer is talking about the principle of faith, and he declares that the principle is only fully seen and fully demonstrated in Jesus. Can you see the difference this makes to the text?

Take the word *author* also. A better translation of the original Greek word used here is *file-leader*. It does not mean, as some translations put it, 'originator' or 'beginner'. It means the one who takes precedence, the head of the procession, leading it in revelation.

What the writer to the Hebrews is attempting to bring out in this word is the picture of Jesus leading the great procession of those who witness to the power of faith.

It is indeed a wonderful procession that spans the ages from Abel onward: but look, hold your breath, for one races past them all and makes his way right to the front of the procession.

And who is he? It is Jesus, the File-leader, the one who has total pre-eminence. Alongside him, the great heroes of faith, such as Enoch, Noah and Abraham, pale into insignificance. Jesus is not just another great hero of faith: he is the greatest!

❧ *Blessed Lord Jesus, I am so grateful that I can have faith in you when my faith in everyone else fails. For you and you alone are worthy of faith. All honour and glory be to your precious and peerless Name. Amen.*

He defies all comparison

FOR READING AND MEDITATION – HEBREWS 1:1–12

'"You have loved righteousness and hated wickedness; therefore God ...
has set you above your companions ..."' (v.9: NIV)

To run the race of faith, we must see our Lord and Saviour, Jesus
Christ as the File-leader of faith, the one who has pre-eminence.

In Hebrews 11, we saw many fine illustrations of faith. They worshipped, walked and worked by faith. Now turn to Jesus. What do
you see? No one worshipped God, walked or worked for God as did
Jesus. He moves to the head of the procession. Abraham's faith was
at work as he 'obeyed and went, even though he did not know where
he was going' (Heb. 11:8). Again, turn to Jesus – and what do you
find? Such obedience. It brought him, not into an unknown country,
but to a grisly Cross.

Joseph, after his death, was embalmed and laid to rest. So was
Jesus – but because of who he was and what he had wrought through
his life, the grave could not hold him. He arose!

Moses, because of his sin, was forbidden to enter the Promised
Land. Jesus not only accomplished an exodus far greater than anything Moses dreamed of, but actually brought Moses to –

*Stand with glory wrapt around
on the hills he never trod
and speak of the strife that won our life
with the incarnate Son of God.*

✎ *My Saviour and my God, I know that you are far more wonderful than
any description or title that is given you. I am so thankful. Amen.*

The vindicator of faith

FOR READING AND MEDITATION – HEBREWS 12:2

'Let us fix our eyes on Jesus, the author and perfecter of our faith ...' (NIV)

The real meaning of the word 'finisher' or 'perfecter' in the original Greek is 'vindicator'. Jesus is not only pre-eminent as the File-leader of faith – the one who leads the procession – but he is pre-eminent also as the Vindicator of faith – the one who establishes it as an abiding and eternal principle. Faith in God leads inevitably to faith in man. Faith in man? Perhaps you find that difficult to accept. Jesus thought man was worth dying for.

'The Cross for evermore,' said one great theologian, 'indicates the value that Jesus put upon man.'

What does God see in you and me? Perhaps it is his image in us, the hallmark of the divine, which, though blurred and damaged, is yet worthy of redemption.

Whatever it was, we know this – Jesus believed in man. His faith, however, was also faith in the future. He looked forward with confidence to the day when all the nations would be gathered before him, and he would judge the world.

Cast your mind back now to the text with which we began: 'The just shall live by faith.' Now ask yourself: has Jesus vindicated that principle? Has he illustrated and exemplified it in a way that puts it beyond all possibility of misunderstanding? My heart says 'Yes'. How about yours?

Blessed Saviour, my heart too, says 'Yes'. You have taken faith and vindicated it in a way that no one else could do. You are its fulfilment and its fullness. Blessed be your glorious Name for ever. Amen.

The joy set before Him

FOR READING AND MEDITATION – HEBREWS 2:5–18, 12:2

'... who for the joy set before him endured the cross,
scorning its shame ...' (Heb. 12:2, NIV)

Consider the phrase, 'who for the joy set before him'. What was this 'joy'? Was it his return to heaven? I think not. Faith is confidence in 'things hoped for, the evidence of things not seen'. The vision that sustained our Lord was not merely that of getting back to his Father's throne, but of re-establishing in the universe the rule and reign of God.

In order to achieve that, however, a pathway had to be trodden: 'Jesus ... endured the cross, scorning its shame.' Is there any phrase more full of infinite majesty and beauty? Nothing was more shameful than dying upon a cross, yet Jesus willingly gave himself to it in order that you and I might be redeemed. A God like this can have my heart forever!

Now we reach the culminating phrase: he 'sat down at the right hand of the throne of God'. Try and write that sentence against any of the names in the list of heroes of faith in Hebrews 11 – and what happens? It just doesn't fit! This statement can only be applied to Jesus. As we see him seated there on his Father's throne, we realise that, in words like this, faith has its last and unanswerable argument. Let this word sink deep into your heart: 'Looking away from all that will distract to Jesus.'

✎ O blessed Master, you know how often I have stumbled because my eyes have been on others. From now on my concentration will be only on you. I will glance at others, but gaze at you. Amen.

How are we saved?

FOR READING AND MEDITATION – EPHESIANS 2:1–10

'For it is by grace you have been saved, through faith –
and this not from yourselves, it is the gift of God...' (v.8: NIV)

The first question asked whenever the subject of faith is discussed is this: is there any difference between the faith we use in our natural lives and the faith we use in believing God? Faith is one of God's gifts to us. When he created us, he built into us the ability and capacity to believe.

Belief is a habit of life: we have to believe to live. In a sense, we can't go through a single day without faith. When we board a bus we have faith – faith that the driver is able to do his job. When we go to a restaurant we have faith – faith that the food is wholesome and properly prepared.

Why do people not use this God-given ability to believe in Christ? As the Scripture says: Satan has 'blinded the minds of the unbelieving' (2 Cor. 4:4, NASB). If I understand conversion correctly, what happens is this – through anointed preaching or witnessing, the Holy Spirit unfolds to the mind the reality of the Gospel.

Once this is understood, the individual then reaches out by faith to take hold of Christ, and is saved. Conversion is a combination of the human and the divine. It is both activity and receptivity. You do it – and he does it.

Father, thank you for showing me that faith is both receptivity and activity. I do the believing and you do the saving. What a partnership! Amen.

Faith and the gift of faith

FOR READING AND MEDITATION – 1 CORINTHIANS 12:1–11

'To another faith by the same Spirit . . .' (v.9: NIV)

Why do we need an additional gift of faith as described in 1 Corinthians 12:9? The faith spoken of here is a special faith, to be used for supernatural purposes. Paul lists nine 'special abilities', three groups with three gifts in each.

The first enables a person to supernaturally know – the word of wisdom, word of knowledge and discerning of spirits. The second enables a person to supernaturally do – faith, working of miracles, and gifts of healing. The third group enables a person to supernaturally speak – tongues, interpretation and prophecy.

What, then, is the 'special ability' called 'faith'? It is a divine gift, given only to certain people or on certain occasions, in order to accomplish supernatural exploits. Paul demonstrated this gift in Acts 27:22 when he decreed, by faith, that there would be 'no loss of life among you, but only of the ship' (RSV).

Every Christian has faith – individual faith. God has also made it possible for us to access a supernatural realm, beyond our ability to conceive. This faith, operating through certain members of the Body of Christ, issues forth in mighty signs, wonders and miracles. How sad that, with such a need for God's power to be seen at work today, this gift is not more in evidence.

O Father, now that I see the resources that are available, I feel my prayer must match the possibilities. Launch your whole church, I pray, into a greater orbit of spiritual power than we have ever known before. In Jesus' Name I ask it. Amen.

Faith versus the faith

FOR READING AND MEDITATION – ACTS 6:1–7
'So the word of God spread ... and a large number of
priests became obedient to the faith.' (v.7: NIV)

What is the difference in Scripture between the phrases 'faith' and 'the faith'? Faith has to do with believing: the faith has to do with beliefs.

This passage shows how, following the descent of the Holy Spirit at Pentecost, the church began to emphasise certain beliefs. So clear was their emphasis on things such as the birth, life, death, resurrection and ascension of our Lord that these doctrines became the foundation of the Christian faith.

When Paul returned to Lystra, Iconium and Antioch in order to encourage the converts, we are told that he exhorted them to 'continue in the faith, and that we must through much tribulation enter into the kingdom of God' (Acts 14:22, AV). Again Jude, in the third verse of his short epistle, says: 'I felt I had to write and urge you to contend for the faith.'

The phrase 'the faith', when used in the New Testament, refers to the systematic declaration of certain Biblical truths. These form the corporate basis of our beliefs as Christians. The tragedy is that with some, becomes based on doctrine for their individual faith, rather than on a personal commitment and trust in Christ. If we mistake the faith for individual faith, we are in deep trouble.

✎ *Father I see how easy it is to make this mistake, and to believe that because I understand Christian doctrines, I am a man or woman of faith. Help me to see that the faith can never be a substitute for personal faith. In Jesus' Name. Amen.*

Faith and faithfulness

FOR READING AND MEDITATION – GALATIANS 5:16–26

'... the fruit of the Spirit is ... faith ...' (v.22: AV)

Is there any difference between ordinary faith and the faith listed as one of the fruit of the Spirit? Most translations use the word *faithfulness* in preference to *faith*, (Greek: *pistis*) although some prefer the word *fidelity*. The thought that flows through this word is not so much of a person being strong in his ability to believe, but of one who is trustworthy, reliable and dependable.

Individual faith is the venturing of the whole personality in trusting one who is worthy. The gift of faith is the supernatural ability to believe for a miraculous manifestation of God's power.

Faithfulness, or fidelity, is one of the nine characteristics growing as the natural outflow of the Spirit who abides within. The first two, love and joy, have a miracle quality and not a moral one – the third, patience, has a moral quality and not a miracle one.

When Paul speaks of 'the works of the flesh' in verses 19–21, he calls them 'works', but when he speaks of the moral qualities in the life of the believer, he refers to them as 'fruit'.

What is the difference? 'Works' is something manufactured, not natural; 'fruit' is something that grows as a natural outcome. Every Christian has faith; not all Christians have faithfulness. Faith needs work if it is to grow; faithfulness does not need work, but is the natural outcome of abiding in the Vine.

Father, I am so grateful for the miracle qualities that faith brings, but no less for the moral qualities coming as I abide in Jesus, the Vine. I want to grow, not only in faith, but also in faithfulness. Amen.

Faith versus works

FOR READING AND MEDITATION – JAMES 2:14–26

'. . . so faith without deeds is dead.' (v.26: NIV)

If faith is of such prime importance, why is it that James lays such an emphasis on works?

The apostle James began a controversy which has gone on for centuries. The problem is caused when his words are compared with those of the apostle Paul in Galatians 2:16: 'A man is not justified by works of the law but through faith in Jesus Christ . . . because by works of the law shall no one be justified' (RSV).

Putting James in opposition to Paul is a popular pastime with some Christians, and on one occasion even the great Martin Luther fell into this trap.

James and Paul do not contradict each other – they complement each other. Paul writes that works cannot result in faith, while James writes that faith must inevitably result in works. James goes on to make the point that 'a person is justified by what he does and not by faith alone' (v.24). Contradictory? No.

James' point is that the only faith which can be accounted as righteous, is that faith that comes to fruition in works. If works are the basis of our faith, then it is competitive. If works flow out of faith, it is complementary. Works can never produce faith, but faith inevitably produces works.

Father, help me not to fall into the trap of taking an effect and turning it into a cause. My faith must not be manufactured through my works, but manifested through them. Help me to make this distinction. For Jesus' sake. Amen.

Positive confession

'... whoever says to this mountain, "Be removed and be cast into the sea," and does not doubt ... he will have whatever he says.' (v.23: NKJ)

In order to have faith, must we not do more than believe? Should we not also speak out words of positive confession?

The thinking behind this question is related to a form of Christian teaching known as *positive confession*. This says we shall have whatever our mouth speaks out. So refusing to accept a negative situation and declaring it to be a positive one, will generate sufficient faith to bring about a dramatic change in our circumstances. Closely related is the teaching stating one should testify to healing whether the facts support it or not, since testifying 'before the fact' generates the faith to produce the fact.

Faith and confession are definitely linked together in Scripture. We see it in today's text: 'Whoever says to this mountain, "Be removed ..."' Jesus often spoke out in faith to situations. He spoke to a tree and it withered; he spoke to a storm and it ceased; he spoke to a corpse and it came to life. The important thing, however, is this: confession does not create faith, but only releases it. The words 'he will have whatever he says' are dependent, not merely on what we say, but on the principle 'have faith in God'. It is only after faith is present that it can be confessed. Positive confession is fine as long as it is used to release faith, and not create it.

O God my Father, I see that deliberately twisting your Word is not the only way to fall into error. It can be done also by overemphasis. Save me from this, I pray. In Jesus' Name. Amen.

Faith and prosperity

FOR READING AND MEDITATION – DEUTERONOMY 32:1–18

'Jeshurun grew fat . . . he became heavy and sleek.
He abandoned the God who made him . . .' (v.15: NIV)

If every believer used his faith to become prosperous, would this not convince unbelievers?

This question arises out of another overemphasis – the issue of 'prosperity'. This states, 'when we are rightly related to God's principles and know how to exercise our faith, then we can have everything we want – in abundance'. *You possess what you confess,* or *Name it and claim it.*

Has God given us the ability to believe simply in order to get everything we want? I doubt it. God has promised to supply all our needs (Phil. 4:19), but it is our needs, not our wants. Read the context: 'I know what it is to be in need, and I know what it is to have plenty' (Phil. 4:12). Paul accepted all levels of God's provision for his life, realising that God would give him what was best for him at the time.

I do not believe in the 'poverty syndrome' – the more we skimp on things the more spiritual we are – but neither do I believe in the possession of things for their own sake.

Those who push God hard to let them become prosperous may find they finish up like Israel: 'And he gave them their request; but sent leanness into their soul' (Psa. 106:15, AV).

Heavenly Father, I'm shaken to the core to realise that if I want my own way strongly enough – then you will let me have it. Teach me how to be positive, but not to go beyond your will and purposes. For Jesus' sake. Amen.

The first step

FOR READING AND MEDITATION – 2 THESSALONIANS 1:1–12
'We ought always to thank God for you …
because your faith is growing more and more …' (v.3: NIV)

If our faith is to expand, we need to see that faith is not something fixed, but that it can develop and grow. Many Christians have no expectation of growth. They point to the text: 'God has dealt to each one a measure of faith' (Rom. 12:3, KJV), and infer from this that our calling is to go through life functioning within our appointed and preordained circle. But take another look at the text at the top of this page – this time in a different translation: 'My brothers … I always thank God for you … Your faith has made such strides' (J.B. Phillips). The Greek word used here is *huperauxano*, meaning 'to increase above the ordinary degree'.

A missionary who found it difficult to grow trees in his garden was told by an expert, 'Dig a very deep pit, put in a layer of fertiliser, then one of ordinary earth, then another layer of fertiliser, followed again by a layer of earth – and so on to the top.' This, he said, gives the growing tree something to reach after. Its roots get to one level, and feel the call of the deeper richness. In the same way, your faith must be rooted in the truth that you are designed to be a growing person, or else it will remain dwarfed and immature.

❧ *Father, help me to see that not only my faith, but my whole personality, is in the grip of a divine intention. I am made to grow. For Jesus' sake. Amen.*

Firm up the decision

FOR READING AND MEDITATION – COLOSSIANS 2:1–10

'... just as you received Christ Jesus as Lord, continue to live in him,
rooted and built up in him ...' (v.6: NIV)

Make a conscious decision to give yourself to the task of cultivating your faith. Prayer has been defined as 'constantly bringing the whole of life into the light of God's presence for cleansing and decision'. Note 'constantly', for that is the secret. You prayed earlier: 'Lord, increase my faith', but now, in the light of the Scriptures and the challenges you have faced, it is time make an act of positive decision. 'Character is decision,' said a philosopher. So decide now to give yourself fully to this task.

Cultivation of faith does not mean trying in your natural strength. The essence of cultivation is relaxation. A good musician never tries too hard – he lets go and lets the music get into his fingertips, so that he does not play the music, but the music plays through him.

It is the same with God. Don't use him – let him use you. Walter Rauschenbusch says, 'My faith grows in the great quiet of God.'

Moffatt translates 2 Peter 1:5: 'Furnish your faith with resolution'. Faith is first, resolution second. Christianity is not primarily resolution, a whipping up of the will. It is primarily faith, a surrender of the will. Faith is not struggling and striving: it is letting go and trusting.

Father, I see that if I am to grow in faith, it is not by anxious effort, but by quiet trust in your infinite resources. Today I make this decision – not to use you, but to let you use me. Help me, dear Father. Amen.

Keeping the right balance

FOR READING AND MEDITATION – LUKE 18:35–43

'Jesus said to him, "Receive your sight; your faith has healed you."' (v.42: NIV)

Get a proper perspective on how much God wants to do in your life, and how much he wants you to do.

We need to face the thorny question of the sovereignty of God and the freedom of man. Many Christians have unbalanced views about these two concepts.

If you are overbalanced on God's sovereignty, then you will tend to sit back and let God do it all. If you are overbalanced on freedom of the human will, then you will try to do it all yourself – and get nowhere. Error, more often than not, is truth out of balance.

I believe God built an amazing faculty when he designed us with the ability to believe and trust.

Faith is trust in another, and yet it is an attitude of our own. It develops self-reliance and other-reliance at the same time. If it were mere passivity, it would not develop self-reliance. If it were mere activity, it would not develop other-reliance.

This truth, I believe, is written into such statements as: 'According to your faith will it be done to you,' and 'Your faith has healed you.' He retains his place as Creator, but invites us to create with him and become, in a sense, mini-creators. God develops us, as he gives to us.

Father, how can I ever sufficiently thank you for helping me to develop my confidence in you and yet, at the same time, my confidence in myself. Help me always to keep these two factors in their right proportion. For your own dear Name's sake. Amen.

Think, man! Think!

FOR READING AND MEDITATION – MATTHEW 6:25–34

'If that is how God clothes the grass of the field …
will he not much more clothe you, O you of little faith?' (v.30: NIV)

Have you ever noticed how, in the Scriptures, faith and thinking are linked together? Dr Martin Lloyd Jones claims that faith is primarily … thinking.

> *This is what Jesus is attempting to show here: that faith requires thought. 'Look at the birds,' says Jesus … 'think about them … draw your deductions. Look at the flowers … think about them … draw your deductions. Look at the grass in the fields … think about it … draw your deductions.' The whole trouble with a person of little faith is that he doesn't think. He allows circumstances to bludgeon him, and fails to consider the evidences of God's goodness and care.*

This principle can be applied in other areas of life as well. Look at your Bible – a miracle, not only of inspiration, but of preservation. Think about it. Look at the bread and wine at Holy Communion – think about them. Those visible reminders of Christ's death are designed to make us think. They call us to remember, and the more we consider them and what they represent, the more our faith increases. Don't just read the Bible or celebrate Communion – think.

O Father, what a fool I've been to take so much for granted. In future, help me not just to see the evidences of your goodness, but to think about them. For the more I think – the more I grow. Amen.

Be alert to this danger

In cultivating faith, take care that you don't become so preoccupied with the subject of faith that you lose sight of the object of faith – God.

Some have almost deified faith itself, believing that their faith can do or provide all things and be more than a match for all circumstances. Faith, even natural faith, has such power that it can produce the most amazing results.

Dr Ernest Holmes says, 'The idea that faith has only to do with our religious experience is a mistake. Faith is a faculty of the mind that finds its highest expression in religion ... but faith is an affirmative mental approach to reality.'

If there is one thing that has been nagging at me, it is that some may become so preoccupied with faith that they will lose sight of God. There are already signs that the church is being influenced by the twin evils – humanism and secularism – putting man at the centre of things and not God. We must be careful that in upgrading faith, we do not downgrade God.

'When we shift our faith from God to anything else,' says Judson Cornwall, 'we tend to think and exercise faith for, rather than faith in. Faith for makes us things-oriented, rather than God-oriented.'

Father, I realise that I have come to one of life's supreme choices. Don't let me fumble at this place, for if I do, then everything goes to pieces. Help me to keep you as the focus of my faith – not things. For Jesus' sake. Amen.

Faith on an ego trip

FOR READING AND MEDITATION – GALATIANS 2:20
'I have been crucified with Christ ...' (NIV)

Make sure your ego is where it should be – at the feet of our Lord Jesus Christ. Why? Because if your ego is not fully surrendered to Christ, you can easily use faith to embark upon an ego trip.

If we cannot say with Paul, 'I have been crucified with Christ and I no longer live, but Christ lives in me', then we lay ourselves open to the misuse of faith.

Psychologists say all of us have a need for power. And nothing panders to our basic need for power more than faith.

Faith produces within the personality a feeling and an awareness of power. We can either use that power to meet our own ego needs, or use it to honour and glorify the Lord.

An evangelist known for his daring faith and ability to produce astonishing miracles, told me in a moment of honest confession, 'There is something within me that enjoys ordering God around ... that delights in being the focus of attention. Can you tell me what it is?'

I responded to his honesty with equal candour and said, 'Yes, you are using your faith partly to meet your ego needs, especially the need for power.' He fell on his knees, confessed his failure to God, and rose to an even greater ministry than before.

Gracious Master, help me to get this matter of my ego sorted out once and for all. I want my faith not to be ego-centred, but Christ-centred. Grant it, Lord Jesus. Amen.

A good idea – or God's idea?

FOR READING AND MEDITATION – 1 KINGS 17:1–6
'Then the word of the Lord came to Elijah …' (v.2: NIV)

Get close to God in prayer and through his Word, so you hear his specific directions for your life.

Elijah said there would be 'neither dew nor rain … except at my word.' Did Elijah think it up, and then use his faith to bring it to pass? No, of course not. Throughout Elijah's life, we read: 'Then the word of the Lord came to Elijah.' On Mount Carmel he says: 'I have done all these things at your word' (1 Kings 18:36, RSV).

Elijah heard from God first, before putting his faith into action.

Jesus, when challenged about why he healed the man at the pool of Bethesda on the Sabbath, said: 'The Son can do nothing by himself; he can do only what he sees his Father doing' (John 5:19).

What is he saying here? That he looked up to heaven to see what God wanted – and then became the extension of God's will here on earth. He saw what God was doing – and then did it with him.

If we follow this principle, it will deliver us from that most awful of maladies – presumption. Get close to God. Know not only the *logos* – his general will revealed in the Bible – but also the *rhema* – his specific word revealed for you.

𝒩 *O God my Father, how desperately I need to learn this lesson. Help me to live so near to you that I will be able to discern between what is just a good idea, and what is God's idea. For your dear Name's sake. Amen.*

Taking action

FOR READING AND MEDITATION – PSALM 42

'Why are you downcast, O my soul?
'... Put your hope in God, for I will yet praise him...' (v.5: NIV)

The next step in developing your faith is to act on the faith that you have and as surely as day follows night, faith will grow in you. 'Before you ask for more faith,' says a well-known evangelist, 'be sure you are putting to use the faith you already have.'

How good are you at practising the faith you already have? For example, when God clearly asks you to do something you don't feel like doing – how do you respond? Do you take a step of faith and do it anyway? If you don't, how can you then ask for more faith? When God asks you to make a sacrificial offering toward some special project – what is your response? Do you say, 'But I have needs of my own'? If that is the case, how can you ask for more faith? And what happens if one day God doesn't seem as real to you as he does at other times – how do you respond? Do you allow your feelings to dictate to you and refuse to pray or praise God, or do you take a step of faith and say as David did: 'Why are you downcast, O my soul? ... Put your hope in God, for I will yet praise him'?

Will you not take the decision to do that right now?

Oh Lord, forgive me for the many excuses I have not to act when you ask something of me. Help me not to listen to my emotions, but to take action and put my trust in you. Amen.

Stepping out

FOR READING AND MEDITATION – MARK 3:1–6

'He stretched it out, and his hand was completely restored.' (v.5: NIV)

A great new adventure awaits you in the realm of faith, but you must act on what you already have. In the Gospel of Mark we find a perfect example of this: Jesus asked the man with the withered hand to stretch it out – the one thing he couldn't do. And yet as he responded with the grain of faith that he had, his hand was made whole in the process of obedience.

'Faith,' said someone, 'is like a muscle; the more it is exercised, the stronger it will get.' Make up your mind that, from now on, you are going to get in some spiritual exercise. Find out what God wants you to do – and then do it.

As you launch out you will think you are stepping out into a void, but that void will turn to rock beneath your feet. Many saints have walked this path before you and can testify to the truth of this statement. Don't wait any longer – take that step and you'll see!

Lord Jesus, I do not see everything, but I see you. Let that suffice me. Today I shall take the step I know you want me to take. I will supply the willingness – you supply the power. Now – here goes!

Faith under test

FOR READING AND MEDITATION – MATTHEW 15:21–28
'Then Jesus answered, "Woman, you have great faith!
Your request is granted" ' (v.28: NIV)

Expect your faith to be toughened in the fires of testing. Look how Jesus put the Canaanite woman's faith to the test.

After a sharp clash with the Pharisees who were offended at his teachings, Jesus withdrew to the area of Tyre and Sidon. Travelling through the country with his disciples, he was approached by a woman whose daughter was possessed by an evil spirit. She pleaded with Christ to deliver her. But here is the astonishing thing: 'Jesus did not answer a word' (v.23).

How did she handle this silence? She did not react with cynicism; no root of bitterness sprang forth; no hasty words were blurted out in retaliation. She responded by showing her faith to persevere and persist. It was this, I think, that led Jesus to say of her, 'O woman, great is your faith!' (RSV). What a compliment. This Canaanite woman had received nothing, but she continued to have faith and hope.

Do you need to have answers and explanations for all the difficulties God allows to overtake your life? If so, then you need to discover the security of living by faith. God wants to bring you to the place where you can trust his love, even though you cannot comprehend his purposes.

✎ *O Father, thank you for reminding me that your silences are not designed to topple my faith, but to toughen it. If my faith has to be tested, then help me to come out triumphant. For Jesus' sake. Amen.*

Not the end – the beginning

FOR READING AND MEDITATION – MARK 11:24

'"... whatever you ask for in prayer, believe that you have received it, and it will be yours."' (NIV)

One thing has become clear – faith is the principle by which we live. If we do not live by faith, then we just do not live.

Several years ago, while in the United States, my wife and I decided to visit an exhibition. To enter we had to drop a coin into a turnstile. A lady ahead of us dropped her coin into the slot and then stood back waiting for it to open. But it didn't, even though she had inserted the correct coin. The attendant said, 'Now push against it.' She did – and immediately she was through. It needed the slight, but aggressive 'push' of faith to open.

This is a parable. Many have come into the Christian life, having paid the price of surrender, and they remain standing at the turnstile waiting to go through. You need to press against the promises held in God's Word, and walk through them into his wider purposes.

Let the text that I have chosen today serve as a divine summary of all we have been saying: 'Whatever you ask for in prayer, believe that you have received it, and it will be yours.' 'Have received', not 'will receive'.

Faith sees it as already done. All that is needed is that slight push on the turnstile.

O God my Father, this is not the end but the beginning. Help me to move out from here into a life of faith that is grander and greater than anything I could ever have imagined. For Jesus' sake. Amen.

Three days long ago

FOR READING AND MEDITATION – 1 CORINTHIANS 15:1–11

' . . . Christ died for our sins according to the Scriptures . . .
he was buried . . . he was raised on the third day . . . ' (vv.3–4: NIV)

I have looked at the Easter story from many different perspectives over the years. Now I have chosen to view it as providing us with the anchor points we need to hold fast in the midst of life's storms.

Max Lucado tells of several young men spending a few days on a houseboat. On the radio they heard that Hurricane David was about to devastate their area, so they set about tying the houseboat to some trees that skirted the bank. An experienced sailor came by and said, 'Tying your houseboat to the land is not going to help. The wind will whip the trees out of their sockets. Your only hope is to anchor deep. Put out anchors in all directions, leave the rope slack . . . and pray.'

The chances are that many reading these lines are caught in a storm, or are about to be, and so it is absolutely imperative that you know how to anchor your life. In those three days from cross to re-surrection, God built anchor points that will hold you safe and secure in any storm. Three days. Not long enough for a man to build a house, but long enough for God to lay down some ledges to which you can hook your anchors and ride out every storm.

⊸ *My Father and my God, may the wonder of all that you did for me at Calvary come home afresh to me as I contemplate once again the Easter story. Give me a new glimpse of your glory I pray. In Jesus' Name. Amen.*

Fixed!

FOR READING AND MEDITATION – PSALM 112:1–10

'... a righteous man will ... have no fear of bad news;
his heart is steadfast, trusting in the Lord.' (vv.6–7: NIV)

The Easter story can be looked at from many angles. This time, however, I feel impressed to view the cross and resurrection not from a theological perspective alone, but as a bedrock to which we can attach our anchors when the tidal waves of adversity roll over us.

'There is nothing that can turn black and white theology into technicolour,' says one writer, 'as much as problems.'

Some years ago I got caught in a storm when my wife died after suffering with cancer. There was no time to sit and philosophise on the mystery of pain and suffering. No time to meditate on the great truths. Time only to drop the anchors, sit tight, and hope they would hold. I am glad to tell you they did.

Am I talking now to someone in the midst of a spiritual storm – or perhaps about to enter one? You want to know that when you drop your anchors they will fasten to some solid point. That the hull of your heart will not be splintered if no anchor point is found. I tell you with all the conviction of which I am capable that when you understand what God did for you on that first Easter, never again will your anchors drag through the sand. You will be fixed to the things that are fixed!

 O God, unveil to my understanding the significance of those three days long ago so that I might be able to drop my anchors into the depths of the encouraging and reassuring revelation. This I ask in Jesus' Name. Amen.

Calvary – a fixed point

FOR READING AND MEDITATION – ACTS 27:27–38

'Fearing that we would be dashed against the rocks,
they dropped four anchors . . . and prayed for daylight.' (v.29: NIV)

Every mariner knows that when a strong wind threatens to hurl his boat onto the rocks, the best thing he can do is to drop anchor. And the best anchor points are those sunk deeply in solid bedrock.

When the boat on which apostle Paul was sailing was about to be dashed on the rocks, the captain 'dropped four anchors . . . and prayed for daylight'. He knew that when his anchors gripped, the boat would be able to ride out the storm. This is what we must learn to do when, with titanic fury, the storms of life break upon us – we must be fixed to the things that are fixed.

The cross is a fixed point; an anchor point sunk in solid bedrock. The gospel is not the invention of the last century; it is the message once delivered to the saints.

For 2 000 years men and women have found it holds them fast. Many a storm has beaten upon it. There have been dark ages in which only a few have fastened themselves to it, and multitudes perished because they passed it by. Still it stands! Still it serves! And those who cast their anchor at its base will, as the Scripture says, 'never be put to shame' (1 Pet. 2:6).

✒ *O Father, my spirit responds with joy to the truth that no matter what storms may sweep into my life, I have a safe and secure anchor point in Calvary's cross. All honour and glory be to your Name forever. Amen.*

The storm-breaker

FOR READING AND MEDITATION – JOHN 16:17–33

'"In this world you will have trouble. But take heart!
I have overcome the world."' (v.33: NIV)

The truth of the Easter story is that something was accomplished during those three days long ago that has a direct relevance to every single one of us born into the world.

How does what happened at Calvary, and the resurrection, relate to us when our marriage looks as if it's over, redundancy strikes, our children are sick, a loved one is dying, tests prove that surgery is required, and so on? What connection is there between what happened on that first Easter and when hope runs out?

The whole Easter story sounds very gripping when the sun is shining and there are no dark clouds scudding overhead, but what about when the hurricane strikes, when the waves crash in on the beach of our lives and suck our joy out to sea?

It is a strong conviction of mine that the message of the cross relates to every possible human condition, but it is never as powerful and effective as when a person is engulfed in a storm. For you see, that is what the cross is all about. It is the story of a Man who allowed a storm in all its fury to break upon him, so that it may not break with all its fury on us.

✎ *Lord Jesus Christ, I realise that storms will come, but because of Calvary I have some solid anchor points to ride out any storm. Teach me to know them and to rely upon them. For your own dear Name's sake. Amen.*

Tragedy and triumph

FOR READING AND MEDITATION – MARK 15:33, 16:1–8

'"Don't be alarmed … You are looking for Jesus the Nazarene,
who was crucified. He has risen!"' (v.6: NIV)

What was involved in those three days that changed the world? They were no ordinary days. They were the most critical days in history.

They begin with our Lord's own disciple planting the kiss of betrayal on his cheek. His fellow countrymen bayed for his blood. Friends ran for cover. He was slandered, mocked, beaten and finally strung up on a cross to die. Thorns ripped open his scalp; his lungs screamed with pain; the cut, crushed nerves mounting in fierce agony. But death was not ready. His soul had to wrestle with the awful spectre of sin. His own Father turned his back on him, leaving him all alone. A soldier plunged a spear into his side, unaware that by doing so he was fulfilling the divine plan.

As he died, the earth rumbled and graves split open, uncovering the dead rising. As sorrowful followers of Christ walked home, in the temple, the veil was torn from top to bottom.

Kind hands took him down from the cross and laid him in a sepulchre. Our crucified God rested for hours and hours on a cool bed of rock. And then … and then … as Alice Meynell the hymnwriter says,

> *All alone alone alone,*
> *he rose again behind the stone.*

꙰ *Loving God and heavenly Father, you have the last word in everything. And your last word is not death, but resurrection. I belong not just to Good Friday but Easter Sunday. Amen.*

When unbelief prevails

FOR READING AND MEDITATION – PSALM 22:1–11
'My God, my God, why have you forsaken me?' (v.1: NIV)

Let's focus on the cross and the resurrection. The two are really one. Without the cross there could have been no resurrection, and without the resurrection the cross would have no real meaning.

The first anchor point the cross gives us is the security it offers whenever we doubt that God loves us.

During a dark moment many years ago I confided in a fellow minister, 'I don't think God really loves me or else he would not have let this happen to me.' He looked surprised and then said somewhat disgustedly, 'If you feel like that then you ought, in all honesty, to resign from the ministry.' I thought it was a cruel and insensitive remark. What he didn't seem to realise was that sometimes, when a storm sweeps in, the turbulence of our emotions affects our rationality. There is nothing to be ashamed of in this. The greatest saints of the ages have experienced it.

Despite his unhelpful words, however, my storm-tossed soul was able to find an anchor point in the cross. It is the one spot in the universe where the love of God can never be doubted. A God who would give his own Son to redeem me, just simply has to be love.

O God, whenever doubts concerning your love come sweeping in, help me see they can all be answered in the cross. There, at Calvary, in the Person of your Son, you died for me. Only love eternal would have done this. Amen.

The first temptation

FOR READING AND MEDITATION – GENESIS 3:1–13
'Now the serpent was more crafty than any of
the wild animals the Lord God had made.' (v.1: NIV)

It was doubt concerning God's love that brought the first sin. To understand the thrust of this temptation you have to hear in Satan's words the insinuation against the love and goodness of God.

What the devil was really saying was: 'If God loved you then he would not have restricted you in the way he has.' There is no anger in the devil's voice, no demonic demonstrations – just a question.

Whenever anything the least bit negative happens in our lives, you can be sure that Satan will pounce on it with glee. 'Ah,' he says, 'surely if God loved you he would have prevented this from happening. Isn't he the strong and all-powerful One? If it was not his might that stopped him intervening then what was it? It must be one thing only – he doesn't really love you.'

Remember Satan's strategy is not to convince you, but to confuse you. He rarely offers arguments; he simply raises questions. Eve allowed a doubt of God to develop into a dislike, and then into disobedience. We cannot stop doubt coming into our hearts, but we can stop it lodging there. The next time Satan tries to get you to doubt God loves you, point to the cross. He has no answer to that!

✒ O God, help me be alert to the wiles and strategies of Satan. May I take in my hands the shield of faith so that I might be able to quench every one of his fiery darts. Teach me how to doubt my doubts and believe my beliefs. In Jesus' Name. Amen.

God's greatest word

FOR READING AND MEDITATION – JOHN 3:1–16

'"For God so loved the world that he gave his one and only Son ..."' (v.16: NIV)

Many years ago, I sat down to prepare a sermon on the theme of God's love. I began to go through the Bible book by book to find references on the theme. You can imagine my surprise when I discovered the first four books of the Bible make no mention of God's love at all. I relaxed when I came to Deuteronomy (sometimes called The John of the Pentateuch), for here are several references to God's eternal love. However, reading through the first three Gospels I was again surprised – there are no clear references to God loving us in Matthew, Mark or Luke. There is an incidental reference to God's love in Luke 6:32–36, but no clear or direct statement. Once again, it is evident from these three books that God loves us, yet the statement is not directly made.

Then in John's Gospel I read the first New-Testament declaration of God's love. It was like a burst of sunlight in the darkness, and it simply overwhelmed my soul.

C.H. Spurgeon once said that if all of the Bible was lost to us except John 3:16, that there is enough divine revelation in this one verse to present the gospel to the whole world.

Gracious Father, it is as if your heart is uncovered in these matchless words of John 3:16. Help me meditate on this thought throughout this day. I would put my heart up against your heart, feel its beat and catch its rhythm. In Jesus' Name I pray. Amen.

The motive behind Calvary

FOR READING AND MEDITATION – JOHN 3:16–21

' "For God so loved the world that he gave his one and only Son . . ." ' (v.16: NIV)

There is more of the gospel packed into these 26 words than in all other literature. I have been preaching and expounding on John 3:16 for over 40 years, and I feel, as did the Queen of Sheba concerning Solomon's Temple: 'The half was not told.'

Tennyson's lines about the flower in the crannied wall come to mind:

> If I could understand
> what you are, root and all, and all in all,
> I should know what God and man is.

The glory of the cross is shown in the motive that lies behind this verse. And that motive 'God so loved . . .'

When you see that the cross is not the cause of God's love, but that God's love is the cause of the cross, then it takes on a new perspective. God does not love us because Jesus died, but Jesus died because God loved us.

We must not leave out the little word 'for'. Read it like this: 'The Son of Man must be lifted up . . . for God so loved the world.' God loved us so much that he gave up his only Son for us. But for the love of God, this lifting up would never have taken place.

✎ *O God, I see and feel that this verse is charged with the new wine of the kingdom. Help me not to sip of it; help me to drink deep draughts of it. In Jesus' Name. Amen.*

You want proof?

FOR READING AND MEDITATION – GALATIANS 2:11–21

'. . . the Son of God . . . loved me and gave himself for me.' (v.20: NIV)

Why, in the light of such a clear unfolding of divine love, should we ever find ourselves doubting it? Perhaps because our souls cry for something more than a verbal revelation of love; we need something vital. We hunger for proof.

One of my favourite forms of study is to read the lives of the saints. Saint Augustine, Saint Bernard, Saint Teresa, and so on. What interests me is that although the ways in which they came to the awareness of God's love differ, the place of revelation was always the cross. And no wonder! For there the heart of God is unveiled.

Saint Teresa, for example, went one day into her private oratory, where she noticed a picture of our Lord being scourged. She had looked at it a hundred times, but in a moment of blinding revelation she saw it as she had never seen it before.

One of her biographers says of her, 'She saw God suffering – suffering for love and suffering for her. It struck her to her knees, sobbing in pain and wonder, and when she arose, she arose a new soul.'

Those who would doubt the love of God need only to draw nigh to Calvary. There the revelation is more than verbal. It is vital. We have the proof.

O God, bring me again to the cross so that I might see love. Hold my sin-dulled gaze there until, in blinding revelation, I see still more of its length and breadth and depth and height. In Jesus' Name I ask it. Amen.

Light in the darkness

FOR READING AND MEDITATION – GENESIS 15:1–19

'When the sun had set . . . a smoking brazier with a blazing torch
appeared and passed between the pieces.' (v.17: NIV)

Abraham found God's promise that his descendants would be as
numerous as the stars somewhat staggering – but nevertheless he
believed. But he asked for some reassurance with promise number
two: 'All this land will be yours.' And a little help was given. Abraham was instructed to take some animals and birds, cut them in
half, and arrange the halves opposite each other.

After doing this, he was engulfed by a great darkness and fell
into a deep sleep. Suddenly, Abraham saw a smoking brazier and a
blazing torch passing between the carcasses. The invisible God had
drawn near to confirm his previous promise and seal his covenant.
He was saying in effect: 'May what has happened to these animals
also happen to me if I do not uphold my word' (Jer. 34:18).

What has all this got to do with the cross? Well, whenever like
Abraham, you are engulfed in the darkness of doubt, and God seems
very far away, remember that the hands that carried the fire pot
and blazing torch 2 000 years earlier, and brought light into the darkness, are the hands that were crucified for you. So when next the
darkness descends, go out to the cross. Stand in awe before the tree
and let all your doubts and hesitancies be extinguished in the
flame of Calvary's love.

*O God, though you have a thousand ways of reassuring me that your
promises are true and that I am the object of your love, no way captures my
heart more than the cross. I shall be eternally grateful. Amen.*

How did you feel, God?

FOR READING AND MEDITATION – ROMANS 8:28–39

'He who did not spare his own Son, but gave him up for us all . . .' (v.32: NIV)

A minister tells of taking his little girl to school the first day. Free of any concern as they drove along, she fell silent as they pulled up at the school gates.

'Daddy, I don't want to get out.' He fought a Herculean urge to say, 'Okay, let's forget it and go home.' 'Darling,' he said, 'I'll go in with you and stay for a while.' Of course, once she was in the classroom she soon forgot that he was there.

As the father walked back to his car, today's verse came into his mind. Reflecting, he prayed, 'Is this how you felt, God? Is what I feel now anything like what you felt when you gave up your Son?' If so, he thought, it explains so much: the proclamation of the angels to the shepherds – a proud Father announcing the birth of his Son. The voice at Jesus' baptism: 'You have represented me to absolute perfection.' And how his heart must have felt when the Saviour cried, 'Father, take this cup away.'

How God felt about his Son going to the cross is only conjecture, but this we know for sure – he gave him up for you and me. What an anchor point this gives us when assailed by doubts. He gave his best for us, says Paul, why then should we doubt his love?

✎ *Father, I see the cross is living proof that you care. Help me cast my anchor at its firm foundations. You provide the anchorage, I must avail myself of its security. Amen.*

The God who is there

FOR READING AND MEDITATION – ISAIAH 44:1–8

' "This is what the Lord says – he who made you,
who formed you in the womb …" ' (v.2: NIV)

The poet Whittier put it beautifully when he wrote:

> *Here in the maddening maze of things,*
> *when tossed by storm and flood,*
> *to one fixed ground my spirit clings,*
> *I know that God is good.*

The cross provides us with that 'fixed ground'. At Calvary we do not just hear that God is love; we see it. We have living proof.

But we must turn now to another problem that assails many of God's people with hurricane force – of whether the great God who sustains the universe has a personal interest in every detail of our lives. I have met many in my time who, while accepting the fact that God loves them, believe that the affairs of their individual lives are too trivial for God's notice. They know they are saved, but they are not convinced that the Almighty takes an interest in every detail of their lives. Are you one who thinks like this? Then come to the cross. I hope to show you that what God did for you on Calvary is convincing proof that he knows you more intimately and more perfectly than you know yourself.

O Father, help me walk through life knowing that your thoughts are ever towards me. Open up your word to me that shows so clearly you are a God whose love runs down to the tiniest details. In Jesus' Name I pray. Amen.

Is anything too trivial?

FOR READING AND MEDITATION – GENESIS 16:1–16

'"You are the God who sees me . . ."' (v.13: NIV)

A godly woman, mother of three missionaries and a member of my church, had a small but difficult problem. I offered to pray with her. 'Oh, there is no need to pray over this; I am sure the Lord doesn't have time to deal with such an insignificant matter.'

I questioned her carefully, and found that her view of God was quite unworthy of him. She thought of God as sitting on the circle of the heavens, wrestling with the great problems of humanity, with no time to give his attention to what she considered was an unimportant and inconsequential matter. I asked her, 'Do you think God knows your name?' Her gaze dropped to the floor and she said, 'I doubt it.' My heart went out to her.

Many go through life with only a vague understanding of God's willingness and readiness to become involved in the smallest details of our lives.

Samuel Chadwick, speaking of the Creator's personal interest in every one of his children, said, 'The divine attention to detail is amazing. Nothing is too trivial for Omniscience. Come straight to God ... lay all questions before him and he will make it plain to you what is his will.'

ꙮ *Father, drive from me all doubts and fears I may have concerning your willingness and readiness to engage your mind with mine. And help me understand that there is no problem or difficulty I may ever have that you will not enter into with me. Amen.*

Admittedly it's hard

FOR READING AND MEDITATION – PSALM 32:1–11

'I will instruct you and teach you . . .
I will counsel you and watch over you.' (v.8: NIV)

Many things make it hard for people to believe in the active care and concern of God in their daily lives. When the astronomer tells us that the nearest star is millions of miles away, and that the total number of stars in the universe is akin to the total number of grains of sand on all the seashores of the world, our minds tend to be terrified. God seems very far away. The bewildering vastness of space makes it seem naive to ask: does God really have a personal interest in me?

We are going through a phase when even some who believe in a personal God see him as somewhat limited and restricted. Rabbi Kushner's book, *When Bad Things Happen to Good People* became a bestseller. Why? Because it presents a view of God as a God who is good and who loves his creation, but is less than omnipotent. This view of God is popular with many of today's theologians.

How does Scripture deal with the issue of whether we can expect the Creator and Sustainer of the universe to notice the needs of individual persons on this microscopic earth? The Lord simply says not to worry, '. . . I will guide you with my eye' (v.8, NKJ).

✎ *Gracious Father, it makes sense that if I am a child of an Eternal Purpose, then your all-seeing eye is going to follow me every step of the way. I see I am in an uncertain age. Help me hold on to this reassuring truth. In Jesus' Name. Amen.*

Why some struggle

FOR READING AND MEDITATION – LUKE 12:22–26

' "Consider the ravens: They do not sow . . . yet God feeds them.
And how much more valuable you are than birds!" ' (v.24)

Neither the vastness of space nor the conclusions of theists can fore-close the discussion. Who made vastness a standard of value? A baby means much more than a mountain; a baby can love. Men and women are more than the stars; men and women can think. As one writer points out, 'Astronomy and geology may conspire to prove the utter insignificance of man, but man is still the astronomer and the geologist.'

And what right do modern-day theologians have to regard their views as higher than Scripture? The Almighty God declares over and over again in his Word, the Bible, that he is a God who takes a loving and active interest in the affairs of every one of his children.

I think the reason why some Christians struggle with the idea of a caring God is because they have built their idea of God too closely on a human model. It is hard to believe he can both sustain the world and take a Father's care of his children. In today's world we think so much in business terms, of leaving the small details to subordinates, and are quietly scornful of the idea that God's care runs down to trivialities. 'Be still,' he says, 'and know that I am God' (Psa. 46:10).

My Father and my God, I am thankful that you have a family and that I am part of that family. Because of this, I have the assurance of my heavenly Father's constant love and care. I am so deeply, deeply grateful. Amen.

Thoughts that never stop

FOR READING AND MEDITATION – PSALM 139:1–24

'How precious to me are your thoughts, O God! . . .
When I awake, I am still with you.' (vv.17–18: NIV)

The Bible is filled with instances of God involving himself in the day-to-day affairs of his people. Think of Abraham's slave seeking Rebekah, of Moses, Samuel and the prophets. Of Philip and the Ethiopian eunuch, or Ananias and Saul, Peter and Cornelius. All these stories are substantially false unless God's care and guidance runs down to trivialities. All through the ages, men and women have claimed that God came to them and involved himself in the details of their lives. The psalmist exults that God knows everything about him, and that the Almighty's thoughts are always toward him.

Some years ago, I found myself talking for quite a while to a young girl who, every so often, looked at her watch, closed her eyes and went quiet for about 30 seconds. The third time she did it I asked her if there was anything wrong. 'Oh no', she said, 'but my boyfriend and I have this pact. On the half hour we stop what we are doing and think about each other.' 'How odd,' I thought, but as I considered the matter I changed my mind and thought, 'How romantic.' According to our text for today, God does not think about us on the hour or on the half hour – his thoughts are continually towards us. Hallelujah!

✎ O Father, what joy fills my soul as I reflect on how continuously your thoughts are toward me. There is never a moment when you do not think of me. And all your thoughts are good. Thank you, my Father. Amen.

Graven hands!

FOR READING AND MEDITATION – ISAIAH 49:8–18
'"See, I have engraved you on the palms of my hands;
your walls are ever before me."' (v.16: NIV)

Isaiah was prophesying that the time would come when the city of Jerusalem would be a mass of mouldering decay. Ransacked by the Babylonians, several decades of neglect would result in the sad sight Isaiah saw in his vision. The walls were flat, but yet God, speaking through the prophet, says, 'Your walls are ever before me.'

What did he mean? There were no walls. The walls were a memory of the past, or a dream of the future. But God saw them. God declares he cannot forget his people, because he has graven them on the palms of his hands. They are indelibly marked where they cannot be overlooked. God's chosen people need never fear that the Almighty will forget them.

Leap centuries and see the fulfilment of the prophet's word. On the summit of a hill called Skull, Roman soldiers take the Son of God, condemned to death by the religious rulers. They spread his hands across a roughly hewn cross, and fasten them to the beams with nails.

Because of this, you can never be forgotten, never be overlooked. Let it stagger you if you will … you are graven on the palms of his hands.

❧ *Lord Jesus Christ, I see now what all this means – because of Calvary I can never be forgotten by you. You are as much aware of me as you are the wounds in the palms of your hands. Blessed be your wondrous Name forever. Amen.*

Those blessed wounds!

FOR READING AND MEDITATION – JOHN 20:24–31

' . . . Jesus came and stood among them and said, "Peace be with you!" ' (v.26: NIV)

Slip into the Upper Room with the frightened disciples, meeting behind closed doors for fear of the Jews. Presently, another figure appears in their midst. At the end of a brief conversation with Thomas, he says, 'Put your finger here,' at the same time spreading forth his hands. 'See my hands . . . stop doubting and believe.'

Oh those blessed wound prints, the most precious evidence of everlasting love and care. He has graven you upon the palms of his hands. The Great God who sustains the universe thinks continually of you. The Almighty can never forget you or overlook you. It's just not possible. So when next the hurricane of unbelief comes crashing into your life and you find it so hard to believe you are of any consequence in heaven because you are of such little consequence on earth, throw your anchor into the dark depths that surround the cross. You will find a firm anchor point for your soul.

The Lord of life watches over you. God made you, and his tender mercy is over all his works.

See where before the throne he stands
and pours the all prevailing prayer,
points to his side, and lifts his hands
and shows that you are graven there.

✎ *Gracious loving and redeeming God, help me never to forget that when I feel overlooked or forgotten by you, it is an illusion. I can never be forgotten by you. For I am graven in the palms of your hands. Thank you, my Father. Amen.*

All can fall

FOR READING AND MEDITATION – PSALM 130:1–8

'But with you there is forgiveness; therefore you are feared.' (v.4: NIV)

We look now at the third anchor point at Calvary – that when we do fall into sin, forgiveness is to be found at the cross. Preaching one day I said, 'All of us stumble and fall into sin at times.' One of the elders came to me at the close of the service and urged me never to use that phrase again.

'There are some of us in this church,' he said, 'who haven't sinned in years, and we find it an affront when you give others a different impression.'

I felt deeply sorry for the man. There were clear evidences of pride at work in his life, of which he was seemingly unaware. Gently, I drew his attention to it, giving instances of how and where it surfaced. I fully expected his resignation, but he flung his arms around me, and wept on my shoulder for half an hour.

So I say again; all of us stumble and fall into sin at times.

Sometimes others may not know about it, sometimes (if it is attitudinal) we may not know about it. But always – God knows about it. That is why, as the old saying goes, it does not behove the best of us to look askance at the worst of us.

O God, help me face, as this man did, the truth that unacknowledged sins may be lurking in my heart. It is only in your light that I can see light. I draw near to you so that I might be fully cleansed and made fully whole. In Jesus' Name. Amen.

Too broad a category

FOR READING AND MEDITATION – 1 JOHN 1:1–10
'If we claim to be without sin, we deceive ourselves
and the truth is not in us.' (v.8: NIV)

want to pick up on the thought I touched on yesterday, namely that
all of us stumble and fall into sin at times. Many see themselves at
a place in the Christian life where it is not possible to sin. I do
believe we can develop a relationship with God whereby we find it
possible not to sin; but I do not believe we can ever reach a stage in
our Christian lives here on earth where it is not possible to sin.

Those who claim to live lives free from sin usually have very
broad categories for evil: adultery, stealing, fornication, lying, de-
frauding, blaspheming – things easily be seen and identified.

If we define sin as narrowly as this, then of course it is possible to go for years without sin.

But sin is subtle as well as obvious, and if we do not understand this we can fool ourselves that all is well when it is not.

A statement I once read that impressed me deeply is this: 'There
is only one sin – the sin of making ourselves God – all the rest are
sins.' I will come back to this tomorrow, but for today, let that intriguing thought lie upon your mind. And resist the temptation to
turn the page.

*O God, I would enter a life of complete frankness and open honesty. I want
to live with no hidden closed caverns in the depths of me. I long so much to
be 'a child of light'. Help me, dear Father. In Jesus' Name. Amen.*

The law of love

FOR READING AND MEDITATION – JOHN 13:31–38
'"Love one another. As I have loved you,
so you must love one another."' (v.34: NIV)

The sin from which all other sins devolve is self-centredness. And
not just self-centredness in itself, for even non-Christian philosophers condemn self-centredness as detrimental to effective living.
The real sin is that by being self-centred, we keep God out of the
part he reserves for himself – the centre of our being.

One of my concerns with modern-day Christianity is that we
define sin too narrowly. We look for the obvious things and then
because we do not see those things at work in our lives, say, 'I am
free from sin.'

I argue that the purpose of living is to reflect the ethos of the
Trinity in the way that each person relates to the others in glorious
other-centredness. This is a category of living we don't hear much
about in our churches.

Would you say that whenever we violate the law of love, identified so clearly in this Scripture, we are committing sin? I would.
We might shun the obvious sins, but then go on to violate the law
of love with impunity. When I look at my life and think of it in terms
of the broad categories of sin, there is not much that is wrong. But
when I see how very often I fail to love as I am loved, my heart is
ashamed – and I have to repent.

✎ *Lord Jesus Christ, you who modelled what it is like to love as you were
loved, teach me to do the same. And when I fail, help me recognise my failure and lean upon you in deeper dependency. Amen.*

Self-deception

FOR READING AND MEDITATION – 2 SAMUEL 12:1–10

'Then Nathan said to David, "You are the man!"' (v.7: NIV)

he reason I wish to expose the subtle nature of sin is that we might
more wonderfully enjoy the completeness of God's salvation, particularly the joy of a full and free forgiveness.

My concern is that we might know just what kind of sins go on
in our hearts so that we can bring them out, repent of them, and
experience the gift of God's forgiveness.

How easy it is to deceive ourselves that there is no sin in our
being when there is. It is not hard to understand how this happens.
A defence mechanism called 'denial' goes to work to help us ward
off any discomfort or anxiety in our soul, and we go deeper and
deeper into deception.

This is what happened to David. His sins were blatant and obvious. Lust, adultery, treachery and murder. If the 'man after God's
own heart' could allow himself to be so self-deceived about such
obvious sins as adultery and murder, how careful we ought to be
about the more subtle sins of self-centredness, pride, and so on.

Self-deception is dangerous. It can keep us feeling spiritual,
while at the same time choking the life out of our soul.

*O God, If I am self-deceived, help me I pray, for I want to be free of every-
thing that would rob me of your presence and power. Time is short, and living for you is too precious to have it hindered by sin. Make me every whit
whole. Amen.*

What became of sin?

FOR READING AND MEDITATION – PSALM 51:1–19

'For I know my transgressions, and my sin is always before me.' (v.3: NIV)

The reluctance to face up to the gravity of sin has led to the omission of the word from contemporary literature.

Karl Menninger, a well-known American psychiatrist, drew attention to the fact that in today's world, 'one misses any mention of "sin". It was a word once in everyone's mind, but it is now rarely if ever heard. Does that mean,' he asks, 'that no sin is involved in our troubles? Has no one committed any sins? Where indeed did sin go? Whatever became of sin?'

He goes on to look at some of the reasons for 'sin's disappearance. Some things we used to call sin, which were dealt with by the church through confession and forgiveness have now become crime and are handled by the world. Other sins have been redefined in terms of sicknesses, or symptoms, so that punishment is replaced by treatment. 'Collective irresponsibility' enables us to transfer the blame for deviant behaviour from ourselves to society as a whole.

To ignore the reality of sin is dishonest. To tamper with the label and call a serious thing by a light name is utter foolishness. We don't make a deadly thing innocuous by giving it a different name. Poison is still poison – no matter what other label we give it.

O God my Father, I see the folly of minimising sin. Give me a balanced sensitivity to this whole issue so that I might see the seriousness of sin and thus enter more joyously into the freedom of forgiveness. In Jesus' Name. Amen.

The divine anchorage

24 MARCH

Accept with gratitude

FOR READING AND MEDITATION – LUKE 7:36–50

' "Therefore, I tell you, her many sins have been forgiven –
for she loved much." ' (v.47: NIV)

How little we make of forgiveness, generally speaking, in the Christian church. Emil Brunner says, 'Forgiveness is the very opposite of anything which can be taken for granted. Nothing is less obvious than forgiveness.' The more we consider how sin offends the heart of God, the more it is a mystery how he could ever forgive us. He does, through the blood of the cross. We put a lot of emphasis on encouragement, exhortation, enlightenment, and so on, but very little prominence is given to the message of forgiveness.

Yet the essential focus is that the atonement is the foundation of our lives. Life that is built on the atonement, on the wonder of the fact that, despite the enormity and gravity of our sin, God has found a way to forgive us.

The reason I have focused on sin over the past few days is to prepare you to receive an even greater revelation and appreciation of the wonder of forgiveness.

For you see, we will never understand the depth of forgiveness, until we perceive the horror and ugliness for which we are forgiven. If we do not understand that, then our gratitude will be no greater than the tip we leave for a waiter who has served us a good meal.

O God, I feel sad that so often I take your forgiveness for granted, rather than accepting it with gratitude. Help me see just what I have been saved from and saved to – and in viewing the contrast come to an even greater appreciation of my salvation. Amen.

Pardon and power

FOR READING AND MEDITATION – PSALM 86:1–17
'You are forgiving and good, O Lord,
abounding in love to all who call to you.' (v.5: NIV)

What do we do when we find ourselves facing the surging tides of sin, and we are aware that there are things within us that can cause us spiritual shipwreck? We drop our anchor at the cross. There is forgiveness to be found at Calvary's tree.

'He is faithful and just and will forgive us our sins' (1 John 1:9).

This does not mean, however, that because God forgives, you can sin with impunity. If you are a true Christian, there is something in you that wants not to sin. But if and when you do, then make your way at once to Jesus, repent of your sin and claim his full and free forgiveness. A Christian can fall into sin, but does not want to belong to sin.

As a minister prayed with a drunk, he began to sob and said, 'I know I'm in the gutter. But oh! . . . I don't belong there, do I?' The minister put his arm around him and said, 'No, you don't; you belong to God.'

Remember that the next time you fall into sin. You don't belong there. You belong to God. Hurry always to the cross with your sins. Pray not only for pardon, but also for power – the power not to make the same mistake again.

✒ *My Father and my God, how can I ever thank you sufficiently for providing for me the way of forgiveness. Although it is free, it is not without cost. It cost you the pain I need never know – the pain of hell. I am so deeply deeply grateful. Amen.*

Stoicism is not the way

FOR READING AND MEDITATION – 1 CORINTHIANS 12:12–26

'If one part suffers, every part suffers with it . . .' (v.26: NIV)

Just recently, I heard of an American financier, a multi-millionaire, before whom the strongest of men quailed. His frown could cow the most ferocious, and his eye was awful in anger. Yet when his wife died after no more than six months of marriage, this hard, metallic man became distraught and cried out for comfort.

Sooner or later, everyone faces the need for comfort and consolation. When that hour comes, where will we turn? Christians turn to the cross, to the Christ of the cross. I make no apology, therefore, for turning your gaze once again in the direction of Calvary.

The Stoics – those who believe you must stand up to whatever comes without allowing yourself to feel pleasure or pain – claimed that their creed was the only one that can get you safely through life.

Their ideas were summed up by the poet Whitman, who said, 'Under the bludgeoning of chance … my head is bloody but unbowed.' It is a noble attitude – noble, but very lacking. The Stoics feared that unless you shut out love and pity, the world of grief and sorrow would troop in behind.

But if you are a harsh, insensitive person, you are an inadequate person.

Father, steeling myself against life is not the way. I become less of a person by doing so. I want to respond to whatever comes, in the way your Son responded to it. For his dear Name's sake. Amen.

Three worldviews

FOR READING AND MEDITATION – JOHN 6:60–71

' "Lord, to whom shall we go? You have the words of eternal life." ' (v.68: NIV)

What are the attitudes of some of the non-Christian religions towards unmerited sorrow and suffering?

Buddhism's philosophy is this: as long as you are in life, you are in sorrow. You must cut the root of desire, even for life, and then you go into the actionless, passionless state called *Nirvana* – the state, literally, of the snuffed-out candle. Buddhism (in my opinion) probably has the most negative teaching about life that has ever been formulated.

Hindus take the attitude that there is no such thing as unmerited sorrow or suffering. Whatever is, is just. If you are suffering now it is because you have been sinful in a previous existence. A Hindu said to a missionary, 'Jesus must have been a terrible sinner in a previous birth because he suffered so terribly in this one.'

The Muslim attitude is this – whatever happens is the will of God, and we must accept it as the will of God. On the surface, the message looks like the Christian one, but when you probe, you find that Muslims believe both good and evil are the will of God. 'This concept,' says one Christian commentator, 'is as stifling and stunting as it is static.'

None of these philosophies has solid anchor points to which life can be fastened in a storm. They are not the way.

✎ *O Father, sometimes it is only when I put my faith up against others that I can see its supremacy and superiority. So I say with Simon Peter: 'Lord to whom can we go? You have the words of eternal life.' Amen.*

Why Jesus came

FOR READING AND MEDITATION – JOHN 12:20–36
'"Now is the time for judgment on this world;
now the prince of this world will be driven out."' (v.31: NIV)

Jesus accepted the fact of human suffering. He neither explained it nor explained it away. Christ's purpose in coming to this world was not primarily to explain things, but to spell out the 'good news' – that in him we can find life and power to surmount all obstacles.

The gospel may not explain, but it most certainly brings about change – a change of heart and a change of mind. Jesus transforms suffering by using it. He shows us that victims can become victors, tests can be turned into testimonies.

I once heard a preacher say, 'If you come to Christ you will never have any more problems.' I thought of the early Christians, who were in constant trouble, and also of the many Christians I know who are going through the most heartbreaking situations.

It is not right to say to a non-Christian, 'If you come to Jesus you will never have any problems.' But it is right to say, 'If you come to Christ you will find new strength to overcome your problems.' Sometimes people who become Christians have more problems to face than they had before – just because they are Christians. Personally, I would rather face all kinds of problems providing I have Jesus, than have no problems and be without him.

Father, I'll have to change my vocabulary, for quietly I am changing my attitudes. The things I thought might be stumbling blocks I am now seeing as stepping stones. Difficulties are really doors. How wonderful. Teach me more. Amen.

The divine anchorage

Watch the lights!

FOR READING AND MEDITATION – MATTHEW 5:33–48

' "He causes his sun to rise on the evil and the good,
and sends rain on the righteous and the unrighteous." ' (v.45: NIV)

Have you ever thought what would happen if a Christian never ha
to face sorrow or suffering again? What would happen to the uni
verse? It would soon become chaotic and undependable. In the rea
world, the law of the universe is not going to ask if a man or woma
is a Christian or not; it goes to work irrespective of these consider
ations. The world is a hard school, and it helps to know the rules

Suppose Christians were kept from getting knocked over by
car whenever they rushed into a busy street. What would happer
Christians would become champion jaywalkers! And they woul
lose the quickness of decision which comes from coping with
world of changing circumstances.

I will never forget what a policeman told me when I was a littl
boy living in the city of Birmingham. As I ignored the traffic light
and rushed across the road, he said, 'Son, if you want to live long
keep your eye on the lights.' It was good advice and I have neve
forgotten it.

The New Testament does not teach that because we are Chris
tians we will be exempt from sorrow and suffering. It does teach
however, that God will be in the sorrow and suffering, to enable us t
turn it to good account. Everything furthers those who follow Chris

✎ *Father, I know it makes sense, but I confess there is still something in m
that would wish to avoid all sorrow and suffering. There is a lesson I need t
learn here. Help me not to miss it. Amen.*

Can God heal?

FOR READING AND MEDITATION – JAMES 5:7–19

'Is any one of you sick? He should call the elders of the church ...' (v.14: NIV)

God can and does intervene to deliver us from physical sickness and suffering, but it is more the exception than the rule. Not everyone who asks for healing gets healed; that is a simple empirical fact.

Healing evangelists get a bad press nowadays – and some not without good reason – but the honest ones will tell you less than ten per cent of the people who are prayed for receive healing. Does this mean we ought to forget the whole business of praying for people who are sick? No, for we must not measure the results of our prayers only by what we see.

There may be no apparent or immediate physical changes, but who can measure the spiritual changes that come from prayer? Who can see what mighty things God does in the soul of a person when he or she is prayed for, or what goes on in the inner being of those who are the subjects of the laying on of hands?

It is right to ask for deliverance and healing for those who are afflicted, but let us not limit our asking to physical changes only. The soul and the body are inextricably linked, and when we do not see evidences in the body, who is to say something powerful has not happened in the soul?

O Father, give me a balanced view on this perplexing subject of healing. Help me see that all prayer is answered. You say, 'Yes', 'No,' 'Wait,' or 'Here's something different.' Teach me how to accept your answer – without quibbling. In Jesus' Name. Amen.

The cost to God

FOR READING AND MEDITATION – MATTHEW 16:21–28

'"... whoever loses his life for me will find it."' (v.25: NIV)

At creation, God went ahead and designed a world in which there was the possibility of sin and suffering. He could have avoided this by making human beings like puppets, but he chose to create us as moral beings capable of good and evil.

Human parents bring into the world a child upon whom they can lavish their love. In so doing they run a great risk of having a child who might break their hearts. Yet they assume the task – for love's sake.

So God, the Divine Parent, took the same risk in creating us, for there was the possibility we too might break his heart. We did – the cross proves it. At creation he assumed a responsibility for us, and at the cross he discharged it. Only on that basis could he have created us.

Stand before the cross. There God takes on himself all our sin, our sorrow and our suffering, and says, 'I will bear it too.' A God who set himself apart from the pain of the world, would be a God self-centred and miserable.

But the God who would know the joy of a cross, would be a God who would know the deepest joy of the universe – the joy of saving others at cost to oneself.

✎ *My heart is humbled to think that you obey the very law you set for us – the law of self-giving, of going down into death in order to save. May your grace toward me make me more gracious to others. Amen.*

A God with wounds

FOR READING AND MEDITATION – 1 PETER 5:1–11

'. . . I appeal as . . . a witness of Christ's sufferings . . .' (v.1: NIV)

There is no full and satisfying answer to the issue of unmerited sorrow and suffering. C.S. Lewis says, 'We are big enough to ask questions of the universe but not big enough to understand the answers.'

Christians are people who take God on trust and, when lashed by the tempests, we cast our anchors at the cross, and there we find the security we need to ride out the storm.

Even if we cannot understand why God allowed suffering to enter his universe, this we can understand – he bears such suffering himself. Edward Shillito in his poem *Jesus of the Scars*, says:

> *The other gods were strong, but thou becamest weak,*
> *they rode but thou didst stagger to a throne.*
> *but to our wounds only God's wounds can speak,*
> *and not a god has wounds, but thou alone.*

No other God could speak to my condition, for no other God has been there. This is why the cross provides such a sure anchor point – it holds me fast to a God who was willing to suffer for me. A thorn-crowned Man – his pains healing ours, his wounds answering our wounds, his love taking our sin. A God who suffers, a God who cares.

✎ O God, you have the marks of a cross upon you. And those marks are not mere scars – they are the sacraments of your love. Through them I see deeper into the mystery of your heart. And what I see there fires my soul. Thank you my Father. Amen.

Secure against failure

FOR READING AND MEDITATION – 2 CORINTHIANS 6:1–13

'... dying, and yet we live on; beaten, and yet not killed;
sorrowful, yet always rejoicing ...' (vv.9–10: NIV)

The cross provides an anchor point to hold us fast whenever we are tossed about by failure. In human terms the cross seems an unmitigated failure and disaster. Yet when seen from its correct perspective, it was the greatest triumph of the universe.

We need to be reconciled to the fact that failure is one of life's most certain experiences. The first time we tried to walk – we failed. The first time we tried to form a word on our lips – we failed. The first time we tried to drink a glass of milk on our own – we failed.

And failure doesn't stop when we pass from being children to adults. Did you pass your driving test the first time you took it? If you were one of the failures, I imagine no one pointed a finger at you and said, 'You must be a pretty worthless person if you failed your driving test the first time.'

Thomas Edison, inventor of the light bulb, tried endless experiments before finding success. He was told, 'All these thousands of attempts and you haven't learned a thing.' 'Wrong,' said Edison, 'I have learned thousands of ways of how not to do it.' From failure comes experience, from experience comes wisdom, from wisdom comes mutual trust, from mutual trust co-operation, from co-operation united effort, and from united effort – success.

✎ *Heavenly Father, help me put this whole matter of failure into a spiritual perspective for I see that if I don't, my peace may break into pieces. I may fail, but show me how to avoid being shipwrecked by it. In Jesus' Name. Amen.*

You are not a failure

'... that you may know ... the riches of his glorious inheritance ...
and his incomparably great power for us ...' (vv.18–19: NIV)

Thomas Edison did not regard those unsuccessful attempts as futility; on the contrary, he learned from them. 'Failure,' said Edison, talking to his students, 'is the line of least persistence. More people fail through lack of persistence than lack of talent.'

We need to keep in mind that failure does not in any way diminish our personal worth. Failure hurts not just because of the failure itself, but because of what we tell ourselves about the failure. Inside the heads of those devastated and destroyed by failure will be this kind of self-talk, 'I have failed ... and because of that I must be a worthless person.'

Look at the illogicality of that statement, 'I have failed ... (true) and because of that I must be a worthless person (untrue).' The deep emotional upset we feel whenever we have failed comes not from the failure itself, but from what we tell ourselves about the failure. And when we tell ourselves untruths – and believe them – we set ourselves up for experiencing some pretty devastating feelings.

To have failed does not mean that you are a failure. It has nothing to do with your worth as a person. God loves who you are no matter how much or how often you fail. Don't ever forget that.

✎ O God, I see that my greatest failures are my failures to put things in the right perspective. Drive this truth deeply into my spirit that failing does not mean I am a failure. Thank you, my Father. Amen.

A hole in the ground

FOR READING AND MEDITATION – MATTHEW 25:14–30

' "So I was afraid and went out and hid your talent in the ground." ' (v.25: NIV)

No discussion about failure is complete without referring to the fear of failure. Some people will not start the Christian life for fear they would fail. Burying your talent ends in emptiness and futility – a hole in the ground. Living the Christian life involves more than personal responsibility, but response to his ability.

Sometimes fear produces the very failure we fear. Fear feeds on failure, and failure feeds on fear. To overcome this fear of failure hold these truths firmly in your mind:

1. Decide if the objective you are aiming for is what God wants you to be involved in. If not, drop it. If it is, go forward, trusting in him.
2. Realise that although God cannot fail, we sometimes fail to avail ourselves of the resources found in him. When I have failed, the failure was not his, but mine. He was there all the time; I just didn't lean on him in the way that I should.
3. Consider the worst that might happen if you did fail. Can Christ hold you in such a situation? The answer, of course, is 'Yes.'

If failure comes, not only can Christ hold you in that situation, he can enable you to learn from that situation in ways that will increase your effectiveness in the future. So as a Christian – either way you win!

✎ O God, help me to face the question today of whether I may not be multiplying the talents you have given me because I am afraid to fail. May my faith in you drive out every fear. In Jesus' Name I pray. Amen.

Thank you, failure

FOR READING AND MEDITATION – PSALM 10:1–14

'But, you, O God, do see trouble and grief;
you consider it to take it to hand.' (v.14: NIV)

Sometimes failure teaches us more than success. Carl Jung said, 'The counsellor learns little from his successes; they merely confirm him in his mistakes. His failures, on the other hand, are priceless experiences in that they not only open up the way to a deeper truth, but force him to change his views and methods.' When I quote this statement, counsellors in training often confess to being puzzled.

When we appear to be successful we keep going. We feel good, our ego is stroked, people are pleased with us, and life stays on an even keel. But we may not be as successful as we think. Underneath our successes there may be fatal flaws, and if we never discover them, we make no changes.

So it is that we learn more from failure than success.

When I am in a reflective mood, I look back at my own life and see how many of the things I did, although they looked like 'successes', were deeply flawed. Had my life not been balanced with so many failures, I might have continued following my 'successes', and missed some important new spiritual directions. So I say with all my heart – and I am sure you can say the same too – 'Thank you failure; you have been used by God to lead me into a new way.'

✍ *Father, I see that I ought to be grateful for some of the failures you have allowed to happen in my life. I dread to think where I might be were your guiding hand not at work. Thank you, dear Father. Amen.*

Failure – a comma

FOR READING AND MEDITATION – MATTHEW 26:47–56

'"But this has all taken place that the writings of
the prophets might be fulfilled."' (v.56: NIV)

How did Jesus feel the night one of his disciples betrayed him and
the rest abandoned him? Remember he had almost three and a half
years of his time and teaching invested in this small group of men.

Note how Jesus responded to the betrayal by Judas. 'When he
was gone, Jesus said, "Now is the Son of Man glorified ..."' (John
13:30–31). On the surface it looked like he had failed. Yet at that
very moment of failure Jesus says, 'Now is the Son of Man glorified.'

I think the word *now* is very important here. Jesus does not
say 'soon', or 'later', but 'now'. At the precise moment the storm was
about to unleash itself upon him, our Lord dropped his own personal anchor into the reassuring depths of his Father's sovereignty
and love. Betrayal looked like failure, yet Jesus knew a great purpose was being wrought and so he turned the whole thing from
failure to success.

This also applies to the other disciples. They fled in the hour of
his need, and it looked as though the lessons he had taught them
had not gone very deep. Had he failed? Seemingly so. But Pentecost
shows not failure, but fruitfulness. The failure was simply a comma,
not a full stop.

✎ *O Father, help me to see my own failures in this same light – not as a full
stop but a comma. And give me the same attitude as Jesus had, to see that
all things – even failure – can serve. Amen.*

Cosmic optimism

FOR READING AND MEDITATION – COLOSSIANS 1:1–14

'. . . the faith and love that spring from
the hope that is stored up for you in heaven . . .' (v.5: NIV)

The divine anchorage

'Christianity,' said someone, 'is cosmic optimism. It enables us to look out at the universe through optimistic eyes.' I am convinced the Christian is the only one with a buoyant hope and an open door. Christians may be poor material in themselves, but they know they have got hold of ultimate reality in Jesus Christ.

There are failures among Christians, and among sincere Christians too. Not because Christ is a failure, but because we fail to follow his guidance or lay an appropriating hand on eternal resources.

A missionary tells how a vine had reached its delicate fingers up and across a space until it grasped the branch of a pine tree. Then came a storm. The morning after, he saw the vine was a poor drooping thing – the branch was broken in the storm. It was rotten. Many Christians are like that; they fasten themselves on to dead branches, instead of on to Christ. The storm comes and they go down, along with the dead branch.

Where people have held on to Christ the ultimate reality, they have survived the storm of failure. They have even toughened beneath the adversity. When failure comes, it can cause us to cling more firmly to Christ. No failure is failure if it succeeds in driving us to cling more closely to him.

Lord Jesus Christ, you are the one steady place amid a world of difficulties and storms. You will never let me down. Help me to catch your dependableness so that people looking to me for support may not be let down. Amen.

The true victory

FOR READING AND MEDITATION – 1 CORINTHIANS 15:50–58

'But thanks be to God! He gives us the victory
through our Lord Jesus Christ.' (v.57: NIV)

'The most influential person who ever lived on our planet was Jesus of Nazareth and he died an apparent failure.'

Our Lord's death on the cross may have looked like failure, but actually it was a most glorious success. Because of what Christ did on the cross, we are secure. The same one who took the darkness of the world's sin, and brought forth the light of the gospel, is able to take every failure of our lives and make it work in some way for good.

If the gale of failure is threatening to drive your frail ship onto the rocks of despair, drop your anchor at the cross. God has chiselled a ledge in the bedrock of the universe, just for you.

Face the fact that you may fail: but perhaps God, through the failure, is stripping you of everything, that he may give to you Everything. Don't take your eyes off the cross. It was there that God showed his ultimate power. He overcame evil with good and hate by love. He turned what looked like an abysmal failure to a most marvellous victory.

He may not save you from failure, but he will save you in it. You will be the victory. Then although you may never preach a sermon, you can be one.

✎ *Lord Jesus Christ, I see that everything I have is safe in you – even my failures. You turn failure into fruitfulness – fruitfulness in me. I need be afraid of nothing for I can use everything. I am so very thankful. Amen.*

A universal fear

FOR READING AND MEDITATION – 1 CORINTHIANS 3:10–23

'All things are yours, whether . . . life or death . . .
all are yours . . . ' (vv. 21–22: NIV)

The cross provides an anchor point enabling us to remain steady and secure in the face of death. Unless Christ physically returns to take us to be with himself, everyone will one day die.

As George Bernard Shaw once said, 'The statistics concerning death are quite impressive; one person in one will die.'

Did you know why Mahatma Ghandi started his Swaraj movement in India? 'My aim,' he said, 'was the abandonment of the fear of death. So long as we let ourselves be influenced by the fear of death, we can never attain to freedom. We are not yet completely free because we are not prepared to look death quietly in the face.'

William Cory, a minor poet at the beginning of the century, confessed that the fear of death never left him. One day, in a room where a caged canary was bursting with song, he said, 'Yes he's happy; that's because he does not know that he will die.'

As we pause between Good Friday and Easter Sunday, how wonderful it is to know that because of what Christ did on the cross and later in the resurrection, no Christian need ever be intimidated by death. It is death that has died, not he.

✎ O deathless Christ, alive for evermore, why should I be afraid of death? In you is life, and as I am in you, I too shall never die. Help me see death as it really is – a mere transition, a veranda that opens up to the house with many rooms. Amen.

Thirty-three forever!

FOR READING AND MEDITATION – JOHN 20:1–17
'They still did not understand from Scripture that
Jesus had risen from the dead.' (v:9: NIV)

How wonderful it is that we have not only a Good Friday in the Christian calendar, but also an Easter Sunday. The one without the other would render the Christian message meaningless.

During the Battle of Hastings in 1066, the news spread that the intrepid leader, William the Conqueror, was dead. As soon as William himself heard it he rode up and down among the ranks shouting, 'I'm alive! I'm alive! I'm alive!'

What a gripping and graphic picture this is of what an infinitely greater Conqueror did on that first Easter Day.

Following our Lord's execution on Good Friday, the news spread throughout the ranks of his disciples that the one they had followed was dead. But on Easter Sunday, he burst through the bars of death and announced to his disciples, 'I'm alive! I'm alive!' Don't believe, I beg you, that Christ rose from the dead spiritually and not physically. If Christ's resurrection was only a spiritual one, then only the spiritual is redeemed. The material world is left out of redemption – a part of the incarnation but not the resurrection.

Of course, our Lord had a different body when he came out of the tomb than when he went in, but it was a physical body nevertheless. Thirty-three forever!

O risen Lord, let us hear your voice as we have never heard it before, shouting, 'I'm alive! I'm alive! I'm alive!' And because you live, I live also. Hallelujah! Amen.

Love like a river

FOR READING AND MEDITATION – JOHN 20:19–23

'. . . Jesus came and stood among them and said, "Peace be with you!"' (v.19: NIV)

Picture the Upper Room following our Lord's resurrection. Prior to his arrival on the scene, the disciples were frightened, confused and bewildered. Their most courageous act, so it seems, was to lock the door. I can picture them trying to avoid each other's gaze as they reflected on the news that the Master was alive. All must have looked within themselves.

As Max Lucado writes, 'Nagging their memories were the promises they had not kept. When the Roman soldiers took Jesus, Jesus' followers took off. With the very wine of the covenant on their breath and the bread of his sacrifice in their stomachs, they fled.'

Suddenly, they hear a voice: 'Peace be with you!' What would he say to them? Would he berate them for their disloyalty and unbelief? Would he turn on them and lash them with a where-were-you-when-I-needed-you kind of speech? No. He simply lavished upon them his love.

It was that, I think, which unlocked the doors of their hearts. He looked into the eyes of his betrayers and instead of denouncing them – he encouraged them. This is the kind of love that burns in our Saviour's heart – a love that never diminishes, even when unreciprocated.

O my Saviour, when I remember the many times your love has gone unreciprocated in me, my heart is ashamed. Yet you go on loving me. How can it be? Help me, I pray, to be more open and responsive to your love. For your own dear Name's sake. Amen.

Freedom from fear

FOR READING AND MEDITATION – HEBREWS 2:10–18

'. . . and free those who all their lives were held in
slavery by their fear of death.' (v.15: NIV)

What are the main elements that underlie a great fear of death? My
study of the issue revealed three things:

First, the physical fact of dying.

Second, the fear of finality.

Third, the fear of judgment.

Take first the physical fact of dying. People say, 'I fear the pain
that may accompany my dying.' But doctors are convinced that, with
some exceptions, what is called 'the agony of death' is felt much more
by the bedside watchers than by the one who is passing over.

Take also the fear of finality, the dreadful thought that death is
indeed the end and there is nothing beyond. For a Christian, of
course, this fear has been laid to rest in the resurrection of our Lord.

The last element in the fear of death is the fear of judgment.
This is not as common in our day as it was even 30 or 40 years ago,
as the theme of judgment to come is not frequently heard in most
modern-day pulpits.

But no one who knows Christ need fear judgment. He is our
Saviour, our Surety, our Physician, our Life-giver, our Redeemer
and our Friend. Too good to be true? Too good not to be true!

*O Living Christ, I am grateful that you are not a road with a dead end;
you are the living way. Take from my heart right now all unhealthy fear. Remind me again that through Calvary and the resurrection it was death that
died, not you. Amen.*

Jesus is the resurrection

FOR READING AND MEDITATION – 2 CORINTHIANS 5:1–10

'. . . as long as we are at home in the body
we are away from the Lord.' (v.6: NIV)

When the famous agnostic Robert Ingersoll died, the order of funeral service gave this solemn instruction, 'There will be no singing.'

Not like the funeral of John Wright, a member of our staff whose face shone with the love of Jesus. We grieved, but we also sang. Why? Because the Scripture says: 'We do not ... grieve like the rest of men, who have no hope' (1 Thess. 4:13).

Some Christians think we should never grieve: others believe we should never sing. There is a place for both. We grieve for the loss, and it is right to feel sorrow. But we know that the soul of a Christian goes to be with the Lord, so we sing.

A funeral director said, 'I have noticed that Christianity seems to make a great difference in death. Christian people seem to know how to take it better.'

When Martha met with Jesus following the death of her brother, Lazarus, Jesus said something quite astonishing: 'I am the resurrection and the life' (John 11:25). But Jesus had not yet died and been resurrected. How could he say that? Well, you see, Jesus is not the resurrection because he rose from the dead; he rose from the dead because he is the resurrection. Does death have the last word with Jesus? Not on your life!

✒ *O Father, how clear it all is now – death is just the gateway to a fuller life. It is the pause in which you change my body from a mortal to an immortal one. Blessed be your wondrous Name forever. Amen.*

Many infallible proofs

FOR READING AND MEDITATION – ACTS 1:1–11

'. . . he showed himself to these men and gave many
convincing proofs that he was alive.' (v.3: NIV)

How do we know Jesus Christ rose from the dead? The word *convincing* – *tekmerion* in the original Greek – is used nowhere else in the New Testament, and means 'infallible'. What are some of the infallible proofs that leave us in no doubt that Jesus Christ rose again from the dead?

The first is the empty tomb. Some said the disciples had snatched Jesus' dead body from out of the tomb, and were only pretending that he was alive. Well, a hoax does not evoke hallelujahs, nor does body-snatching produce transformed lives. Like produces like.

The second is the fact of the Christian church. D. L. Moody, the famous American preacher, wrote, 'The church of Christ is not a monument to a dead Lord; it is an argument for a living Lord.'

The third is the day he dedicated, the replacement in public worship of the seventh day of the week by the first day? Referring to this fact, Athanasius, in the fourth century, said, 'We keep no Sabbaths; we keep the Lord's Day as a memorial of the beginning of the new revelation.' But perhaps the greatest of all proofs is the one an old man gave to a couple of irreligious youths when they asked him why he believed Jesus rose from the dead. 'Well,' said the old man, 'I was talking to him this morning.'

✎ *Lord Jesus, had you stalled at the last ditch, had you been beaten at the barrier of death, then we would be stalled – eternally. But now we go over the barrier with you. Nothing can stop us. Hallelujah!*

Him one swell Guy

FOR READING AND MEDITATION – 2 TIMOTHY 1:1–14

' . . . Christ Jesus . . . has destroyed death and has brought life
and immortality to light through the gospel.' (v.10: NIV)

Fear no longer. Jesus is alive! It was said of the writer Ralph Waldo
Emerson, 'He did not argue; he simply let in the light.' The same
can be said of Jesus. He did not argue the point of immorality; he
showed himself alive.

A class of Japanese children in Hawaii were learning of the death
of Jesus. One little boy jumped up crying, 'Not fair . . . him one swell
Guy.' A little girl pulled him back and said, 'It's OK. Wait for the end
of the story. He didn't stay dead.'

Those three momentous days from Good Friday to Easter Sunday made a difference to the universe. They mark the moments when
our Navigator, the Lord Jesus Christ, descended into the deepest
waters to leave some solid anchor points for his followers.

The next time you feel overcome by the thought of dying, just
cast your anchor into the Easter waters. Remind yourself that the
best Man who ever lived went down through death and came back,
and the first thing he said was, 'Fear not.' He has never let us down
in one single area of life. Will he let us down in death? Impossible.
And if death, the final enemy, has been vanquished, what can the
little enemies along the way do to us now?

*Father, I cast my anchor in the Easter waters and rejoice that your Son,
the Lord Jesus Christ, has 'brought life and immortality to light'. In him death
is impossible and eternal life so gloriously possible. Blessed be your Name forever. Amen.*

Devil defiers

The divine anchorage

FOR READING AND MEDITATION – REVELATION 12:1–17

'"They overcame him by the blood of the Lamb . . ."' (v.11: NIV)

The Easter message gives us a solid rock from which to withstand the attacks of the devil. So whenever you feel under attack from Satan, drop your anchor at the cross. Calvary spells defeat for the devil, and although he may not wish to acknowledge it, you must point him to it – if necessary, again and again and again.

Five names are given: 'the dragon', 'the serpent', 'Satan', 'devil', and 'the accuser'. 'The dragon' carries with it the thought of monstrosity – something ill-formed and unlike anything human. In the word 'serpent' there is the idea of cunning, slyness, and craftiness. 'Satan' implies opposition – an evil adversary. 'Devil' means deceiver and slanderer. 'The accuser' carries the thought of someone who makes lying accusations.

However, look at the weapons we have to fight with: the blood of the Lamb, the testimony of those to whom the blood has been applied, and the sacrificial spirit which carries them even unto death. Although we will never be able to avoid the attacks of the devil, through Christ and his triumph on the cross we are well able to withstand them.

The devil is a defeated foe. God knows it, the devil knows it, but you too need to know it.

Yes Father, I do know it, but I want to know more. Teach me how to stand against the wiles of the devil, and may I come through these next few days understanding more of the resources that are available to me. Amen.

Knowing the enemy

FOR READING AND MEDITATION – 1 JOHN 3:1–10

'The reason the Son of God appeared was to destroy the devil's work.' (v.8: NIV)

What sort of work is the devil engaged in? The first is to call into question a revelation from God. God said to Adam: 'When you eat of it you will surely die' (Gen. 2:17). The devil asked: 'Did God really say that?' (Gen. 3:1). The same devil is at work in the world today. 'How can you be sure the Bible is true and is from God?' he asks.

Another aspect of his work is to deny the truth of God's revelation. When the devil found he could not get Eve to deny the fact that God had spoken, he suggested that what God had said was not true. 'You will not surely die' (Gen. 3:4).

A third aspect is to cast doubt on the benevolence of God: 'God knows that when you eat ... your eyes will be opened, and you will be like God, knowing good and evil' (Gen. 3:4). The cunning insinuation behind this remark was, 'God is trying to keep something from you that is for your good; there is more to know.'

Surely the devil has come to you with similar thoughts. But knowing where they come from is your security.

Doubt is our adversary's chief weapon. Trust in God is our biggest defence.

O Father, I see how important it is that I know something of how the devil works. Help me to trust you even in the face of massive doubt. Remind me at such times that there is a safe and sure anchor point at the cross. In Jesus' Name I pray. Amen.

More of the Satanic ploy

FOR READING AND MEDITATION – JAMES 1:1–18
'... each one is tempted when, by his own evil desire,
he is dragged away and enticed.' (v.14: NIV)

Bringing about the fall of Adam and Eve was one of Satan's greatest achievements, and he uses the same strategies still.

With Adam and Eve he appealed to their physical, aesthetic, and intellectual nature. '... the fruit of the tree was good for food' (the physical being); 'pleasing to the eye' (the aesthetic being); 'desirable for gaining wisdom' (the intellectual being) (Gen. 3:6). He attacks us through the things we like, not the things we don't like.

Take first the physical. How many does Satan ruin daily by pushing them towards indulgence in food and drink?

We are drawn to the aesthetic. Satan pushes us to become preoccupied with the beautiful and the artistic, until all thoughts of God have been driven out.

And the intellectual. Sometimes people can be lured into sin by their desire to gain wisdom and knowledge. They become brilliant in mind, but use their brilliance to argue God out of existence.

If the devil can induce us to accept any sort of light – intellectual light, scientific light, philosophic light – instead of the light that comes from Calvary, he has us in his grip. He has repeated the victory which he accomplished at Eden.

My Father, thank you for reminding me how the devil approaches me through the things I like rather than the things I don't like. Keep me ever alert to the Satanic ploy and ever close to your heart. In Jesus' Name. Amen.

The power of the blood

FOR READING AND MEDITATION – REVELATION 1:4–19

'To him who loves us and has freed us from our sins by his blood . . .' (v.5: NIV)

How do we overcome Satan? Through the blood of the Lamb. Every accusation Satan levels at us must be met by the blood of Christ.

Point to the blood that was shed for you on Calvary and the accuser cannot say another word. He is immediately silenced. This argument prevails against the devil whenever he approaches God and tells the truth about you.

The truth is that you are a sinner and worthy of death. Because you have sinned you deserve to be banished forever from God's presence. But remember also the truth of God's word, 'If we confess our sins, he is faithful and just and will forgive us our sins and purify us from all unrighteousness' (1 John 1:9).

Martin Luther, it is said, had regular visits from the devil. He declared, 'The devil came to me and whispered, "You are a sinner and you are lost forever." "Not so fast," retorted Martin Luther, "you told the truth when you said I am a sinner, but you lied when you said I am lost forever. I am a sinner trusting in the Lord Jesus Christ and therefore I am saved."'

We are lost, that is true. But, set against this, must always be the truth that we are saved by the blood of Christ.

✑ *Gracious God, I rest not in my own righteousness but in yours. Through the blood of the cross I am saved – and saved for all eternity. How can I ever thank you sufficiently? All honour and glory be unto your Name forever. Amen.*

Christ within

FOR READING AND MEDITATION – COLOSSIANS 1:24–29

'. . . the glorious riches of this mystery,
which is Christ in you, the hope of glory.' (v.27: NIV)

The divine anchorage

At the cross, Paul tells us, Jesus disarmed and triumphed over the devil, and all at his command. First-century Christians had no difficulty believing this; why do we? But it is one thing to believe that Jesus has defeated the devil; it is another thing to live in the reality of it.

A.W. Tozer tells us how to move from theory to experience. 'The secret of overcoming the devil is to hang on to the fact that Christ is in you, the hope of glory. I'm not foolish enough to say I am not afraid of the devil. He has got some judo holds I have never heard of. But he can't handle the one to whom I'm joined; he can't handle the one to whom I'm united; he can't handle the one whose nature dwells in my nature.'

Ah, there's the secret – being in Christ and having Christ in you. It's a mystery, of course, as Paul points out, but it is a mystery which can be experienced even though not fully comprehended.

William Law (John Wesley's one-time teacher) said, 'A Christ not in us, is a Christ not ours.' A Christ above us is not enough. A Christ beside us is not enough. A Christ ahead of us is not enough. Only a Christ within us is enough.

O Father, help me see that I have all I need to combat the wiles of Satan when I have you within. May I walk through this day and every day in the sure knowledge that the one who conquered Satan now lives in me. Amen.

A six-stage victory

FOR READING AND MEDITATION – COLOSSIANS 2:6–23

'. . . having disarmed the powers and authorities, he made a public spectacle
of them, triumphing over them by the cross.' (v.15: NIV)

How did Christ accomplish his victory over the devil? John Stott, in
his book *The Cross of Christ*, talks of six stages.

The first stage is the conquest predicted. The Old Testament
contains most of these predictions, the first being in the Garden of
Eden: 'I will put enmity between you and the woman . . . he will
crush your head, and you will strike his heel' (Gen. 3:15).

The second was the conquest begun – the earthly ministry of
Jesus. Satan made many attempts to get rid of Christ, but they were
all frustrated and foiled. The third was the conquest achieved –
our Lord's ordeal on the cross, a great victory. The fourth was the
conquest confirmed and announced, through the cross and the resurrection. The cross was the victory won, and the resurrection the
victory endorsed, proclaimed and demonstrated.

The fifth is the conquest extended as the church carries the
message and spreads it around the world.

And the sixth stage? The conquest consummated, when Christ
returns, and casts the devil into the bottomless pit. When all evil is
overcome, Christ will hand over the kingdom to the Father, and
God will be all in all.

✎ *O God, help me catch the length, breadth, depth and height of your great
victory over Satan. Help me to live in it, to draw forth into my soul its releas-
ing and liberating power. This I ask in Jesus' Name. Amen.*

Anchor deep

FOR READING AND MEDITATION – 1 JOHN 2:7–17

'I write to you, young men, because you have overcome the evil one.' (v.13: NIV)

Jesus experienced Satan's attacks when he was on this earth – and so do we. Jesus also overcame Satan's attacks when he was on earth – and so can we.

Everyone can live victoriously over the devil – even the young. In and through the cross, our Lord Jesus Christ has established an anchor point that can hold our lives steady and secure, no matter how fierce the onslaughts of the devil.

'Stability in a spiritual storm,' says one preacher, 'comes not from seeking a new message but understanding the old one.'

The most reliable anchor points are the tried and tested truths of the Bible. What our Lord said to Satan when confronted by him in the wilderness was this, 'It is written ...'

This indicates that his confidence was not in clever little statements, or fine phrases, but in the already established Word of God.

That is where our anchor point is also – in the written word of God. This tells us that through the victory of the cross, the devil is defeated and stripped of all his authority. Attach yourself to this anchor point and no wind of Satanic opposition will be strong enough to capsize your vessel or cause it to be cast upon the rocks. Anchor deep, turn your eyes to Jesus on the cross, and hold on.

⚓ *My Father and my God, let the thoughts with which my mind has been engaged these past few days settle within me to become patterns of victory. Never again will I allow myself to be defeated by Satan. For in you I am more than a conqueror. Amen.*

An unshakable kingdom

FOR READING AND MEDITATION – HEBREWS 12:14–29

'. . . since we are receiving a kingdom that
cannot be shaken, let us be thankful . . .' (v.28: NIV)

How do we remain steady when around us we see evil gaining the upper hand? We find a safe and secure anchor point at the cross.

Since the mid-sixties, the world has changed considerably. Evil appears not only to have increased, but also to have blunted the conscience of many. This raises the question: how far can evil go? Does the moral universe bend to evil?

Well, because of the cross, the answer is 'No!' Perhaps not to-day, perhaps not tomorrow, but the third day – No! On the third day, evil breaks itself upon the facts of life.

I draw a parallel between the day of resurrection, when the wrongs done to Jesus were made right, and the fact that one day in the future evil will break itself on the very nature of reality. Only truth has the moral universe behind it. There is nothing behind evil but evil. The word *evil* in English is the word live spelled backwards. It suggests to my mind that the universe is not built for evil but for life – abundant life, that is.

The kingdom of God is the only kingdom that will survive, for it is the only kingdom that has within it the elements of truth and righteousness.

Heavenly Father, I stand amidst shakeable kingdoms, but I stand with my feet in the one unshakable kingdom. Passing events cannot swamp me, for I am anchored to the Rock of Ages. I am so thankful. Amen.

Truth prevails

FOR READING AND MEDITATION – 2 CORINTHIANS 13:1–10

'For we cannot do anything against the truth, but only for the truth.' (v.8: NIV)

How far can evil go? So far and no further. It can crucify the Creator of the universe on a cross. Force went a long way on that first Easter, but it only went two days. The third day God raised his Son from the dead.

One of the elements of evil is a lie. How far can lies go? Well, lies took the truthful Son of God and pinned him to a tree.

Three days later, however, the lies were overcome by truth. The universe is not built for the success of a lie.

I read that the Tamils of South India say, 'The length of the best concocted lie is just eight days.' They mean that in eight days a lie goes to pieces – broken by the very nature of a moral universe.

When the diminutive Joseph Goebbels was propaganda minister for the Nazis during the World War II, the Germans used to say, 'Lies have short legs!' Lies may seem to be good in the short run, but they are bad in the long run.

A lie, you see, has nothing behind it but itself. The universe makes a lie break upon itself.

So how far can lies go? A long way, some might say, but really not very far. They can go the first day, the second day, but the third day – No!

❧ *O God, what confidence this gives me to know that nothing can work successfully against the truth. May my life bear witness to that truth, today and every day that I remain here on the earth. In Jesus' Name I pray.*

The terrible meek

FOR READING AND MEDITATION – MATTHEW 5:1–12

' "Blessed are the meek, for they will inherit the earth." ' (v.5: NIV)

In the play *The Terrible Meek* by Charles Ram Kennedy, one of the soldiers at the crucifixion says to Mary the mother of Jesus, 'I tell you, woman, this dead Son of yours, disfigured, shunned, spat upon, has built a kingdom this day that can never die. The living glory of him rules it. The earth is his and he made it. He ... has been moulding and making it through the long ages. Something has happened up here on this hill today to shake all our kingdoms of blood and fear to the dust. The terrible meek, the fierce agonising meek, are about to enter into their inheritance.'

The last word in human affairs is not lies, not violence, not force, not intimidation, not fear, but love. If you feel overwhelmed by what you read in the newspapers or see on television, keep in mind that they are now in the first and second day.

A third day is coming when evil will be swept from the universe and the kingdom of God will be ushered in. Today meekness might seem like weakness, but it will not be long now before the meek, the terrible meek, will enter into their inheritance.

Loving heavenly Father, forgive me for my impatience, yet when I see 'truth on the scaffold and wrong on the throne' I want to do something about it today. But teach me how to have patience with the patience of God. In Jesus' Name. Amen.

Jesus is King – now!

FOR READING AND MEDITATION – HEBREWS 2:1–9

'But we see Jesus . . . now crowned with glory and honour . . .' (v.9: NIV)

One of the great missionary hymns begins, 'Jesus shall reign where'er the sun doth his successive journeys run.' Isaac Watts, the hymn writer, was looking forward to a time when the rule of Christ would be unchallenged by the whole universe, but the New Testament teaches us that our Lord reigns now.

The writers of the epistles (Paul and Peter particularly) emphasise that the Kingship of Christ is not something to speculate about establishing in the future, but something to enjoy in the present. The writer to the Hebrews says: 'But we see Jesus . . . now crowned with glory and honour.' 'We see,' not 'we shall see'.

It was not a faint hope that Jesus would occupy the throne one day that sustained and inspired the early Christians, but the sure knowledge that Christ was on the throne then – crowned, glorified, and triumphant.

You and I need a similar assurance. We too need to see that Christ reigns in the midst of world confusion. Why he allows it to happen is beyond our comprehension, except that God knows exactly what he is doing.

Just as he was in charge of events when his Son lay in the darkness of the grave, so he is in charge of events now. Reason may not believe it, but faith most surely does.

✎ *O God, help me hold on to this truth, that you are not struggling to make your way to the throne – you are there now. And crowned with glory and honour. In the face of all that might contradict this truth – I believe. Amen.*

Half-gods are no gods

‘"But seek first his kingdom and his righteousness . . ."' (v.33: NIV)

do not consider myself to be a prophet in the predictive sense, but feel 'the spirit of prophecy' upon me as I write.

Surely it is clear to all Christians that we are living in a day when nations are being shaken and when strange things are happening before our very eyes. Totalitarianism, Fascism, Nazism, Communism have broken down. Fascism made the state supreme, Nazism made the race supreme, Communism made the ordinary people supreme. All these systems are half-gods.

A minister tells how after the last war, he spoke to some prominent German leaders on today's text. As he described the loving totalitarianism that characterises Christ's kingdom, they pounded their fists on the seats. 'Why did you do that?' he asked. They said, 'You seemed to sense why we turned to Nazism. Life for us was at a loose end – compartmentalised. We needed something to bring life back into wholeness, into total meaning and goal. We thought Nazism could bring that wholeness. But it let us down, let us down in blood and ruin. Now we see that what we were seeking for was the kingdom of God. We chose the wrong totalitarianism.'

I think what we are witnessing in our day is the shaking of earthly kingdoms in order that the unshakable kingdom might appear.

Father, can it be that what I am witnessing in the earth are the birth pangs of a new order? Are you about to usher in the fullness of your kingdom? Make me prayerful, expectant, ready and spiritually alert. Even so, come Lord Jesus. Amen.

Don't go on appearances

FOR READING AND MEDITATION – ROMANS 8:18–27

'. . . we . . . groan inwardly as we wait eagerly for our adoption as sons,
the redemption of our bodies.' (v. 23: NIV)

What are we to do when we feel overwhelmed by the evil that seem
to be mounting in our world?

Appearances must be treated with suspicion. Good Friday ap
peared to end the miraculous ministry of the Man from Galilee an
crush the life out of the Son of God, but Easter Sunday saw him ste
forth in all the power of a resurrected life.

If Easter means anything, it means that God always has the las
word. Men might appear to have it today, but all we need to do is t
wait until tomorrow, or the day after tomorrow, and there – th
third day – we see that the last word is God's.

I remind you again of the words of Charles Ram Kennedy, fic
tional, but in keeping with reality, 'I tell you, woman, this dead Sor
of yours, disfigured, shunned, spat upon, has built a kingdom thi
day that can never die.'

Those who cast their anchor at the cross, and are willing to b
patient with the patience of God, will find that evil is destined to
break itself upon the facts. The first day and the second day are ques
tion marks. But the third day is an exclamation mark. And how!

*O God my Father, help me walk through this world, evil though it ma
be, with the confidence that everything is under your control. Mystifyin
though it is to me, I know there is a purpose in everything. Help me hold o
to that – always. Amen.*

A gale warning

ocus on these gripping words in Hebrews 2:1: 'We must pay more careful attention, therefore, to what we have heard, so that we do not drift away.' The most foolish thing a sailor can do is to neglect dropping his anchor into solid bedrock. He has to pay attention to the anchor, or be cast upon the rocks.

Over the years I have observed that the ones who get shipwrecked are those who, though they hear the advice, fail to heed it. Christians are overcome because they neglect putting into operation the principles they have been taught.

There is only one thing that can save the hull of your heart from being battered against the rocks when the storm of doubt or devilish opposition bears down upon you. You must deliberately, purposefully and painstakingly remind yourselves of the truths I have covered, and use them in the same way that a sailor uses an anchor. Every anchor point I have talked about in these meditations was embedded in the rock during those dark hours between Good Friday and Easter Sunday. I assure you those anchor points are sturdy enough and strong enough to withstand the fiercest hurricane or storm. Use them.

Father, help me not merely to hear but to heed your warning. Shake me out of any lethargy that might have gripped my soul, and drive the truths I have learned these past few weeks deep into the core of my being. In Jesus' name I pray. Amen.

Danger! Fire!

FOR READING AND MEDITATION – LUKE 12:49–59

'"I have come to bring fire on the earth,
and how I wish it were already kindled!"' (v.49: NIV)

Two kinds of fire burn in this universe – one demonic, the othe
divine. These two tongues of flame compete passionately for ou
attention; both seek to engulf us, both seek to set us ablaze. An
the truth is this: the fire we allow to consume us will determine ou
spiritual destiny – both here and hereafter.

Let me draw your attention to two contrasting biblical texts. I
the first our Lord tells us: 'I have come to bring fire on the earth
and how I wish it were already kindled.'

The second is found in James 3:6: 'The tongue also is a fire,
world of evil among the parts of the body. It corrupts the whole per
son, sets the whole course of his life on fire, and it itself set on fire b
hell.' As we listen to Christ speaking of casting his holy, heavenly fir
on earth, and to James describing the appalling mischief wrought b
a tongue sent on fire by hell, we see that we do indeed live out ou
lives between two fires.

The question each of us must ask ourselves is this: what kin
of fire has hold of me – hell fire or holy fire? There is no neutra
ground. You and I will be consumed either by the fire that ravage
or the fire that redeems. Which one will it be?

✣ O Father, I do not hesitate – I want to be consumed by your fire. Help m
throughout the days of this special study to come closer than ever before t
the heavenly flame. In Christ's name I ask it. Amen.

A framework of fire

FOR READING AND MEDITATION –
HEBREWS 12:25–29; MATTHEW 25:34–41

'For our "God is a consuming fire."' (Heb. 12:29, NIV)

'Depart . . . into the eternal fire.' (Matt. 25:41, NIV)

an Macpherson points out that our physical existence on this earth s set within two great natural fires: a fire above us in the heart of he sun, and a fire beneath us in the heart of the earth. The sun, say ur scientists, is a vast ball of incandescent matter spinning through pace at a tremendous speed and flinging off from its surface long ongues of flame. They also tell us that if it were possible to sink a haft through the cold, hard crust of our planet to the centre of the arth, we would come across a blazing inferno 'seething and boil-ng in the great womb of the world'. But how different in their action pon humanity, says Macpherson, are these two huge fires. The fire rom above is creative, vitalising, beneficent; the fire from beneath s convulsive, frightening, catastrophic. One expresses itself in the elicate beauty of a violet; the other in the awful destructiveness f a volcano.

Permit me to draw a spiritual application from this. The fire that omes from heaven is genial, vivifying and beautifying; the fire hat comes out of hell is threatening and destructive. Which fire vill we give ourselves to? Which fire will we choose to influence us? have made my choice – it is the fire from heaven. How about you?

Father, help me to choose to turn my whole being towards the fire that omes out of heaven. Let its influence affect every part of my being. In Jesus' Jame. Amen.

Redeemed from fire by fire

FOR READING AND MEDITATION – MALACHI 3:1–12

'... For he will be like a refiner's fire ...' (v.2: NIV)

The redeeming fire

There are two kinds of fire in the universe – one divine, the other demonic; one of heaven, the other of hell.

Some time ago I came across a poem by T.S. Eliot which relates in a powerful way to our theme. He says in *The Four Quartets*:

> *The only hope, or else despair*
> *lies in the choice of pyre or pyre –*
> *to be redeemed from fire by fire ...*
> *we only live, only suspire*
> *consumed by either fire or fire.*

'To be redeemed from fire by fire ...' Eliot is thinking of the fact that some fires can be overwhelmed and overpowered only by a fiercer flame. Take the fires of passion, for example – only a higher passion can meet and master a passion that is lower and unworthy. T.S. Eliot was right; Scripturally, evangelically right, when he said that man must be redeemed from fire by fire. As Dr John Mackay, has put it, 'The issue facing us in this twentieth century is simply this: fire – or Fire!' We must choose between the fire that ravages or the fire that redeems.

✎ *O Father, grant that the flame of your Spirit in my heart may burn with such fierce heat and intensity that no lesser fire will be able to survive it. In Christ's Name I pray. Amen.*

The only hope ...

FOR READING AND MEDITATION – HEBREWS 1:1–7

' "...He makes ... his servants flames of fire." ' (v.7: NIV)

The only way an evil, destructive flame can be put out of the heart is by the kindling of a hotter, purer fire. And the only fire that burns with a flame so hot that no lesser fire can survive it is the fire that comes out of heaven.

Many years ago I conducted a crusade in the city of Belfast, Northern Ireland. Hours prior to the opening moments of the crusade, riots broke out in the city and a number of buildings was set on fire. People were reluctant to leave their homes, so the crusade had to be cancelled.

As I left the city a friend of mine shook my hand and said, 'I am sorry things have turned out like this. In Northern Ireland it's going to be a race between Christianity and political ideology. Whichever makes its message a flame of fire will win.'

I am glad to note that despite the riots, the fires and the bombings, Christians in Northern Ireland show evidence of being more on fire for God today than they have ever been.

The only way hatred will be quelled is by being engulfed in the fire of God's love, burning in the hearts of those who are redeemed. The only hope for this mixed-up, confused and violent generation is to be redeemed from fire – by fire.

Father, I see so clearly that the only way the fires of hell that are burning in this world can be quenched is when we Christians are set alight by Holy Spirit fire. Let your fire burn in me – this day and every day. Amen.

This rabble of the passions

FOR READING AND MEDITATION – GALATIANS 5:16–26

'The acts of the sinful nature are obvious:
sexual immorality, impurity and debauchery . . .' (v.19: NIV)

Fire, or fire? We must settle either for the fire that ravages or the fire that redeems. Take first the fire of unregulated instincts and appetites.

In his youthful days, the mystical English poet, John Donne, sported the family crest, which consisted, oddly enough, of a sheaf of snakes. One writer says, 'It was an appropriate symbol of the vipers of passion which, unholy and unruly, nested in his bosom.'

The day came, however, when John Donne met Jesus Christ and the fire of unregulated passion that burned in him was engulfed by the heavenly flame. He changed the family crest with its coiled serpents to one in which was depicted the form of the crucified Saviour.

Emerson writes of nature supplying man with such a large source of energy in that strange basement powerhouse of his appetites and instincts that he is in perpetual danger of running amok. He writes, 'To secure strength she implants cruel hunger and thirst which so easily overdo their office and invite disease . . . we live in youth amidst this rabble of the passions.'

A fierce phrase. It lifts the lid on the fatal flames that are engulfing countless multitudes. Tragically, the fires that were intended for the furnace chamber to run the ship have broken out into the stokehold and are destroying it.

Father, I see that the only way to be released from 'this rabble of the passions' is to be engulfed with a stronger and purer passion – your passion. Infuse into me that passion. In Jesus' Name. Amen.

Reprobate instincts

FOR READING AND MEDITATION – ROMANS 1:18–32
'Therefore God gave them over in the sinful desires of
their hearts to sexual impurity . . .' (v.24: NIV)

Probably the most powerful of the instincts and appetites is the sex drive. The sex instinct, under the control of the Holy Spirit, and expressed only in accordance with his will, is a power for good. In many people, however, the sex drive is out of control and they are quietly destroying their lives.

Paul speaks of an unregulated sex drive in this passage. When translating Romans 1:28 *Moffatt* uses the phrase 'reprobate instinct' – it is an instinct naturally right, but turned reprobate.

Millions around the world are being engulfed in the fateful flames of Aids, because their sex drive is out of control.

On television the other day I watched a practicing homosexual trying to convince the audience that the sex appetite is the same as our appetite for food. He said, 'God has given us the sex appetite in the same way as our appetite for food and we do ourselves harm if we do not indulge it.' What nonsense! There is a great difference between the appetite for sex and the appetite for food. We cannot live without food, but we can live without sex.

Sex is a fire. Used wisely within the moral guidelines set down by God, it can be a blessing; used unwisely, as happens so frequently in today's world, it will burn.

O Father, help men and women to understand that your moral guidelines are not given to repress us but to release us. And give me victory over my own appetites and desires. In Jesus' Name I pray. Amen.

The song of all songs

FOR READING AND MEDITATION – ECCLESIASTES 12:8–14

'…Fear God and keep his commandments,
for this is the whole [duty] of man.' (v.13: NIV)

God must be first – not sex. If any man could have made sex work his way, it was Solomon. He had everything: position, wisdom, youth, opportunity – and a philosophy about sex.

He puts it startlingly clearly in the opening verse of his Song of Songs. How does it begin? 'Oh for a kiss from your lips!' (Song of Songs 1:1, MOFFATT). Nothing wrong with that – but is it the song of all songs? The chief emphasis in life? Some would say, 'Yes'. Freud would agree.

Other philosophies could be stated in the same way: 'The song of all songs – oh for a well-fitted bank account!' 'Oh for constant praise and approval!' But if life is only these, it will run into a dead end. Solomon started out by saying that the chief emphasis is sex but ended up by saying: 'I denied myself nothing my eyes desired … Yet when I surveyed all that my hands had done … everything was meaningless …' (Eccl. 2:10–11).

Why did life turn dead on his hands? It was because he was seeking the wrong thing first. No age has emphasised sex more than this age and no age has enjoyed it less. There is no shame in sex but there is shame in the wrong use of sex.

◁ *Father, I am thankful for the fire that you have put within the drive of sex, but help me to keep that fire under control. Baptise me with heavenly fire. In Jesus' Name I pray. Amen.*

The worst thing about anger...

FOR READING AND MEDITATION – ESTHER 1:1–12

'... Then the king became furious and burned with anger.' (v.12: NIV)

We look now at another fateful flame that burns like an incendiary in the human heart – the fire of uncontrolled hatred and anger. Every day millions are being consumed by the flames of hatred and anger and they do not realise it. The worst thing about anger is being the person who holds the anger.

In an experiment to discover the effect of anger, doctors put a tube down a man's nostrils into his stomach to test the contents of his stomach when he was in different states of mind. They found that when he was in a good humour, his digestion worked normally; after they purposely made him angry, his digestion completely stopped. A doctor told me that he could find no physical basis for a woman's vomiting until he discovered she was expecting her mother-in-law. At his suggestion, the visit was postponed – and the vomiting stopped.

When we say of another, 'He burns me up,' it's true: he does. You want to burn him up and all you do is burn yourself up. We say, 'I blew up,' and it's true: we do. You really want to blow up the other person and you only blow yourself up.

Hatred and anger are baleful fires that, if not quenched by the fire of God's love, can kill – literally.

O God, I see that I pass on to my body the health and unhealth of my spirit and my soul. I want to be healthy in spirit, soul and body. Consume me with your fire, that all lesser fires may have no hold on me. In Jesus' Name. Amen.

Anger is poison

FOR READING AND MEDITATION – ECCLESIASTES 7:1–12
'Do not be quickly provoked in your spirit,
for anger resides in the lap of fools.' (v.9: NIV)

A doctor was baffled over the cause of sickness in a baby. One day he entered their home while the parents were quarrelling and saw the mother nursing the child. He threw up his hands and said, 'Now I know what is the matter with your baby – you are poisoning it by ill will.' The poison was in the mother's milk, put there by anger.

We use a variety of words to describe our negative feelings. Take irritation. This is the feeling we get when something upsets us, but it is a feeling that soon passes. Indignation is similar to irritation, but is deeper and stronger and takes longer to pass away. Resentment arises when the mind continues to focus on the irritation or indignation, and will not allow it to pass. The feelings then keep simmering, day after day, or week after week.

These three emotions – irritation, indignation and resentment – can reverberate within us without being expressed.

Hatred and anger are different; these are strong emotions that soon reveal themselves. When irritated or resentful, we may clam up; when angry or hating, we usually blow up. Allowed to increase, hatred and anger develop into rage and fury. These emotions must be recognised, understood and kept under control. If you don't control them, they will control you.

O God my Father, I realise that if I live with my hates I will not be able to live with myself. Let your heavenly fire burn in the deep parts of my being. For Jesus' sake. Amen.

Being angry – yet without sin

'He looked round at them in anger and, deeply distressed at their stubborn hearts, said to the man, "Stretch out your hand." ' (v.5: NIV)

The Incredible Hulk is the story of a man who, whenever he gets enraged, turns into a powerful figure who is able to overturn cars, tear down trees and bend steel bars as if they were made of rubber. My concern with this programme is that it may teach children and young people, as well as gullible adults, that the way to tackle problems is by venting anger.

I once shared this opinion in a meeting and afterwards someone came up to me and said, 'But the Bible says it's okay to be angry.' He quoted the first two words of a translation of Ephesians 4:26 that says: 'Be angry, and sin not.' Note the words – 'and sin not'. How can we be angry without committing sin? By being angry at nothing but sin. In the passage before us today we see our Lord demonstrating a fierce but righteous anger. Anger is righteous when it is grief at what is happening to others; anger is unrighteous when it is a grudge at what is happening to oneself. If we are honest, most of our anger is occasioned by self-interest and self-concern – and is thus unrighteous. Jesus was angry – and did not sin. In him the fire of anger was under control.

✎ *O Father, I would be rid of all that corrodes my soul. I see that hatred and anger can eat like acid into my moral nature. Burn into me so that all that is injurious to my being can be burned out of me. In Jesus' Name. Amen.*

The flame of jealousy

FOR READING AND MEDITATION – PROVERBS 6:27–35

'… for jealousy arouses a husband's fury, and he will show
no mercy when he takes revenge.' (v.34: NIV)

In the Old Testament the Almighty decrees: 'For I, the Lord your God, am a jealous God' (Ex. 20:5). Elijah said at Horeb: 'I have been very jealous for the Lord God of Hosts' (1 Kings 19:10, KJV).

God's message to Zechariah was: 'I am very jealous for Jerusalem and Zion' (Zech. 1:14). And the apostle Paul said: 'I am jealous for you with a godly jealousy' (2 Cor. 11:2). These are expressions of the zeal of love.

Not a passion for self, but a great passion for something loved. It was because God loved his people with a full abounding love that he was jealous for them. Ungodly jealousy is different; it is as hateful as the other is praiseworthy, as foul and poisonous as the other is cleansing and pure.

In a small town in Yorkshire, a manager of a mill was so jealous of another man that he brought about the complete closure of the place, putting hundreds of people out of work. A whole community was devastated – just to satisfy his jealousy. Satisfy? Hardly. Within two years he was dead. The newspapers said, 'He died a bitter man.'

Make no mistake – out of all the fires that consume, jealousy is the one with the fiercest of flames.

✍ *O Father, give me the grace and power to deal, and deal effectively, with the ravaging flames of jealousy. Save me from the poison and the passion of it. In Christ's Name I pray. Amen.*

How jealousy works …

FOR READING AND MEDITATION – ROMANS 12:9–21
'Honour one another above yourselves.' (v.10: NIV)

What exactly is jealousy? The pain, or displeasure we feel at the happiness, success or imagined superiority of another. The elation we feel when someone we dislike stumbles and falls. Jealousy is deadly and it never fails to scar and scorch the soul.

It is more common to the middle-aged. The ambitious youth can be surpassed without being too upset because he realises he still has his youth. There are latent powers in him to use. But a man in middle age senses that he does not have as much energy as previously and he falls easy prey to jealousy.

Jealousy gets into the crevices. It is focused on those we know – those who are closest to us. Jealousy is not normally directed against those who vastly outsoar us, but those who just outsoar us, those who compete in the same circle, for the esteem we covet.

The local footballer is not jealous of the nationally famous goal-scorer, but of someone in the same team.

A Latin proverb says, 'The potter is envious of the potter, the smith of the smith.' Jealousy explains why it is easier to 'weep with those who weep' than to 'rejoice with those who rejoice'. The former do not provoke us to jealousy; the latter do.

✎ *Father, give me the courage today to look at those around me, those in the same circle as I, and ask myself: how do I feel when I hear them praised? And if you see in me the tiniest ripple of jealousy, root it out, I pray. In Jesus' Name. Amen.*

John-ward or Jesus-ward?

Jealousy has been the cause of many a downfall. Homes have been divided, wars initiated, businesses ruined, relationships soured.

Jealousy can also invade a heart in which Christ dwells. A prominent evangelist became extremely jealous of D.L. Moody's success. He shared with a close friend that he wished Moody had never been born. Unable to deal with his jealousy, he became so consumed by it that his ministry came to an end.

How different from John the Baptist. One day John's disciples came to him and said: 'Rabbi, that man who was with you on the other side of the Jordan – well, he is baptising, and everyone is going to him.' John replied: 'The bride belongs to the bridegroom. The friend who attends … is full of joy when he hears the bridegroom's voice. That joy is mine, and it is now complete' (John 3:26, 29). In other words: I know my place. I've found my niche, and I'm content in it.

In the passage before us today, Peter seems to have been afflicted by jealousy. He asked: 'Lord, what about him?' Imagine it – he had just come from a wonderful encounter with Christ but there was still a lingering jealousy. Pentecost had not yet burned it out, so he looked John-ward instead of Jesus-ward.

✎ *O Father, help me to rejoice in the joy of all your children; help me to feel success in their successes and to be honoured in all their honours. Help me to love with a creative love. In Jesus' Name I pray. Amen.*

The desire to possess

FOR READING AND MEDITATION – 1 TIMOTHY 6:1–10

'For the love of money is a root of all kinds of evil.' (v.10: NIV)

Another fire that burns with a fierce flame in the human heart is the fire of acquisitiveness – the all-consuming desire to possess riches and material things. The aim of life for many people is to have more and more and more. We live in a material world which depends in part on material things. You cannot preach effectively to a hungry man. Man cannot live by bread alone, but he also cannot live without it.

A minister tells how, working amongst the poor in the slums, he gave a glass of milk to a little girl and said, 'Drink it up.' The little girl looked at him with wide eyes and said, 'What? Can I drink it right to the very bottom?'

What years of deprivation lay behind that enquiry? One cannot despise money or material things, for without them life on this earth would be impossible. But for many, material things grow so large that they push out everything else.

Things cannot satisfy the deep craving for life and meaning, but people still pursue money and possessions with a passion that ought to be reserved only for God. The fire that burns on the altar of their hearts is a false and fateful flame. It has not come down from above; it has come up from below.

✎ *O Father, grant that the fire of acquisitiveness shall have no place in my life. Deliver me from false values and false goals. Help me keep my money in my hands, not in my heart. In Jesus' Name I pray. Amen.*

The greed of pelf

FOR READING AND MEDITATION – LUKE 16:1–15

'"... You cannot serve both God and Money."' (v.13: NIV)

Money as money is not evil. Money speeds on errands of mercy and lends itself to a thousand philanthropies. It feeds the hungry, clothes the naked. A judge said recently at the Old Bailey, 'A couple of pounds very often saves a life and sometimes a soul.' No, it is not money that is the perilous thing – it is the insensate love of it that devours and consumes.

It is sad to see so many men and women allowing their lives to be blighted by the greed of pelf. They become slaves to Mammon. Their faces are stamped with an avaricious look. Sweetness and serenity vanish from their nature; they become as metallic as the coin they seek.

So consuming is the fire of acquisitiveness that burns in their souls that they have to heap more and more fuel. In the flames of the desire to accumulate, all the lovely things of life perish. They can repeat the words of Edna St Vincent Millay:

I cannot say what loves have come and gone
I only know that summer sang in me
a little while and in me sings no more.

When the winter of materialism sets in, it is a very frosty season.

✎ *Father, help me see that you have made us in your image and we cannot live successfully if we try to live in the image of the material. Save me from trying. In Jesus' Name. Amen.*

Never enough!

FOR READING AND MEDITATION – ECCLESIASTES 5:10–20

'Whoever loves money never has money enough;
whoever loves wealth is never satisfied with his income.' (v.10: NIV)

The more fiercely the fire of acquisitiveness burns in the heart, the more blighting it becomes. Men and women are evaluated in terms of how much or how little they possess. A wealthy man I talked to told me that he used to imagine what would be said when the newspapers announced his death and how much money he had left behind. He told me with tears in his eyes, 'For a pleasure like that I sacrificed everything I had – my wife, my children, my whole family.'

It reminds me of the epitaph, 'Here lived a wealthy miser who pulled down crows' nests for fuel. He got the usual reward; half a million half a minute before he died, and nothing half a minute later.'

The peril of riches does not lie in possessing riches: it is the inordinate longing for them that is the deadly thing. A man is consumed with the flames of acquisitiveness when he puts a pre-eminent worth upon money, and loves and longs for nothing else.

Anything which weakens the conviction that our security is only in God is dangerous, and nothing weakens that conviction more than the love of money. Our text for today tells us that 'whoever loves money never has money enough'. And why? It is because he doesn't have the money – the money has him.

O God, help me, for I live in an acquisitive society where worth tends to be judged by wealth. At the same time, I am a Christian and my judgments must be different. Help me to decide the Christian way. In Jesus Name. Amen.

Unpurchasable people

FOR READING AND MEDITATION – LUKE 12:13–21

'"… Be on your guard against all kinds of greed; a man's life does not consist in the abundance of his possessions." ' (v.15: NIV)

In the Ten Commandments, covetousness is put along with murder, adultery, theft and slander. Jesus did not deny that things were important, but said they were not supremely important.

He did not scorn material things, but he knew their perilous ability to get mastery of the soul and consume all our desires. The people who have caught the spirit of Jesus Christ, whose lives have been set on fire by him, are emancipated from slavery to things. They enjoy them, but are not ruled by them.

Professor W.E. Hocking has argued that we cannot have a sound society unless we have a sufficient number of men and women who cannot be bought. He called them 'unpurchasable people'.

The Christian church or, better still, Christ, specialises in producing 'unpurchasable people' as he transforms them from the image of the material into the image of the spiritual.

Did you know that Christ talked more about wealth and money – and its dangers – than about any other thing? But still the fire of acquisitiveness burns in human hearts. It matters not whether it be a political empire or an evangelical empire; where the fateful flames of cosvetousness are allowed to burn, they end up consuming not just the empire, but the people who control it.

✎ *O God, again I pray that you will preserve me from the cravings and desires that can so easily be fanned into a blaze within me. Let your fire absorb all other fires that are within. In Jesus' Name I ask it. Amen.*

How few look really happy

FOR READING AND MEDITATION – 2 TIMOTHY 3:1–9

'... There will be terrible times in the last days. People will be ...
lovers of pleasure rather than lovers of God.' (vv.1–4: NIV)

Freud said that pleasure is the chief hunger in the human heart, and that we will never understand why people behave the way they do unless we see their behaviour in terms of a desire to have that hunger met. People spend night after night in clubs, casinos and race-tracks, at the pub or in front of the television. One might think that these are extremely happy people.

But look at these people the following day. Study their faces and observe their expressions. How few look happy then.

To gain satisfaction from wholesome entertainment is not wrong; it becomes wrong when we allow ourselves to think that pleasure is the chief good of life and its primary aim. The very abandon, not to say fanaticism, with which masses give themselves to the pursuit of pleasure is a sign of the deep, haunting and unbearable discontent that shadows them wherever they go.

Lacking the secret of inner contentment, their boredom drives them to a frenzy – a frenzy which runs here, there and everywhere in an effort to have someone entertain them. All across the world one sees the smoke and flame of this false fire burning with a fierce intensity. How sad that so many are looking everywhere for peace and joy – everywhere except where it can be found.

O God, how can I ever be sufficiently thankful that my search for life ended when I found you? In the flames of your eternal love and joy all lesser fires have been consumed. Blessed be your glorious and wondrous Name. Amen.

Nothing!

FOR READING AND MEDITATION – LUKE 23:1–12

'He plied him with many questions,
but Jesus gave him no answer.' (v.9: NIV)

Hedonism is the doctrine that all that matters in life is pleasure and this ought to be a person's chief aim. King Herod was a hedonist. The historian Josephus tells us that Herod was known all over the Roman empire for his love of pleasure, and he enjoyed nothing more than bringing a new form of entertainment to his palace. Look again at these words, 'When Herod saw Jesus, he was greatly pleased ...'

There were many in Jesus' day who were pleased to see him. Blind Bartimaeus; Jairus, whose daughter was raised from the dead; Zacchaeus was pleased to see him. And Herod was pleased to see him, but Herod's reason was different: 'From what he had heard about him, he hoped to see him perform some miracle' (v.8).

Herod wanted to see Christ out of a desire for pleasure and amusement. What a picture this is of the insensitivity that can develop in the heart of those whose only concern in life is entertainment.

We read that Herod plied Jesus with many questions 'but Jesus gave him no answer'. Christ answered Pilate's questions – so why not Herod's? Our Lord refuses to indulge those who do not take him seriously. Where life is not viewed with soberness, and where pleasure takes precedence over truth, then the lips of our Lord are silent.

Lord Jesus Christ, I take seriously everything you say and everything you do. May there never be any silence between us. For your own dear Name's sake. Amen.

A new dark age

FOR READING AND MEDITATION – TITUS 3:1–11

'At one time we too were foolish, disobedient, deceived and enslaved
by all kinds of passions and pleasures . . .' (v.3: NIV)

Charles Colson, one-time adviser to President Nixon, says that we
are in the midst of a new dark age – a fiercely hedonistic culture.
He points out that when men and women lose the sense of God,
they are drawn to pleasure as a means of filling up the vacuum in
their souls. Look at the entertainments column in any newspaper
and see how the world spreads out its wares. As T.S. Eliot once said,
'Paganism holds all the most valuable advertising space.'

If we do away with God, then we have no framework of reference, no star to steer by, no harbour.

If there is no God then, 'We are only animated bubbles that rise
to the cosmic surface, glisten in the sunlight for a brief space and
then burst, leaving a nasty wet spot on the surface of things.' Or,
'Life is a fretful child that must be played with until it falls to sleep.'

If there is no God, then we go through an endless succession of
meaningless days.

In this age, God is fading out of the minds of men and women.
Like thoughtless children, they believe that the toyland pleasure
will smother their preoccupations. But though the fires of hedonism may burn, unlike the divine fire, they are destined to burn out.

O God, when I see how foolish men and women are to try and fill their
souls with the pleasures that can never satisfy, I feel like crying out to them,
'Turn to Christ.' Use me, dear Lord, to influence some poor lost soul to turn
to you. In Jesus' Name I pray. Amen.

Fire in Parliament

FOR READING AND MEDITATION – JUDE 17–25

'Snatch others from the fire and save them . . .' (v.23: NIV)

The redeeming fire

Another fire that burns fiercely and hotly is the passionate desire to be free of all moral restrictions and restraints. If ever there was a fire that roared out of hell it is this.

I remember very vividly the day when the British Parliament changed the law concerning homosexuality and said that homosexual acts between consenting adults would no longer be regarded as an offence. A friend telephoned me and in a voice shaking with emotion said, 'Selwyn, the flames of hell have reached into our Parliament. This is the first step – soon there will be others. Call your people to prayer.'

I confess that at the time I thought his words and his reaction were a little extreme, but I have come to see how true they were.

After homosexuality came the laws which took a more relaxed attitude towards abortion. Now there are pressures to change these laws still further. And other new laws – laws that violate the commands and demands of Scripture – will soon be written on our statute books. The mania for getting away from the moral guidelines that have buttressed society for so many centuries is so fierce that some men and women have become like firebugs ready to burn down the temple of God and the soul.

O God, forgive us for failing to fight fire – with fire. We see all around us the flames that roar out of hell. May we see also the fire that comes down from heaven. Burn in me, dear Lord – to the glory and honour of your precious Name. Amen.

The Way and not-the-way

FOR READING AND MEDITATION – NUMBERS 32:14–23

' ". . . be sure that your sin will find you out." ' (v.23: NIV)

When the philosopher Kant said, 'Two things strike me with awe: the starry heavens above and the moral law within,' he meant that the laws of those two worlds are equally authoritative and equally inescapable. The God who established the laws that guide the spinning planets is the God who laid down the moral laws that guide and govern our lives on this earth.

Dr. E. Stanley Jones writes there are two roads through life: the Way, and not-the-way. H_2O produces water. You might twist the formula, but in the end, if you want to produce water, you have to surrender to it. Two parts of hydrogen and one of oxygen is the way; everything else is not-the-way. It is the same with life; there is the Way and there is not-the-way. When our lawmakers turn aside from the moral laws that God has established, they go down a way that is not-the-way.

When we obey the Way, we get results; when we disobey we get consequences. We are free to choose, but we are not free to choose the results of our choosing. Now I used to think this text meant: be sure your sin will be found out. Now I think it says: be sure your sin will find you out. When we violate God's moral law the results register in us; we get the consequences – in ourselves.

Heavenly Father, help our lawmakers and politicians to understand that you are the Creator of both worlds – the world above and the world within. I am so glad I have discovered that. Help me to help others understand it. In Jesus' Name. Amen.

What history teaches us ...

FOR READING AND MEDITATION – JUDGES 17:1–13

'In those days Israel had no king; everyone did as he saw fit.' (v.6: NIV)

When we refuse to recognise God as King over the moral order, then a general moral anarchy sets in.

In his great work, *A Study of History*, Toynbee points out that the characteristic of a civilisation on the way out is a widespread contempt for moral law and order. If that is the case, then as far as Britain is concerned, I say – God help us.

The fire of a demonic libertarianism is moving across our land. We are like the people described in the text before us today: 'Everyone did exactly as he pleased' (MOFFATT). The media-makers are presenting to young people an image of life that says, 'Do exactly as you please as long as it does not offend the person you are doing it with.' No mention of whether it is an offence to God.

There are, however, many homes and families who, even though they have no commitment to Christ or Christianity, have a respect for moral law and order.

This could change, for the fires of moral laxity and permissiveness burn fast and furious. The sparks of this generation become the fires of the next.

And we who are Christians must realise that there is only one fire that can engulf the fires of moral laxity and permissiveness; it is the fire of God.

✍ *O Father, send the burning, blazing fire of the Holy Spirit upon us and engulf all other fires. We cannot go on like this much longer, dear Lord. Send us a Pentecost at any cost. In Christ's peerless and precious Name we pray. Amen.*

Wild fanaticism

FOR READING AND MEDITATION – ACTS 7:54–8:3
'And Saul was there, giving approval to his death . . .' (v.1: NIV)

No consideration of the baleful fires burning would be complete without examining those who are caught in the grip of a wild fanaticism. Saul of Tarsus was a fanatic before he met Christ, then his wild nature was curbed and he changed from a fanatic to a fan.

The first modern example of wild fanaticism that comes to mind is that of Nazism. This destructive fire consumed a whole nation and left it in ashes. Such was the lust for power and glory that many of Hitler's followers blindly followed the most horrifying instructions, and brought about the deaths of millions of Jews in the Holocaust. We have witnessed something similar in the flaming contortions of Fascism and seen it go down in humiliation and repudiation.

In Dublin recently I listened to a former IRA member, now a committed Christian, describe how his fanaticism led him to plant bombs which maimed and killed people. He commented, 'I was so caught up in fanaticism and over-zealousness that I could sit and watch the news with my mother, who knew nothing of my involvement with the IRA, and I would sit there just as if I was another person.'

Such is the power of fanaticism – it sears and scars the soul and blinds it to all that is right and good and virtuous. There is fire in fanaticism, you see, terrible, destructive fire.

Oh God, you laid your hand on a fanatic like Saul and turned him into one of the greatest disciples the world has ever seen. Reach out and lay your hand upon someone like that – today. In Jesus' Name I ask it. Amen.

Stalin or the Saviour?

FOR READING AND MEDITATION – ACTS 4:1–12

' "Salvation is found in no one else, for there is no other name
under heaven ... by which we must be saved." ' (v.12: NIV)

Another fanatical cause is Communism. It feeds the ferocity of its
passion partly on the oppressions and grievances of subject peoples
and partly on its thirst and lust for power. Whatever else Communism is, it is no mere theory; it is a burning vision, 'The Devil's twentieth century missionary movement compounded of ruthlessness
and rapture.' What makes it dangerous is not its ideology, but the
fanatical fire that burns in the breasts of its advocates. Prokofiev, a
Russian composer, rhapsodised about Stalin: ' "Stalin" – I say to the
universe; "Stalin" – and I add nothing.'

Can you hear what was being said? Stalin's name was made to
include all things – the party, the country, everything. That's fire –
dangerous fire. In East Germany people rose up to overthrow totalitarianism and demand a more democratic approach to government.
The infamous Berlin Wall has fallen and thousands are crossing
the borders from East Berlin to the West. Are the flames of Communism about to be extinguished? I cannot say.

The thing that intrigues me is that the passion for this movement in East Germany seems to be centred on a Christian church.

Will the fire in the hearts of Christ's followers win over the fires
in the hearts of dyed-in-the-wool Communists? We wait to see.

✎ O God, we sense we are passing through a turbulent but singularly important phase in history. Help me see also that I am in the kingdom 'for such
a time as this'. In Christ's Name I pray. Amen.

The answer to fire – is Fire

FOR READING AND MEDITATION – 1 CHRONICLES 21:18–30

'He called on the Lord, and the Lord answered him with fire
from heaven on the altar of burnt offering.' (v.26: NIV)

veryone is free to commit to a cause. But when people allow them-
elves to act in ways that violate moral and civil law, then their ac-
ions must be repudiated and denounced.

Islam, too, has its share of fanatics. Not all who subscribe to
slam are in this category – but many are. I heard a follower of the
ate Ayatollah Khomeini say on television, 'I will not rest until I see
alman Rushdie (author of *The Satanic Verses*) brought down to
is death.' There's fire in those words – terrible, destructive fire.

Many baleful fires burn in our world. Physical lusts scar and
ear the personality. Fiery emotions of hatred, anger and jealousy
hipwreck the soul. Longings for cheap thrills pervert the judgment.
esires to own and possess things sit in the driving seat of our per-
onalities and take over control. Manias to be free of all moral re-
traints and restrictions burn away at the anchor ropes in the moral
niverse. Mad and fanatical attempts to seize at power blind men
nd women to all that is virtuous and reward them with ashes.

What is the answer to all of this? How can these fires that roar
ut of hell be engulfed and brought into control?

The answer is Pentecost.

*O God, as I prepare to turn my eyes from the fire that comes up from
elow to the fire that comes down from above, prepare my heart to receive
ll that you have for me. Father, I long to be more on fire. Hear my prayer, in
hrist's Name. Amen.*

The rabble – redeemed

FOR READING AND MEDITATION – JOHN 6:60–71

' "The Spirit gives life; the flesh counts for nothing . . ." ' (v.63: NIV)

The redeeming fire

One of the most thrilling things about Pentecost is that it intro duces us to a fire that does not ravage, but redeems.

Look at the list of false fires. See how the flame of the Hol Spirit redeems us from them. Look again at the fire that heade our list – an unregulated and undisciplined sex drive. John Donne the mystical English poet, according to his own testimony, had mind that was 'like a merry-go-round of lustful images'.

Prior to his conversion he said of his family crest, 'It was an ap propriate symbol of the vipers of passion which, unholy and un ruly, nested in my bosom in those unregenerate days.'

Then he came in touch with the 'fire-baptising Christ' an experienced such a mighty baptism in the Spirit that his entire lif was transformed. What brought order and discipline and victor to the 'rabble of passions' that stirred within him?

It was not a scolding from his parents; not resolutions an floggings of the will; it was the incoming of Christ's love in th power of the Holy Spirit. He was redeemed from fire by fire.

Am I talking to someone now whose life is gripped and con trolled by turbulent and evil passions? Open your whole being t the flame of God. You, too, can be redeemed from fire – by fire.

O God, let your fire consume all the dross and the evil desires that ma have their grip on my life. Let your passion either eradicate or bring unde control every other passion. In Jesus' Name I ask it. Amen.

The open road

FOR READING AND MEDITATION – 2 CORINTHIANS 5:11–21

'For Christ's love compels us, because we are convinced that
one died for all, and therefore all died.' (v.14: NIV)

28 MAY

The redeeming fire

I picked up something I wrote on the sex drive 20 years ago, and realised how much I have moved on in my thinking. The kind of advice I used to give was along these lines: sublimate sexual energy by throwing yourself into activity; shun anything that stirs or titillates; pray more; read the Bible more; go for a walk before going to sleep, and so on.

Whilst these ideas contain a lot of sense, they are really only the fences along the side of an open road – the open road is the experience of the passion and love of Jesus Christ alive and moving in one's soul. We can expel a desire only by a higher and stronger desire. The fire of God's love burning in our hearts is the only fire that can engulf and extinguish all other fires. All the prohibitions cannot save us unless the fire of God is at work in our lives.

There are literally thousands of laws on the statute books. The Christian needs only one: 'A new commandment I give to you, that you love one another; as I have loved you, that you also love one another' (John 13:34, NKJ). When your heart is ablaze with the love of Christ, then you are free. 'Love Christ and do what you like,' said Augustine. Dangerous theorising? No, for in loving Christ you will love what is right.

✶ *Lord Jesus Christ, let the fire of your love fall upon my lesser loves so that all my loves may be lost in you and then found again in true and proper expression. For your own dear Name's sake. Amen.*

Don't fight – surrender

The redeeming fire

FOR READING AND MEDITATION – MATTHEW 13:24–30

' "... collect the weeds and tie them in bundles to be burned ..." ' (v.30: NIV)

When it comes to dealing with 'the rabble of the passions', the operative word is not 'fight' but 'surrender'.

To fight the passions involves focusing attention on them. And it is a well-known law of the personality that whatever gets your attention – gets you. Therefore a great number of people fall under the sway and power of the sex drive at the very moment of fighting it.

The strategy is wrong. When you no longer fight your passions but surrender them to God, then your attention is drawn from them to him. You are looking at him – not them.

But does this principle really work? Few people can have had a greater struggle with passions, instincts and appetites than I. In my youth I was nearly shipwrecked by them.

In a desperate state I flung myself at the feet of Jesus Christ and he lit a fire on the altar of my heart that has never gone out. Deeper and deeper into my personality it has gone, searching the motives, scouring the desires, purging the secret places of the soul and burning the imagination clean.

Is not this the function of fire? One of the functions of fire is to consume inwardly. He will burn up the chaff 'with unquenchable fire' (Matt. 3:12).

Father, I see that the closer I get to you, the more likely I am to get burned. But your burning is the very therapy I need. Burn out of me, I pray, everything that is not of you. In Jesus' Name I ask it. Amen.

Pentecost: a prophecy fulfilled

FOR READING AND MEDITATION – MATTHEW 3:1–12

' "I baptise you with water ... He will baptise you with
the Holy Spirit and with fire." ' (v.11: NIV)

John said, 'He will baptise you with the Holy Spirit and with fire.'
Note the words 'and with fire'. All John could do to ratify his disciples' commitment was to plunge them into the cold waters of the
Jordan, but he saw by the Spirit that Jesus would be a Baptiser with
a difference – he would immerse his converts into flaming fire.

What does this strong, strange word of John really mean? Was
it just a picturesque way of describing a spiritual experience?

What do we find in the Upper Room on the day of Pentecost?
120 of Christ's disciples were paralysed by fear. Suddenly the risen
Christ reached down from heaven and plunged every one of his
disciples into the fiery energy of the Holy Spirit.

They watched in amazement as tongues of fire appear on one
another's heads. A strange new power pulsed through their beings,
they spoke in languages never learned, they were instantly transformed. All their hesitancies and trepidations were broken, and they
burst out on to the crowded streets of Jerusalem to spread the news
that Jesus is alive. What happened to their fear?

It was swallowed up in the flame and fire of the Holy Spirit.
They were indeed baptised with the Holy Spirit – and with fire!

*O Father, I cannot be content with a flickering spiritual experience; I
want one that is engulfed in flame. For that purpose I give myself wholly to
you now; give yourself to me. Set me alight, set me on fire. In Jesus' Name.*

There's more!

'... Peter stood up among the believers [a group numbering about a hundred and twenty] ...' (v.15: NIV)

Why were there just 120 present in the Upper Room? In 1 Corinthians 15:6 we read that after the resurrection our Lord appeared to 'more than 500 of the brothers at the same time'. What happened to the other 380?

Some say the missing disciples were detained by the demands of duty. That perhaps the Upper Room could not hold more than 120. The suggestion is made that perhaps they thought they had everything there was to have spiritually in just seeing the risen Lord. This raises the point that many of Christ's disciples living today think the only experience they can have in the Christian life is an encounter with the risen Lord.

Wonderful though this is – there's more. God offers to all those who know his Son not only the joy of regeneration, but also the thrill of a mighty baptism in the Spirit.

To have seen the triumphant Jesus on the other side of the tomb must have been a wonderful and thrilling experience. Any one of the disciples could be forgiven for thinking that there could be nothing more wonderful than that.

The truth was, however, that this was not so. There was more

O Father, help me face this crucial issue of whether I am getting all out of the Christian life that you want for me. Help me not to be content with receiving only your lesser blessings. I want everything you have to give me. Everything. Meet me now. In Christ's Name I pray. Amen.

Do we get all at conversion?

'Then I remembered what the Lord had said: "John baptised with water,
but you will be baptised with the Holy Spirit." ' (v.16: NIV)

Dr Martyn Lloyd-Jones, one of Britain's greatest Bible expositors said, 'I am convinced that there are large numbers of Christian people who are quenching the Spirit by denying these possibilities (of more) in their very understanding of the doctrine of the Spirit.' There is nothing, I am convinced, that so quenches the Spirit as the teaching which identifies the baptism of the Holy Ghost with regeneration. 'So we say, "Ah, well, I am already baptised with the Holy Spirit. It happened when I was born again. It happened at my conversion. There is nothing for me to seek. I have gotten it all." Gotten it all? Well, if you have gotten it all, I simply ask: in the name of God, why are you as you are?'

The attitude I have adopted over the years towards those who disagree with me on the point that the baptism of the Spirit is additional to and different from conversion is to say, 'If you want to believe that you had everything at your conversion, then the question I would put to you is this: what is your spiritual experience like now? Can you say at this moment that your life is on fire for God? If not, why not?'

Lovingly, I say it again, 'There's more.'

✄ O God, help me evaluate my life, not only in the light of the past, but also in the light of the present. I therefore ask myself: am I on fire now? Am I one of your incendiaries? Father, I want so much to be. Give me more of your Spirit - now. In Jesus' Name. Amen.

A life change – life-changing

FOR READING AND MEDITATION – ACTS 9:1–19

'"Who are you, Lord?". . .

"I am Jesus, whom you are persecuting, . . ."' (v.5: NIV)

Making his way along the Damascus Road, the young Pharisee Saul is suddenly dazzled by a light brighter than the noonday sun. He falls to the ground. 'Who are you, Lord?' he cries. 'I am Jesus, whom you are persecuting,' comes the divine answer.

But is that all God has for Saul? By no means. 'Now get up,' says Christ, 'and go into the city.' Three days later, Saul meets Ananias who greets him, 'Brother Saul, [note the word brother: Ananias knows Saul is already converted] the Lord Jesus ... has sent me so that you may see again and be filled with the Holy Spirit.' There is something more for Saul than an encounter with the risen Christ, great and wonderful though that is – there is a mighty baptism in the Holy Spirit.

Saul's life was changed at his conversion, and again at his subsequent baptism in the Spirit. More than that – he became life-changing. In verses 23–25 we read: 'After many days had gone by, the Jews conspired ... But his followers ... lowered him in a basket.'

In a matter of 'many days' after his conversion and filling with the Spirit, he had many followers. This is spiritual fecundity! He was not only on fire for God – he also set other hearts on fire!

✎ *Father, I see that a blazing heart sets others afire. Set my heart afire with your Spirit and with your love so that I may kindle the same fire in others. In the Name of your Son, my Saviour. Amen.*

Fire! Fire! Fire!

FOR READING AND MEDITATION – ACTS 2:29–39

' "The promise is for you and your children . . .
for all whom the Lord our God will call." ' (v.39: NIV)

hristian biography is filled with accounts of those who have under-
one a thrilling baptism of power subsequent to their conversion:
harles Finney, Dwight L. Moody, John Wesley, Oswald Chambers,
amuel Chadwick in England, Blaise Pascal in France, and so on.
hey discovered, as millions more have, that the promise of the
pirit is to 'as many as the Lord our God will call' (Acts 2:39, NKJ).

Blaise Pascal, an exceptional inventor and genius, who died at
nly 39, wrote one of the most brilliant satires the world has ever
nown – *The Letters of a Provincial*. His *Pensées* is one of the most
owerful books on Christian thought that has ever been penned. He
ame to know Christ when he was 25, but it was not until six years
ter that he received a baptism in the Holy Spirit.

The record of this experience was found sewn into his waist-
oat after his death. This is what it said, 'The year of grace 1654,
londay, November 23. From about half past ten at night to about
alf past twelve. Fire! Fire! Fire!'

This is a remarkable document and records an experience that
nswered his deep sense of need. How I pray that many of you will
xperience something similar in your hearts and say, as did Pascal,
he year of grace 2004, June 3. Fire! Fire! Fire!'

*O God, I thank you that I have come to this hour. My heart is open. Come,
oly Spirit, come. Set my whole being alight with your holy fire. In Jesus' Name
pray. Amen.*

A stone in the heart

FOR READING AND MEDITATION – EZEKIEL 11:16–25
' "I will . . . put a new spirit in them; I will remove from them
their heart of stone and give them a heart of flesh." ' (v.19: NIV)

A woman of 70 once said to me, 'I have lived most of my life with a stone in my heart. It has been there ever since the day my mother said to me "I hate you" because I stood in the way of her going to another man.'

I saw the divine fire at work as she surrendered her deeply repressed anger to Christ, and the stone in her heart vanished.

Some years ago a missionary told me a remarkable story. He said, 'I came back from the missionary field a broken man, given up to die. My doctor said, "I don't know what is wrong, nothing I know can help you." A friend said, "I know what is wrong – you have hatred and bitterness buried deeply within your heart. I'm going to lay my hands on your head and pray for you that God will help you."

'Before my friend could move towards me, I broke down and wept. "Yes," I cried, "I'm a bitter and angry man. O God, forgive me."

The missionary continued: 'Suddenly the Holy Spirit fell upon me. I felt him burn up the anger that was deep within me; I got up and have never had a day's sickness since. Now my doctor says laughingly that I am so healthy I am ready for hard labour.'

O God, how can hate have any part of me when I belong to a Man who died upon a tree for those who hated him? Burn in me until all sinful hatred and anger are burned out of me. In Christ's Name I pray. Amen.

The first word in Christianity

FOR READING AND MEDITATION – ROMANS 7:14–25

'Who will rescue me from this body of death? Thanks be to God –
through Jesus Christ our Lord!' (vv.24–25: NIV)

The best way to deal with anger is to have it burned out of you by the Holy Spirit. It is not enough to say, 'I'll try hard not to be angry.'

Not that the Scripture doesn't put a great deal of emphasis on the use of the will. 'Put to death, therefore, whatever belongs to your earthly nature . . . rid yourselves of all such things as these: anger, rage, malice, slander and filthy language from your lips' (Col. 3:5, 8).

Clearly the Bible calls us to use our will. Effective Christian living, however, does not depend only on the exercise and function of the will. Behind our will is our whole nature – our thinking, our feeling. We must be willing to trust the Holy Spirit with this inner part of our being, and allow him to penetrate and burn out the rottenness that dwells within us.

Unless we are willing to get close enough to Christ for him to immerse us in the flame of the Spirit, then all that happens is that the Christian life becomes just an exercise of the will – try harder.

Many get caught up in the 'try harder' syndrome. They do not realise that the first word in Christianity is 'trust', and the second is 'try'. The more you understand what it means to trust, the easier it will be to obey.

✎ *O God my Father, help me comprehend all that you are saying to me this day. Save me from getting these words – trust and try – the wrong way round. In Jesus' Name. Amen.*

The refining fire

FOR READING AND MEDITATION – JEREMIAH 23:25–32

'"Is not my word like fire?" declares the Lord . . .' (v.29: NIV)

Many Christians get caught up in rule-keeping, and what holds them together is the good feeling this gives them. They are, as a friend of mine describes them, nothing more than 'happy Pharisees'.

They are not depending on Christ and the Holy Spirit to do his work within them but on the strength of their will to keep them going. There is a place for the will, but not here. The role of the will in the Christian life is to work out what God has worked in.

Behind most hatred and anger is a touchy, unsurrendered self. When the will is surrendered to Christ and the Holy Spirit, when the divine fire is allowed to burn within, then there is nothing in us waiting to be triggered off by circumstances or what others say.

A self that explodes in hatred and anger is probably diseased with self-centredness. Amazingly, it is easier to 'try harder' than to trust Christ and the Holy Spirit to come with his searching, scorching fire into the secret places of the soul. The wise and understanding, however, say with Wesley,

> *Refining fire, go through my heart,*
> *illuminate my soul;*
> *scatter thy life through every part*
> *and sanctify the whole.*

❧ O Father, make me wise and understanding. Show me the foolishness of self-dependency and break the stubbornness and commitment to independence that lies deep within me. In Jesus' Name I pray. Amen.

I pray for him daily

FOR READING AND MEDITATION – DEUTERONOMY 4:15–24

'For the Lord your God is a consuming fire . . .' (v.24: NIV)

Let me tell you the story of Dr F.B. Meyer and how he was able to allow God to work in him in such a way that jealousy was burned up in his heart.

When Dr Meyer was first introduced to a well-known annual convention, people poured in from all parts of the British Isles to hear his inspired and inspiring addresses. For years no speaker was more welcome. However, over time another speaker appeared – Dr Campbell Morgan, a fine and gripping Bible teacher. As Dr Morgan's Bible studies were scheduled in another hall at the same time as Dr Meyer's, people had to choose. Most chose to hear Dr Campbell Morgan.

When Dr Meyer saw what was happening, he confessed to more than one person that he found himself liable to bouts of jealousy.

Realising that he could not continue like this, he fell on his knees, surrendered himself afresh to Christ and asked that the fire of the Holy Spirit might overwhelm and overpower the flames of jealousy that had began to sear his soul.

Later, a close friend asked him whether he had been able to deal with his jealousy. 'Oh yes,' he replied, 'God has greatly helped me in this; now I pray for him daily.'

Loving heavenly Father, burn out of my system the poison of jealousy and help me to rejoice in the joy of all your children. May the fire of the divine creative love burn brightly on the altar of my soul. In Jesus' Name I ask it. Amen.

Dear brother Paul ...

'... our Lord's patience means salvation,
just as our dear brother Paul also wrote to you ...' (v.15: NIV)

The redeeming fire

'Lord, what about him?' Peter asked, pointing to John, the disciple whom Jesus loved. And Jesus replied: 'If I want him to remain ... what is that to you?' (John 21:21–22).

Jealousy begins with a wrong comparison. To compare ourselves with Christ is a healthy spiritual discipline, but to compare ourselves with others can lead to sin. If they are not as virtuous, we slip into spiritual pride; if they are more virtuous we are tempted to believe that it is only the appearance of virtue. The impulse to comparison must be redirected; it must be focused on Jesus.

I have often wondered how Peter overcame the flames of jealousy obviously at work within him. How did he deal with the emergence of Paul on the apostolic scene? On one occasion Paul confronted Peter rather heatedly: 'When Peter came to Antioch, I opposed him to his face,' wrote Paul (Gal. 2:11).

The Greek text here suggests a strong confrontation. We are not told how Peter reacted either to this rebuke or to Paul's great ministry, but when we read his two epistles we get a picture of a man whose face was entirely turned towards Jesus.

No hint of a lingering jealousy here. Had the fires of Pentecost burned it out? I believe they had.

O Father, if ever the flames of jealousy arise in my heart, overpower them, I pray, with your living fire. I want only the divine fire to burn on the altar of my heart. Grant it shall ever be so. In Christ's Name I ask it. Amen.

Near me ... near the fire

FOR READING AND MEDITATION – LUKE 24:13–35

' "Were not our hearts burning within us while
he talked with us on the road . . .?" ' (v.32: NIV)

A Christian counsellor writes, 'Jealousy is born of ignorance. If your counsellees know all their rival's secret burdens – they would not be so eager to exchange their lot. Explain this to people who are jealous, then the chances are they will be able to conquer.'

Personally, I think that advice is naive and superficial. The fires of jealousy have such a hold that it can only 'be redeemed from fire by fire'.

It is the fire-baptising Christ whose fire is the most powerful, the most searing, the most scorching and the most refining flame the universe knows. It eats through jealousy like acid through paper.

Put all your jealousies in his hands. He can do more about them than you. There is a saying attributed to Jesus which, though un-canonical, nevertheless has the ring of reality about it: 'He that is near me is near the fire.' How could this be otherwise when Jesus is God, and 'God is a consuming fire'?

My advice to those of you who struggle with the whole idea of the baptism in the Spirit, and can't make up their minds whether it comes at conversion or is subsequent to conversion, is: stop worrying about it and get close to Jesus.

You will soon feel the effects of his fiery energy and flame.

✎ *Lord Jesus, forgive me for trying to hold my life together through struggle when I see the keyword for everything is – surrender. As I take a step closer to you now, take a step closer to me. Let me feel the effects of your fire. Amen.*

The final battle

FOR READING AND MEDITATION – HEBREWS 13:1–6

'Keep your lives free from the love of money
and be content with what you have . . .' (v.5: NIV)

Balzac said more than a century ago, 'The final battle for Christianity will be over the money problem and the love of things.'

The more some people have, the more they want. Like some deadly diabetes of the soul, the thirst is not quenched by drinking. The sinister, deadly character of acquisitiveness is that it can buy a soul, bargain for and take integrity, corrupt all decent things and rot a person from within.

How then are the fires of acquisitiveness to be extinguished when once they get hold? I know of only one answer – to draw nearer to the Christ of one burning, cleansing flame. Only touched by him can you overcome the raging fire of acquisitiveness once it begins to burn on the altar of your heart.

I turn again to the note I have been striking day after day – the note of surrender. It is the turntable on which life turns from materialisation to spiritualisation.

The material must be surrendered to God, or we will surrender to the material. I am not talking about the fire of God burning up possessions, but the love of possessions. Mammon can become a master or a message. If unsurrendered to God, it is a master.

Lord Jesus Christ, you who enriched the world without riches, help me to take all my possessions – small or great – and make them the instruments of your purposes. Show me clearly that it is not on my possessions that your fire is to fall – but on me. Amen.

Minted personality

' "The one who received the seed . . . is the man who hears the word,
but . . . the deceitfulness of wealth choke it . . ." ' (v.22: NIV)

Only the passion of God can transcend the passion for things. Jesus talks about two things that choke the growing wheat and make it unfruitful: 'worry' and 'the deceitfulness of wealth'.

Moffatt translates this as 'the delight of being rich'. Jesus does not say that riches are the enemy, but 'the delight of being rich', that is wealth as an end in itself. Wealth or money that has not been surrendered.

If the 'delight' were in what can be done through the riches to help others, it would be a completely different picture. But the riches are an end in themselves and hence Mammon becomes God.

And as we saw, Jesus says, 'You cannot serve both God and Mammon.' But though we cannot serve God and Mammon, we can serve God with Mammon. When acquisitive desire is burned up, then life takes on a sense of stewardship. We feel we are handling our money on behalf of another.

That puts sacredness into the secular, transforms the sordid into the sacred. A minister friend refers to money as 'minted personality'. He was right; when given to God it is just as sacred as the words that fall from dedicated lips.

᚛ *Lord Jesus Christ, you who said, 'I have come to bring fire on the earth,' burn up my every trace of self-interest and self-concern. The only flame I want burning on the altar of my heart is your pure and heavenly flame. For your own dear Name's sake. Amen.*

Gold seekers – or God seekers?

FOR READING AND MEDITATION – 1 PETER 5:1–11

'Be shepherds . . . as God wants you to be;
not greedy for money, but eager to serve . . .' (v.2: NIV)

Throughout the ages, those who have most caught the spirit of their Master are the ones who have been gloriously emancipated from enslavement to things. From Jesus himself to Francis of Assisi, John Wesley, Catherine Booth, sanctity and poverty have known how to live together. None of these men and women of God despised things. What Christian can despise what God has made?

But to a surrendered Christian, things are always servants. Do not think you have to get rid of great wealth and possessions to be a dedicated Christian; you must, however, bring them under his control. Enjoy material possessions and use them, but watch them, for they can consume your being.

American history records the story of two groups who trekked from Omaha towards the far West. One group had written on their wagons 'Gold seekers'; the other group had written, 'God seekers'. For days they travelled in parallel lines and then they diverged – in more ways than one. The gold seekers went on to find their gold, but it passed through their fingers like water. The other group founded a community, which has lived on until today.

Are you a gold seeker or a God seeker? Has the divine fire consumed all acquisitive desires in your heart? If not, why not?

✎ O Father, again I pray that if there be any lesser flame burning on the altar of my heart, engulf it and consume it, and burn in me with your living flame. In Jesus' Name I ask it. Amen.

It all depends on the liver!

FOR READING AND MEDITATION – PHILIPPIANS 1:12–26
'For to me, to live is Christ and to die is gain.' (v.21: NIV)

Edmund Gosse, a man who sought pleasure for its own sake, came to the end of his life and said, 'You speak of the peace which the years bring. But they have brought no peace for me. I am terribly bored. Within me is terror at the idea of this sensual sufficiency coming to an end. I have no idea how the spiritual world would look to me for I haven't glanced at it since I was a child.'

When William James, the great psychologist, was asked, 'Is life worth living?' he answered wittily, 'That depends on the liver!' The ambiguity was intentional. It implied that for life to be worth living there had to be a proper functioning of one's physiology.

Paul endured a great amount of physical discomfort after he became a Christian. He wrote: 'I have worked much harder, been in prison more frequently … I have been constantly on the move … in danger … I have laboured and toiled and have often gone without sleep; I have known hunger and thirst and have often gone without food; I have been cold and naked …' (2 Cor. 11:23–27).

Yet he lived a joyous life.

Why? Because he did not live for pleasure. His heart was set on fire by Jesus Christ. A living interest worked within him – Christ.

Lord, you who walked the earth well amid the sick, strong amid the weak, alert amid the tired, radiant amid the dull, set my heart on fire with your power and your passion. For your honour and glory I pray. Amen.

Our greatest hunger

FOR READING AND MEDITATION – ECCLESIASTES 3:1–15

'He has also set eternity in the hearts of men ...' (v.11: NIV)

Freud said that for a human being to function effectively he must be consumed by the fire of pleasure. The pleasure principle, he believed, was the biggest hunger and drive in the human heart. Many disagreed. Adler, a follower of Freud, said, 'No, it is power that is the dominating hunger of the human heart. That is what men and women are seeking for – to be in control. That is the dominating passion of the human heart.'

The greatest hunger in the human heart is the hunger for God. God has set eternity in our hearts. Augustine put the same thought into his well-known prayer, 'O God, our hearts are restless and they cannot find rest until they find it in thee.' There is nothing wrong with experiencing pleasure; the wrong comes when we allow ourselves to be consumed by it, when we live for that and that alone.

The only way a destructive flame can be extinguished in our hearts is by the kindling of a hotter, purer fire. When we come close to the Christ of the burning, cleansing flame and surrender to him, he casts on the altar of our hearts a fire that consumes all other fires. The desire for pleasure is transformed by the heavenly flame – caught up in a higher and more consuming passion.

❧ *Father, I would be consumed with passion for you and your Son. I know that in my heart there is a desire to experience pleasure, but bring it right now under your complete control. In Jesus' Name I ask it. Amen.*

My, hasn't he changed!

The roots of hedonism – the pursuit of pleasure for its own sake – lie in inner emptiness and boredom. To compensate for boredom there arises a frenzy to find entertainment.

The remedy for this attitude of self-reference is self-surrender. A man who has himself on his hands will soon become bored, will soon tire of himself. But the man who turns himself over to Christ and allows that Man to control his life need never be bored.

Some years ago, a man came into my church and told me he had spent a whole week in Soho, London (a notorious vice spot), tasting every pleasure available. 'And how do you feel now that you have done that?' I asked. 'Pretty bored!' was his reply.

I invited him to repent of his former lifestyle and receive Christ into his life, which he did. Within days he was filled with the Spirit, and returned to the vice spot to share Christ with the very same prostitutes.

I heard one person say of him, 'My, hasn't he changed!' The love of pleasure had been engulfed by a love for Christ. He had been burning with the wrong kind of flame. Now he burned with love for Christ – a different and more powerful fire.

✝ Father, help me see that whenever I am bored with myself, it is because I am living with a wrong self; I need to be set at rights – within. Immerse me in the heavenly flame so that I will burn, not with self-interest, but with God interest. In Jesus' Name. Amen.

Making our hearts a hearth

FOR READING AND MEDITATION – ISAIAH 66:5–16

'See, the Lord is coming with fire . . .' (v.15: NIV)

Decades ago the get-rich-quick purveyors of pornography persuaded some of our befuddled judges and politicians to relax the laws governing this issue. Sexually deprived people, it was argued, had the right to sexual stimulation.

But the moral issues that had been pushed out through the door are now coming back in through the window. Newspapers which once took a lenient attitude to this issue are crying out that pornography must be brought under stricter control. Evidence shows that pornographic literature and films have a direct influence on the increasing sexual abuse and violence that we are witnessing.

Why were people able to open the floodgates to this evil? Why was this fire allowed to roar out of hell in the way it has?

Mainly it was because the fire that consumed the passionate advocates of pornography and moral permissiveness was stronger and fiercer than the fire that burned in the hearts of the Christians who were around at that time.

Oh some voices were raised in protest – but they were few and far between. The reason why the demonic fire rages so fiercely in our modern society is not because the divine fire is unable to combat it and engulf it, but because so few Christians are ready to allow their heart to become a hearth.

O God, make my heart a hearth on which your fire might continuously burn. And may the fire that burns in me be stronger than that which burns in the world. I ask this in and through Christ, my eternal Saviour and Lord. Amen.

Facts – on fire

'Then the disciples . . . preached everywhere, and the Lord worked with them and confirmed his word by the signs that accompanied it.' (v.20: NIV)

The answer to hell fire is Holy Spirit fire. The more powerfully the divine fire burns in you and me, the less powerful will be the impact of the demonic fire upon our society.

In Britain Christians are a small minority: surveys vary between five and ten per cent. But even as few as five per cent of Christians should still provide a nucleus powerful enough to maintain the moral guidelines in our society, and restrain those consumed with a desire to overthrow the commandments of the Lord.

Our power and influence, however, is in direct proportion to the degree with which we are consumed by the heavenly fire. So many of us lack passion. We attempt to meet the passionate arguments of the libertarians with cold logic, forgetting that it is only as ideas become inflamed that they have impact and power.

The facts and the logic must be set on fire by the Holy Spirit.

The disciples had all the facts of the gospel prior to Pentecost – fact number 1: a crucified Christ; fact number 2: a resurrected Christ; fact number 3: an ascended Christ.

Three great and gripping facts, but where did this get them? Behind closed doors for fear of the Jews!

Then came Pentecost and suddenly the facts were set on fire. After that – what a difference!

O God, I am grateful for all the facts that buttress my faith. Again I pray, set everything within me alight. Burn in me, o fire of God. In Jesus' Name. Amen.

The worst form of blasphemy

FOR READING AND MEDITATION – REVELATION 3:14–22

' "He who has an ear, let him hear what
the Spirit says to the churches." ' (v.22: NIV)

I met a man the other day whose job was to insure churches against fire. I told him I was praying that more churches would catch fire. Facetious? Yes, but he saw my point. There are far too many fire-proof churches in Christendom.

We have an example here today. With eyes that 'flashed like fire' (Rev. 1:14, MOFFATT) the risen Christ looked into the midst of the church at Laodicea and shouted, 'Be zealous,' or in other words, 'Get on fire.' The Laodiceans were lukewarm believers and Christ said to them that unless they got on fire he would 'spew' them out of his mouth. Dr. G. Campbell Morgan says, 'Lukewarmness is the worst form of blasphemy.'

Our Lord did not say that he would spew anyone out of his mouth for being too hot. Too much fire is better than lukewarmness. It is much easier to calm people down than to stir them up.

The cause of Christ has been harmed more by lukewarm Christians than by those who are too hot. If you are in a church where the fire has died down to a few glowing coals, ask God to breath on those coals again.

If your own fire has died down, rake off the ashes and stir up the gift of God within you. But whatever you do, don't be lukewarm.

✎ O God, end this 'lukewarm, wishy-washy, mumbling religion' that fills so many of our churches. Lord, set us on fire. We are sick of our disgusting indifference and you are sick of us. Send a Pentecost – at any cost. In Jesus' Name. Amen.

Fiery Christianity

FOR READING AND MEDITATION – JAMES 5:13–20
'Whoever turns a sinner from the error of his way will save him
from death and cover over a multitude of sins.' (v.20: NIV)

Carol Santiago, a New York girl, became a convert to Communism on
a visit to the Philippines. She eventually married a young man who
had been a minister but also become a Communist.

Later her husband was killed and she was left alone with two
small children. She was taken in by a Christian couple and it was
then that she came across her first dose of what she called 'fiery
Christianity'.

At first she was contemptuous of the couple's prayers, hymns
and Bible reading. Then one day her little child was ill. The couple
prayed and the child was instantly healed. She said, 'When I witnessed this, tears came to my eyes and for the first time in my life
I admitted to myself that there might be a God.'

The kindly deeds of the Christian couple piled up on the door-
step of her soul and their red-hot zeal for the Lord Jesus Christ made
a profound impression. One day at the supper table she asked the
couple to help her find the Saviour. They did – and within minutes
she passed from death to life. Now she is busy bringing others to
Christ. When people ask her why she does that which as a Communist she would have despised, her mind goes back to that Christian
family. Warm, flaming love in action.

*O Father, grant that I, too, may exhibit this fiery brand of Christianity
which your Son has died to make available to me. And may my fire set some
other soul on fire. In Christ's Name I ask it. Amen.*

A righteous fire

FOR READING AND MEDITATION – ISAIAH 30:27–33
'The Lord will cause men to hear his majestic voice ...
with ... consuming fire ...' (v.30: NIV)

Fanaticism leads people to sacrifice all things that stand in the way of their cause. But this is not the case with those who are on fire with the Holy Spirit. Christ calls us to fiery discipleship, but not to wild fanaticism.

I have talked to many Christian people who were involved in one kind of cause or another. Some of them burned with such zeal for their cause that they were willing to do anything to advance it – even going as far as to kill and destroy.

I asked one such person, 'What is the difference between the fire that burns in your heart now and the fire that once consumed you?' He thought for a few minutes and said, 'The fire of God is in harmony with all the principles of the universe; it is a righteous fire.'

I thought that his answer was very profound. He saw that the fire of God is a fire that burns against evil, but at the same time honours all that is righteous and true. Someone truly on fire for God will not become so consumed with the cause of Christ as to ignore or violate moral laws just to see the cause advanced. The fire that falls from heaven kindles not only the Spirit's glowing ardour, but a love for truth and righteousness that brings honour and glory to Jesus Christ.

Thank you, dear Father, that you inflame me not merely with zeal for a cause, but with zeal for all that is virtuous and true. I am so grateful. Amen.

To and for him

' "The fire must be kept burning on the altar continuously;
it must not go out." ' (v.13: NIV)

Paul wrote to the Corinthians: '… we are of the opinion and conviction that if one died for all, then all died; and he died for all, so that all those who live might live no longer to and for themselves, but to and for him who died and was raised again for their sake' (2 Cor. 5:14–15, AMPLIFIED).

There you have the secret of zestful and impassioned living: 'to and for him'. His cross becomes the altar of our soul where the fire never goes out, as it never went out in the Holy of Holies in the Temple of Jerusalem.

Where the divine fire is at work there will be no wild fanaticism but a strong and daring faith.

Beware of those Christians who say they are on fire for God but pursue their particular ideas with fanatical zeal. When I looked up the meaning of the word *fanatic* in my dictionary I was interested to read this: 'A fanatic is someone who is filled with excessive and mistaken enthusiasm, especially in religion.' The compilers of the dictionary obviously thought that the church or religion has the biggest share of fanatics.

The true fire, the heavenly fire, the fire of deep devotion to Jesus Christ, burns with a flame so hot that no lesser fire can survive it.

✎ *My Father and my God, grant that just as fire aspires upward, so may the flame of devotion that you have set alight in my heart rise ever upward in praise and adoration. In Jesus' Name. Amen.*

Honest to God

FOR READING AND MEDITATION – PSALM 51:1–13

'Surely you desire truth in the inner parts;
you teach me wisdom in the inmost place.' (v.6: NIV)

The redeeming fire

There may still be some who say: I see the need, but I cannot say that my life is on fire for God. I still need some further help in drawing close to this Christ of burning, cleansing flame. How do I go about it?

First, be absolutely honest with yourself. Face the question of whether you have actually experienced Jesus Christ as the giver of life and the forgiver of your sins. It may be that Christ has never been admitted into your life.

Maybe you are religious, but have never had a personal encounter with the Lord. If this is the case, I urge you to bow your head wherever you are and invite Christ into your life as Saviour and Lord. You may be a committed disciple of Christ but have no drive in your spirit. 'The church is full of people,' said one preacher, 'whose commitment is safe and limited.'

Honesty may compel you to confess that your discipleship is far from the unlimited discipleship of some first-century Christians, who were unreservedly abandoned to Jesus Christ. They could say with Paul, 'Neither count I my life dear unto myself' (Acts 20:24, KJV).

Take a moment right now honestly to appraise your spiritual life and ask yourself, 'Is my life a dull habit or an acute fever?'

✎ *O Father, help me to be honest. There are fears within me that cause me to draw back, but deep down I want to be truly yours. I know you want to draw closer to me: help me draw closer to you. In Jesus' Name. Amen.*

The road to recovery

FOR READING AND MEDITATION – REVELATION 2:1–7
'Remember the height from which you have fallen!
Repent and do the things you did at first . . .' (v.5: NIV)

he next step is that of repentance. Believe me, whenever we come
hort of what God expects and provides for our spiritual lives, the
ault is always ours – never his. Your spiritual condition is low not
ecause God has let you down or failed you in some way. It is that
e do not trust him to work things out in his own way.

The truth is that God knows what he is doing and can never
ail us. When it looks as if he has failed, or doesn't respond to us in
he way we like, it is because he is working out a plan that is hid-
en from us but fully revealed to him.

Trust is a hard thing for a Christian, and it is here that so many
f us fail – myself included. First we must repent of our lack of trust,
nd confess that we have been holding our lives together in our
wn strength instead of depending on Christ and the Holy Spirit.

When the church at Ephesus left their first love, our Lord showed
hem the way back: remember, repent and return.

I appeal to the hundreds of thousands reading these lines all
ver the world – join me in this prayer of confession and repen-
ance. There is no other road to spiritual recovery.

*O Father, forgive me that I have depended on myself instead of on you. I
onfess that I prefer self-management and self-sufficiency to trusting you. I
epent of that right now, and turn to you afresh – meet me afresh. In Christ's
Jame I ask it. Amen.*

We are coming to a King

FOR READING AND MEDITATION – LUKE 11:1–13

' "... how much more will your Father in heaven
give the Holy Spirit to those who ask him!" ' (v.13: NIV)

Alexander the Great's subjects could approach him at any time. A extremely poor man came to him with a request that seemed impertinent. He wanted a farm for himself, a dowry for his daughter and an education for his son. To the amazement of the court, Alexander granted every one. He said, 'I get weary of these people who come to see me asking for a gold piece. That man treated me like king. He asked big.' That is how God likes to give. He has nothing bigger or better to bestow than the Holy Spirit. John Newton writes,

> Thou art coming to a King;
> large petitions with thee bring.

You parents, ask yourselves what are the most joyous moments o your lives. Are they not when you can give your children somethin they long for and that you know is good for them?

It is the same with God. He is more eager to give you the Holy Spirit in all his fullness than you are to receive. It is terribly important for you to understand this eagerness of God to give, for if you have doubts about it, you will not come to him in confidence. You asking will be short-circuited from the start.

✒ I remind myself of the words of your servant, John. Let them go deep int my soul: 'This is the confidence we have in approaching God: that if we ask any thing according to his will, he hears us' (1 John 5:14). In Christ's Name. Amen

'Where is this place?'

FOR READING AND MEDITATION – JOHN 7:25–39

' "...'If anyone is thirsty, let him come to me and drink." ' (v.37: NIV)

ome of God's gifts are given indiscriminately – like the sunshine
d the rain. Not so the Holy Spirit. Before he is given there must
e a real desire to receive him.

Dr Paul Rees tells of a man who approached a speaker at a con-
rence on the theme of the Holy Spirit. 'My heart is so hungry,' he
id, 'I need what you have been preaching about. God knows, I
eed the power of the Holy Spirit in my life.' After a few questions,
e speaker said to the man, 'I believe I know where you could
ter into real deep blessing.'

'Where?' 'Come with me,' said the speaker and they went out of
e gates towards the mountains, a long way off. Every so often the
an would ask, 'Where is this place where I am to receive what I
ant?' 'Oh, it isn't very far,' his companion would say, 'just a little way.'

At last the man said, 'Listen, I can't bear this any longer. I've got
have a meeting with God. I want my life to be set on fire by the
oly Spirit. I must have it now.'

The friend said, 'This is the place right here.'

So together they knelt and right there, where the man had come
the point of desperation, he received his personal Pentecost.

Lord Jesus Christ, I think I see now the truth behind your words: 'Blessed
re those who hunger and thirst ... for they will be filled.' Help me to be both
efinite and desperate in my quest for a deeper experience of the Spirit. In
sus' Name. Amen.

A prayer for power

FOR READING AND MEDITATION – ACTS 4:23–31

'After they prayed, the place where they were meeting was shaken.
And they were all filled with the Holy Spirit . . .' (v.31: NIV)

What else do we need to do to be set on fire by the Holy Spirit? W must ask. Recently I came across a prayer by Dr Frank Laubach:

'Lord, end this wishy-washy, lukewarm, mumbling religion and set us on fire. Put the divine fire in us before the demonic fires destroy us and our world. Take away our small thoughts and our small loves. Make us big as the world in vision. Take away our weaknesses. Fill us with the strength of Jesus Christ. Help the sleeping might of the nation in which I live be awakened into glorious action by the Holy Spirit. We are sick of our disgusting indifference and we know that you are sick of us. Do not spew us out of your mouth, but set us on fire. God of courage, sweep aside our pitiful timidity. Make us divinely unafraid. Help Christendom to rise, not in fine sounding words but in deeds and in fire and in truth; change our defeat, in this battle for freedom and for Christ, into glorious victory. Give us a Pentecost at any cost. Send a Pentecost right now and begin it in me. Keep your promise, Lord Jesus Christ, and baptise us with the Holy Spirit and with fire. The altar is ready, the offering is laid. Now, Lord, send the fire.'

O Father, what more can I add? I make this prayer my very own. I hav asked, so now come and set me and the whole of your church world-wide o fire with the Holy Spirit. In Jesus' Name I ask it. Amen.

Maintaining the glow

FOR READING AND MEDITATION – MATTHEW 9:27–38
' ". . . According to your faith will it be done to you." ' (v.29: NIV)

What must we do to maintain the glow of God at the centre of our soul? Come back once again to the word I focused on earlier – *trust*. The divine fire is not ours to create, but it is ours to receive. We cannot work it up, we can only open ourselves to it.

We must be willing to break with all known sin, inward and outward, and ready to commit ourselves to living moment by moment in utter dependency on Christ.

It means taking God at his word: 'According to your faith will it be done to you.' Once you have opened your life to him and all sin has been put aside, then you must believe that he is now at work in you.

Believe that he is now engulfing that false fire that burned on the altar of your heart.

Believe that he is now burning up that false self that has made you an in-growing rather than an out-going person.

Believe that he is commissioning you and energising you to make your contribution to the biggest business in the world – making Christian disciples everywhere.

Believe also that 'the one who is in you is greater than the one who is in the world' (1 John 4:4). Heaven's fire is much more powerful than hell fire.

Believe it – and as faith functions, the fire will burn.

Father, I ask that not only will the divine fire burn within me but that it will go on burning within me. I would throw my all upon this altar fire. Keep me burning; keep me burning. In Jesus' Name. Amen.

Lips only too ready

FOR READING AND MEDITATION – JOHN 4:27–38
' "... open your eyes and look at the fields!
They are ripe for harvest." ' (v.35: NIV)

'If it were true that the ego had been brought up under the cross,'
said Sam Shoemaker, 'and nailed there with Christ, we shou[ld]
come away with our hearts on fire and our faces shining and o[ur]
lips only too ready to make known the wonders of his grace.'

There you have it: 'lips only too ready'.

One of the functions of fire is to extend itself outwardly. Fir[e]
spreads. The same is true of spiritual fire. Someone who is on fi[re]
is someone who does everything possible to bring others to th[e]
faith. Gamaliel Bradford once wrote, 'The true religious idealist, th[e]
true purveyor of the gospel, no sooner receives the light for himse[lf]
than he is seized with a passion for distributing it. As we see wi[th]
Moody or Booth, the instantaneous result of conversion is the impulse to concern others, to share as widely as possible the greate[st]
joy and benefit that this world or any other has to give.'

Do you realise that some of the great evangelists of the futu[re]
have not been converted yet? They are out there in the world at th[is]
very moment waiting to be won to Christ – through us. If we do[n't]
go out in fiery discipleship to win them, this could affect the futu[re.]
I find that a deeply challenging and a deeply sobering thought.

✎ *O Father, help us not to fail future generations by keeping the fire to ou[r]
selves – warming our own hearts but ignoring the needs of others. Give [us]
'lips only too ready'. In Jesus' Name we ask it. Amen.*

What is fire-lighted evangelism?

FOR READING AND MEDITATION – 1 PETER 3:8–16

'. . . Always be prepared to give an answer to everyone who asks you
to give the reason for the hope that you have.' (v.15: NIV)

he fiery discipleship which Christ offers us all will affect our every-
ay relationships. Fire-baptised businessmen will burn with such
assion for Jesus that their clients will say, 'What is so different about
ou?' Fire-baptised nurses will go about their tasks in such a way
hat patients will be compelled to ask, 'What is it that so powerfully
otivates you?' Fire-baptised housewives will relate to their neigh-
ours in such a manner that when an invitation is given to an evan-
elistic coffee morning they respond. Fire-baptised students will
pply themselves to their studies in a way that marks them out as
tudents who know where they are going.

Fiery discipleship means more than shouting 'Jesus saves' or
ushing gospel leaflets into people's hands; it means guided pene-
ation into the lives of those we relate with day after day after day.

It means laughing with them as well as praying for them; cry-
g with them as well as inviting them to church; going out of our
ay to let them know we care as well as putting their names on a
rayer list. There will be failures – but there will be victories too,
ictories that a placid, timid, unimaginative, complacent Christian-
y will never, never win!

O God, burn so powerfully in me that all those with whom I come in con-
ct will recognise that someone else lives in me. And when the right moment
mes to share you with others – help me to take it without hesitation or fear.
Jesus' Name. Amen.

More fire!

FOR READING AND MEDITATION – LUKE 3:7–18

' "He will baptise you with the Holy Spirit and with fire." ' (v.16: NIV)

Permit me to gather up the essential elements of what we have been saying. There are two kinds of fire in this universe: one divine, the other demonic; one heavenly, the other hellish. And the only way we can be saved from the fire of hell, is by surrendering ourselves to the fire that comes from heaven. The fires that ravage can only be extinguished by the fire that redeems. As T.S. Elliot put it, 'We only live, only suspire, consumed by either fire or fire.'

This is why there must be more fire in our church services and our prayer meetings, more fire in our pulpits and our pews, more fire in our family devotions – more fire in our evangelistic outreach, our missionary support, in our business and professional activities, more fire in our fight against poverty, immorality and permissiveness. Fire! More fire! Christ's kind of fire – for our intellect, emotions and will, for our homes, our churches, our businesses and our nations. So with Amy Carmichael let us look once more at the fire-baptising Christ, draw as closely as we can to him and say:

> Give me the love that leads the way,
> the faith that nothing can dismay,
> the hope no disappointments tire,
> the passion that will burn like fire.
> let me not sink to be a clod:
> make me thy fuel, Flame of God.

In Christ's peerless and precious Name I ask this. Amen.

A call to arms

There are in existence two orders and two kingdoms, locked together in mortal combat. One is the kingdom of God and the other is the kingdom of the devil. And Christians are on the cutting edge of that conflict.

Many Christians are pacifists when it comes to earthly warfare, but no one can be a pacifist when it comes to spiritual warfare.

Once we enlist in the army of God, we need to train in the art of offensive and defensive spiritual warfare. At certain times in the Christian life, we will find ourselves in a battle that demands fierce hand-to-hand combat with the forces of darkness, and unless we know how to handle these situations, we shall easily be overthrown.

The Bible shows us that the devil and his minions are bitter enemies of God. Because they are powerless against the Almighty, they turn their concentrated attention on those who are his followers – you and I. The word *against* occurs six times in all in this passage. This shows that when a person comes over to Jesus Christ, he is immediately identified as being for God, and against the devil.

There can be no compromise on this issue, no peaceful co-existence pact. To be for God is to be against the devil.

Gracious Father, help me get my perspectives clear. Train me in the art of spiritual warfare so that I will be able to resist every onslaught of the devil and come through every conflict victoriously. In Jesus' Name. Amen.

Is there a personal devil?

FOR READING AND MEDITATION – JOHN 8:36–44

'"He was a murderer from the beginning …"' (v.44: NIV)

Surprisingly, some Christians do not believe in a personal devil. A modern-day theologian writes, 'Let us put to sleep this idea of a personal devil who walks about with a pitchfork seeking to tumble people into hell. Evil is not a personality but an influence – it is just the darkness where the light ought to be.'

While I agree that the picture of a personal devil with pitchfork and horns is not found in Scripture, the concept of a personal devil is found everywhere in Scripture. Many of the names given to him denote personality: Satan, deceiver, liar, murderer, accuser, tempter, prince of the power of the air, and so on.

Men don't believe in the devil now, as their fathers used to do.
They reject one creed because it's old, for another because it's new,
but who dogs the steps of the toiling saint, who spreads the net for
  his feet,
who sows the tares in the world's broad fields where the Saviour sows
  his wheat,
they may say the devil has never lived, they may say the devil has gone,
but simple people would like to know – who carries his business on?

Take it from me, whether or not you believe in the devil, he most certainly believes in you.

⚔ *Father, help me see that it is to Satan's advantage for me not to believe in him. Show me the strategies I need to overcome him. In Christ's Name. Amen.*

Satan – an influence or an intelligence?

FOR READING AND MEDITATION – MATTHEW 4:1–11

'Then Jesus said to him, "Away with you, Satan!
For it is written . . ." ' (v. 10: NKJ)

The names given to the devil in Scripture show him to be a real personality. In this passage, Jesus is seen in direct confrontation with the devil, engaging in conversation with him. Some liberal theologians explain this in these terms – Christ (they say) was having a conversation with the dark thoughts that arose from within his nature, so any 'devil' that was present was subjective, not objective.

If we allow that Christ had dark thoughts within his nature, then the whole scheme of redemption tumbles like a pack of cards, for a saviour who is not perfect could never fully atone for our sins.

Actually, it is to Satan's advantage to get us to believe that he is not a personal being. For if there is no personal devil, there can be no personal resistance.

Don't allow yourself to be deceived into thinking that the term devil is a synonym for the evil influence that is in the world. The devil is more than an evil influence; he is an evil intelligence. Only when we recognise this fact will we be motivated to take steps to effectively resist him.

Father, help me see that the first step in spiritual warfare is to 'know the enemy'. For until I know and understand my enemy, I will not be able to defeat him. Deepen my knowledge of these important truths, I pray. In Jesus' Name. Amen.

Who cleft the devil's foot?

FOR READING AND MEDITATION – ISAIAH 14:9–15; EZEKIEL 28:11–19

'For you have said in your heart . . . "I will be like the Most High." '
(Isa. 14:13–14, NKJ)

The seventeenth-century poet John Donne wrote that there were two things he could not fathom: 'Where all the past years are, and who cleft the devil's foot'.

The books of Isaiah and Ezekiel give us a very clear picture, however, of what has been called 'The Rise and Fall of the Satanic Empire'. Jesus, while he was here on earth, said to his disciples: 'I saw Satan falling from heaven as a flash of lightning' (Luke 10:18 TLB). Lucifer (Satan) was created as a beautiful and morally perfect angelic being. 'You were the perfection of wisdom and beauty' (Ezek. 28:12, TLB). 'You were perfect in all you did from the day you were created' (Ezek. 28:15, TLB).

He was upright, brilliant and had an enormous capacity for achievement. God entrusted Lucifer with the highest offices in the universe: 'I appointed you to be the anointed guardian cherub. You had access to the holy mountain of God . . . O overshadowing cherub' (Ezek. 28:14 –16, TLB). In his heart, however, arose a rebellious thought, 'I will be like the Most High' (Isaiah 14:14, TLB).

Five times that phrase *I will* is used in this passage. Two little words, I will. They reveal what lies behind the awful blight of sin – a created will coming into conflict with the will of the Creator.

✎ O Father, now that I see the real issue that lies behind sin – a created will colliding with the will of the Creator – help me constantly to align my will with your will. In Jesus' Name I ask it. Amen.

The strength of satanic forces

FOR READING AND MEDITATION – JUDE 1–13

'... the angels who did not keep their positions of authority ... these he has kept in darkness, bound with everlasting chains ...' (v. 6: NIV)

Lucifer aspired to take over the throne of God and usurp the position of his Creator. Once that happened, Lucifer was expelled from heaven, together with the other angels who had shared his rebellious attitude. This is the fall from heaven that Jesus told his disciples he had witnessed.

Satan, apparently losing little of his administrative skill, marshalled these fallen angels to work against God and his creation. We do not know how many angels fell with Satan, but doubtless it must have been a colossal number. When Jesus asked a demoniac: 'What is your name?' (Luke 8:30), the demons answered: 'Legion.' If they were telling the truth, the man was controlled by thousands of demons. A Roman legion contained 6 000 men! Little wonder, then, that Paul warned the Ephesians they were involved in tremendous spiritual conflict: 'We are not fighting against people made of flesh and blood, but against persons without bodies – the evil rulers of the unseen world, those mighty satanic beings and great evil princes of darkness who rule this world' (Eph. 6:12, TLB).

One of America's founding fathers said, 'If men will not be governed by God, then they will be ruled by tyrants.' How sad that people actually choose to be governed by Satan rather than by God.

O God my Father, I am so thankful that I am under the sway of your eternal and everlasting kingdom. May I come more and more under its sway hour by hour and day by day. In Jesus' Name I pray. Amen.

The Second Coming of Satan

FOR READING AND MEDITATION – 1 TIMOTHY 4:1–16

'… in the last times some in the church will turn away from Christ and become eager followers of teachers with devil-inspired ideas.' (v. 1: TLB)

If we are to be effective in the art of spiritual warfare, we must s that mankind's fiercest foe is not death or disease, but the deceiv we know as the devil. He is behind all our individual woes and i ternational wars. He instigates all our crime and violence. He writ the script for human sorrow.

I think it is safe to say that in this generation, the devil is ge ting more exposure than he has had since the beginning of recor ed time. Not so many years ago, *The Exorcist* broke all box offi records. It has been followed by a spate of films and television show on the subject of the paranormal – so much so that someone ha described this age as the Second Coming of Satan.

In songs, in art, in the theatre, Satan is making his presence fe in a new and powerful way. And now the so-called science of par psychology has given him admittance to the halls of academia. Ho sad that some colleges and universities present accredited cours on Satanism, but bar any reference to the teachings of Jesus Chris

Make no mistake, the devil is on the march. But don't let th thought trouble you too deeply, for the Scripture shows it to be march to oblivion (Rev. 20:10).

O God, I am so grateful for the assurances of Scripture. They come to m at the moment I most need them and hold me fast when the strongest cu rents threaten to sweep me away from my spiritual moorings. Thank yo dear Father. Amen.

Danger – the devil at work

FOR READING AND MEDITATION – 1 PETER 5:1–11

'... Your enemy the devil prowls around like a roaring lion ...' (v. 8: NIV)

A woman came up to me in a meeting and said, 'I think you are giving too much credit to the devil. He is such an insignificant person compared to God that we ought not even mention his name.'

However, we cannot go through life without coming into direct contact with Satan and his forces. It is unrealistic to think that many of the problems confronting us daily have no devilish strategy behind them. Dr Martyn Lloyd-Jones said, 'I am certain that one of the main causes of the ill state of the church today is the fact that the devil is being forgotten ... we have become so psychological in our attitude and thinking. We are ignorant of this great objective fact – the being, the existence of the devil, the adversary, the accuser and his "fiery darts".'

Does the thought of doing battle with the devil frighten you? Then heed the words of Corrie ten Boom, 'The fear of the devil is most likely from the devil himself.'

God has given us all the protection we need to defend ourselves against the attacks of Satan. When we know how to avail ourselves from this protection, we will no longer be afraid of the devil – rather, he will be afraid of us.

O God, as I go deeper into this subject, I am becoming increasingly aware of the intensity of the spiritual battle in which I am engaged. Dispel every fear that may arise in me and show me the way to power and victory. In Jesus' Name I pray. Amen.

God's armour – our only protection

'Put on the whole armour of God, that you may be able to
stand against the wiles of the devil.' (v. 11: NKJ)

The armour of God

God has provided armour for us in Christ. The spiritual armour of
God is our only protection against the wiles of Satan. But it will do
us no good unless we avail ourselves from it in its entirety.

Let's concentrate on the first of these two vital issues. Constantly
before us is the fact that such is the might and power of Satan that
nothing apart from the armour of God will protect us from his
onslaughts. Mark that and mark it well. There are many Christians
who have tried to stand against Satan in their own strength and
have found themselves victims. Satan gets us to believe we can resist
him in our own strength, but when we think that – we are finished.

In my time I have seen many believers lulled by Satan. We never
live more dangerously than when we depend on our spiritual experience and understanding of Christian doctrine to protect us from
the fiery darts of the enemy.

One thing and one thing only can protect us from the attacks
of Satan. That is the spiritual armour which God has provided. You
see, in the devil we are dealing with a foe that is inferior in power
only to the Almighty himself. Therefore, nothing less than the protection that God provides is adequate for our need.

✎ *O Father, I need to get this matter straight, for I see that if my dependence
is on anything other than you, then I am sunk. Drive this truth deep into my
spirit this day. In Jesus' Name. Amen.*

How not to be a wobbly Christian

FOR READING AND MEDITATION – ROMANS 13:8–14

'Therefore let us cast off the works of darkness,
and let us put on the armour of light.' (v. 12: NKJ)

The armour of God

We are exhorted to put on the whole armour of God – not just a few of the pieces we think are most suitable. This is something of crucial importance. We are not to pick and choose in this matter.

If we are to be steadfast soldiers in the Lord's army, if we are to avoid becoming what John Stott calls 'wobbly Christians who have no firm foothold in Christ', then we must put on the entire equipment which God provides for us.

We cannot, we dare not, select parts of the armour and say, 'I don't really like the helmet of salvation, but I don't mind wearing the breastplate of righteousness.' The moment you say, 'I need the breastplate, but I don't need the helmet' you are defeated. You need it all – the whole armour of God.

Our understanding of what is involved in spiritual defence against Satan is extremely inadequate – we just don't have sufficient knowledge of what is involved. It is God alone who knows our enemy, and it is God alone who knows exactly how to protect us.

So learn this lesson now before going any farther – every single piece of God's armour is essential, and to select some and leave the others is to take the route to failure and defeat.

O God, deliver me from the attitude of pride that seeks to put my ideas ahead of your ideas. You know more about what I need to protect me from the enemy than I do. Help me ever to trust your judgment. In Jesus' Name I ask it. Amen.

The belt of truth

FOR READING AND MEDITATION – PSALM 119:145–160
'You are near, O Lord, and all your commandments are truth.' (v. 151: NKJ)

Paul, in listing the six main pieces of a soldier's equipment, illustrates the six main ways to defend ourselves against Satan's power – truth, righteousness, steadfastness, faith, salvation and the Word of God. Most commentators believe that Paul was chained to a soldier as he wrote the letter (Eph. 6:20). The sight of him would have kindled Paul's imagination.

The list begins with the belt of truth. Why does the apostle start with such a seemingly insignificant item? Why did he not begin with one of the bigger and more important pieces of equipment?

The order in which these pieces are given to us is an inspired order, and if we change the order we make our position extremely perilous. The reason why many Christians fail to wield the sword of the Spirit effectively is because they have not first girded their waist with truth. If we reverse the order, we succeed only in weakening our spiritual defence.

It is very important that we grasp this. Girding our waist with truth is always the place to start whenever we are under satanic attack. If you don't start right, then you will not finish right.

So let this thought take hold of you: you cannot do battle with the devil until you first gird your waist with truth.

℣ *Gracious and loving Father, help me to absorb this thought into my inner being this day so that it will stay with me for the rest of my life: I cannot do battle with the devil until I first gird my waist with truth. Amen.*

The power and importance of truth

FOR READING AND MEDITATION – PSALM 51:1–17

'Surely you desire truth in the inner parts ...' (v. 6: NIV)

Girding the waist was always a symbol of readiness to fight. The officers in the Roman army wore short skirts, like a Scottish kilt. Over this they had a cloak or tunic secured at the waist with a girdle. When they were about to enter into battle, they would tuck the tunic up under the girdle so as to leave their legs free and unencumbered for the fight.

What does Paul's phrase, 'gird your waist with truth' really mean? The word *truth* can be looked at in two ways: one, objective truth, as found in Jesus Christ, and two, subjective truth as found in the qualities of honesty and sincerity. The Puritan, William Gurnall, points out that whether the word implies truth of doctrine or truth of heart, one will not do without the other.

I personally believe that in Ephesians 6, Paul is emphasising subjective truth – truth in the inner being. You see, when we are deceitful or hypocritical, or resort to intrigue and scheming, we are playing the devil's game. What Satan despises is transparent truth – he flees from it.

Having our waist girded with truth, then, means being possessed with truth, guided by truth and controlled by truth. No truth – no power over Satan.

O Father, I see that you have set standards by which I rise or fall. When I fulfil them I rise, when I break them I fall. Give me the strength I need to fulfil all your laws, especially the law of truth. In Jesus' Name. Amen.

Under the searchlight of truth

FOR READING AND MEDITATION – PSALM 139:1–24
'Search me thoroughly, O God, and know my heart!
Try me and know my thoughts.' (v.23: AMPLIFIED)

The mental health experts tell us that being willing to face the truth about ourselves is an important part of our growth toward maturity; the same is true in the spiritual realm. How easy it is to hide from the truth and imagine ourselves to be truthful when not.

Sigmund Freud made an interesting contribution to our understanding of human personality when he documented with true genius the incredibly subtle ways in which we lie to ourselves. Psychologists call them 'defence mechanisms', but a more Biblical view of them would be 'lying mechanisms'.

We would all much prefer to be called defensive than dishonest. But whenever we allow ourselves to be self-deceived, we not only impede our spiritual growth – we also lower our defences against Satan. He thrives on deception, and if he can push us toward self-deception, he maintains a definite advantage over us.

Many of us might react with horror to the suggestion that we may be dishonest, for we would not dream of doing or saying anything that was not according to the truth. Yet it is possible to be honest on the outside, and hide from truth on the inside. All of us, even mature Christians, are capable of hiding from truth.

✎ *O Father, I see that if I am to overcome Satan, then I must know truth inwardly as well as outwardly. Search my heart today, dear Lord, and bring to the surface the things within me that are untrue. In Jesus' Name I ask it. Amen.*

Three forms of dishonesty

FOR READING AND MEDITATION – 1 JOHN 1:1–10

'If we claim to be without sin, we deceive ourselves
and the truth is not in us.' (v.8: NIV)

Is it true Christians can inwardly resist truth? Let me identify three defences we use. The first is projection. We are to blame for something, but we project the blame on to someone else so that we can feel more comfortable about ourselves. It may sound simple, but all dishonesty deprives – even simple dishonesty.

Secondly, denial. How many times do we refuse to face that we may be angry? When someone says, 'Why are you angry?' we reply with bristling hostility, 'I'm not angry!' We fail to recognise what others can plainly see. And denial is a form of inner deceit and dishonesty. Thirdly is rationalisation. We do this whenever we persuade ourselves that something is what it is not. C.S. Lewis points out that when our neighbour does something wrong, he or she is 'bad', while when we do it, it is because we did not get enough sleep, or someone gave us a rough time, and so on.

All defence mechanisms deprive us of inner honesty. Apart from hindering our spiritual growth, they lower our defences against Satan. Over and over again in Scripture we are bidden to open up to honesty. The more honest we can be, the more spiritually powerful and effective we can be.

Lord Jesus, help me to open up to honesty. For I see that the more honest I am, the more authority I can wield over Satan. I want to be able to say, as you said, 'The ruler of this world is coming, and he has nothing in me.' For your own dear Name's sake. Amen.

Without truth – we get nowhere

FOR READING AND MEDITATION – HOSEA 10:12

'...it is time to seek the Lord...' (NKJ)

Clinton McLemore says, 'Whenever any one of us embodies and promotes personal honesty, we are knowingly or unknowingly doing God's work.' Ask yourself right now, 'Am I an honest person?' If there are areas of your life where you are not sure, then spend some time before God in prayer today asking him to help you root out all dishonesty and insincerity.

Honesty is our first line of defence against Satan. If we are not honest, or not willing to be honest, then the devil will soon disable us. We live in an age which, generally speaking, evades the truth. We seem to take it for granted that advertisements distort, contracts contain fine print that no one draws our attention to, and professionals conceal one another's malpractices. Few domains of life are uncompromised, few social structures are not tainted.

The Christian church is not without blame either. Consider the endless and often angular manoeuvrings of some church boards and committees. God put the church in the world but somehow the devil has put the world in the church.

'It is time to seek the Lord.' If we don't get things straightened out at the start, then how can we hope to be victorious in the war against Satan? Sin, at its root, is a stubborn refusal to deal with truth.

⊲ *O God, forgive us that we, your redeemed people, sometimes pursue our own interests and allow truth to be dragged in the gutter. Help us, dear Lord. For without truth we have no power. Amen.*

The breastplate of righteousness

FOR READING AND MEDITATION – PSALM 132:1–18

' "May your priests be clothed with righteousness;
may your saints sing for joy." ' (v. 9: NIV)

A soldier's breastplate extended from the base of the neck to the upper part of the thighs, covering many important parts of the body, particularly the heart.

Some commentators suggest the breastplate covered only the front of the chest and provided no protection for the soldier's back. A Christian, they say, should face the devil and never turn his back to expose a part that is unguarded.

Interesting idea but it must not be given too much credence, for the soldier's breastplate often covered his back as well as his front. A soldier's breastplate covered mainly his heart. The spiritual application of this is that in Christ we have all the protection we need against negative or desolating feelings – the heart being seen as the focal point of the emotions.

What an exciting thought this presents. By putting on the breastplate of righteousness, we have the resources to deal with all those debilitating feelings that tend to bring us down into depression and despair – unworthiness, inadequacy, fear, and so on.

When I once mentioned this to a friend who asked me what I thought the breastplate of righteousness was for, he said, 'It sounds too good to be true.' I replied, 'It's too good not to be true.'

Gracious Lord and Master, how can I sufficiently thank you for providing a defence against this most difficult of problems – emotional distress. Show me how to apply your truth to this part of my personality. In Jesus' Name. Amen.

Nothing wrong with Christ

FOR READING AND MEDITATION – ROMANS 8:31–39
'Who then will condemn us? Will Christ?
No! For he is the one who died for us . . .' (v. 34: TLB)

Paul points out in 2 Corinthians 6:7 that our personal righteousness can be a definite defence against Satan. In Ephesians 6, however, the emphasis is not on our righteousness in Christ, but Christ's righteousness in us.

How does putting on the breastplate of righteousness act as a spiritual defence against the wiles of the devil? What about those people who have definitely surrendered their lives to Christ but who still feel they are not good enough to be saved.

Why do they have such feeling? The answer is simple – they have taken their eyes off Christ and his righteousness and have focused on themselves and their righteousness. And in doing that, they play right into the devil's hands.

You see, the devil can find all kinds of flaws and blemishes in your righteousness, but he can find nothing wrong with the righteousness of Christ. The way to withstand an attack like this is to put on the breastplate of righteousness. In other words, remind yourself and Satan that you stand, not on your own merits but on Christ's. This may sound simple, even simplistic to some, but I have lived long enough to see people latch on to it and come from the depths of emotional distress to the heights of spiritual exaltation.

Lord Jesus, help me to latch on to it too. Make it crystal clear to my spirit that although the devil can find many flaws in my righteousness, he cannot find a single flaw in yours. I rest my case – on you. Thank you, dear Lord. Amen.

The tyranny of the oughts

FOR READING AND MEDITATION – ROMANS 5:1–11
'Therefore, having been justified by faith, we have peace
with God through our Lord Jesus Christ.' (v. 1: NKJ)

Satan delights to whip up the feeling that we are accepted by God only when we are doing everything perfectly. This gives rise to perfectionism – a condition afflicting multitudes of Christians.

The chief characteristic of perfectionism is a constant overall feeling of never doing enough to be thought well of by God. Karen Horney describes it as 'the tyranny of the oughts'. Here are some typical statements of those who are afflicted in this way, 'I ought to do better', 'I ought to have done better', 'I ought to be able to do better'.

There is nothing wrong with wanting to do better, but in the twisted thinking of perfectionists, because they ought to have done better, they will not be accepted or thought well of by God. They believe their acceptance by God depends on their performance; they constantly try to develop a righteousness of their own, rather than resting in the righteousness which Christ has provided for them.

If you suffer from this condition, then it's time to put on your spiritual breastplate.

You need to remind yourself that the way you came into the Christian life is the way you go on. Depend on Christ and his righteousness, not on yourself and your righteousness. You are not working to be saved; you are working because you are saved.

✎ Lord Jesus, I see that when I stand in your righteousness, I stand in God's smile. But when I stand in my own righteousness, I stand in God's frown. Help me move over from frown to smile. In your dear Name. Amen.

Paul's breastplate in place

FOR READING AND MEDITATION – 1 CORINTHIANS 15:1–11
'But by the grace of God I am what I am ...' (v. 10: NIV)

Satan attacks subtly by drawing our attention to what other Christians may be saying or thinking about us. The apostle Paul used the breastplate of righteousness as his spiritual defence when Satan targeted him with this particular form of discouragement. Paul's background was anti-Christian, and he could never get completely away from that. He had been the most hostile and brutal persecutor of the church, and he must therefore have constantly run across families whose loved ones he had put to death.

How did Paul react to criticism? Did he succumb to discouragement? Did he say, 'What's the use of working my fingers to the bone for these unappreciative people? They don't do anything but hurl recriminations in my face!' This is what the devil would have liked him to do. But look at what he does. He says, 'By the grace of God I am what I am.'

Can you see what he is doing? He is using the breastplate of righteousness. He is saying, in other words, 'I don't need to do anything to protect myself; what I am is what Christ has made me. I am not standing in my own righteousness, I am standing in his.' What a lesson in how to use the spiritual breastplate! You and I need to learn this lesson too.

✎ O God, day by day I am catching little glimpses of what you are trying to teach me – that the more I depend on your righteousness and the less I depend on my own, the better off I will be. Help me to learn it – and learn it completely. Amen.

How to handle confusion

FOR READING AND MEDITATION – ROMANS 8:29–39

'... nothing will ever be able to separate us from the love of God demonstrated by our Lord Jesus Christ ...' (v. 39: TLB)

Deep in the centre of our being is a compulsive demand to be in control and to live in a predictable, understandable world. Confusion presents a serious challenge, and is the enemy of those who like to have clear answers for everything. Satan, knowing this, steps in whenever he can to take full advantage of it.

Whenever Satan sees that we are not wearing our spiritual breastplate, he comes to us and says something like this, 'Look at the great problems that are all around you – earthquakes, famines, violence, cruelty to children ... how can you believe in a God of love when these things are going on in the world?' Sometimes he presses home with such power and force that you cannot make sense of it, you cannot understand and you have no clear answers. There is only one clear answer against such assaults; it is to put on the 'breastplate of righteousness'. You might not understand particular happenings or give any explanation. But you do know that the God who clothed you with his righteousness and saved you from a lost eternity must have your highest interests, and those of his universe, at heart.

Hold on to that, and your heart will be protected from despair, even though your mind struggles to comprehend what is happening. You can live in peace even though you do not know all the answers.

Father God, I see that I can experience security in my heart even when my mind cannot understand your ways. Hidden in Christ and his righteousness, I am safe. I am so thankful. Amen.

Satan as an angel of light

FOR READING AND MEDITATION – PHILIPPIANS 1:1–11

'. . . he who has begun a good work in you will complete it . . .' (v. 6: NKJ)

When everything is going wrong, the devil moves alongside and whispers, 'Do you still believe that God is love?' 'Yes,' you say. Then he transforms himself into an angel of light and tries another tactic. 'Well', he says, 'you may say that God is love, but it is obvious that he does not love you. If he did then he would not allow you to go through these difficult situations.'

There is only one protection against such an assault; to put the 'breastplate of righteousness' firmly in place. Nothing else will avail. Point him to the truth of Romans 8:28: 'We know that all things work together for good to those who love God.' Notice, Paul does not say, 'we understand', but 'we know that all things work together for good to those who love God, to those who are called according to his purpose' (NKJ).

This brings you directly to the theme of justification by faith, the righteousness of Christ. Rest on that, and that is all you need. Say to yourself, 'He has set his love upon me and saved me. I will have courage. I do not know what is happening to me now. I cannot fathom it. But if he has begun his work in me, then I know he will go on to complete it.'

✒ *O God, what wondrous power there is in your Word. I can feel it doing me good even as I read and ponder it. Give me a greater knowledge of your Word, for only through that can I maintain an advantage over the devil. In Jesus' Name. Amen.*

What happens when we sin?

FOR READING AND MEDITATION – 1 JOHN 1:5–10, 2:1–2
'If we confess our sins, he is faithful and just to forgive us our sins
and to cleanse us from all unrighteousness.' (v. 9: NKJ)

The Hebrew *Satan* means 'adversary', and the Greek word *devil* means 'slanderer'. This is the nature of the Evil One – he is never happier than when he is engaged in pointing the finger of scorn and accusation at us whenever we have sinned or failed.

It is part of the doctrine of the church that a Christian may sometimes fall into sin. We are saved, but we are still fallible. God forbid that we should fall into sin, but if we do, we must remember that we have 'an advocate with the Father, Jesus Christ the righteous'. You can be sure, however, that when you fall into sin, the devil will come to you and say, 'You were forgiven when you became a Christian because you sinned in ignorance, but now that you are a Christian you have sinned against the light. There can be no forgiveness for you now. You are lost – and lost for ever.'

The answer to this, as with all of Satan's accusations, is to put on the 'breastplate of righteousness'. Remind him that God's righteousness not only covers us at our salvation, but continues to cover us for time and eternity.

Never allow the devil to use a particular sin to call into question your whole standing before God. That is something that has been settled in heaven, not in the debating chamber of the devil.

My Father and my God, my heart overflows at the revelation of your full and free forgiveness. Help me not to take it for granted but to take it with gratitude. In Jesus' Name I pray. Amen.

The shoes of peace

FOR READING AND MEDITATION – PHILIPPIANS 1:12–30

'... stand firm in one spirit, contending as one man
for the faith of the gospel ...' (v. 27: NIV)

Shoes are absolutely essential to a soldier. Imagine a barefoot soldier. The rough ground would tear his feet to pieces and render him unfit for duty. But with a stout pair of shoes, he would be ready to face anything that came.

Markus Barth says that the shoes a Roman soldier would have worn in Paul's day were more a sandal. They were known as *caligae* (half boots) consisting of 'heavy studded leather soles tied to the ankles or shins with more or less ornamental straps'. These equipped the soldier to stand solid, preventing his feet from slipping or sliding.

What did Paul have in mind when he penned the words, 'Stand therefore, having ... shod your feet with the preparation of the gospel of peace'? The *New English Bible* brings home the point of the passage in a most effective way, translating it thus: 'Let the shoes on your feet be the gospel of peace, to give you firm footing.'

The shoes we are to put on are the gospel of peace – the tried and tested truths of the gospel. Their purpose is to prevent us from slipping and sliding when we do battle with our wily and nimble adversary, the devil.

What are you like when under attack from Satan? Firm and resolute or unsteady and unsure?

O Father, I see that if I am to stand firm and resolute when under enemy attack, my feet must be securely shod. Show me what is expected of me, dear Lord and help me apply it. In Jesus' Name I pray. Amen.

Don't miss the point

FOR READING AND MEDITATION – 2 TIMOTHY 2:1–15
'Be diligent to present yourself approved to God ...
rightly dividing the word of truth.' (v. 15: NKJ)

23 JULY

The armour of God

Some claim that having our 'feet shod with ... the gospel of peace' means that we should be ready to carry the gospel to others. That fits with Romans 10:15, which says: 'How beautiful are the feet of those who preach the gospel of peace,' but not, in my opinion, what Paul wrote in Ephesians 6:15.

In Ephesians 6 the apostle here is dealing with the Christian's engagement with the devil. 'We do not wrestle against flesh and blood, but against principalities, against powers ...' (v. 12: NKJ).

Paul was an evangelist and had a strong evangelistic spirit, but he was not thinking here of evangelising. He was picturing a Christian under attack by Satan, and warning us that unless our feet are firmly shod, we can easily be knocked down and disabled.

If we relate this phrase to evangelism, we miss the point of his exposition. No one would deny the importance of always being ready to share Christ with others, but the readiness Paul is referring to here is the readiness to stand firm on the truths of the gospel.

Don't get into a fight with the devil in your bare feet. Make sure you are well shod, for if you are not, he will most certainly get the better of you.

O Father, I am so grateful that you breathed into your servant Paul to write these illuminating words. They are inspired, for they inspire me. Continue to teach me, dear Lord. I am hungry for more and more of your truth. Amen.

Nothing to hold on to

FOR READING AND MEDITATION – 1 CORINTHIANS 16:1–18
'Watch, stand fast in the faith, be brave, be strong.' (v. 13: NKJ)

The *Amplified* says: 'Be alert and on your guard; stand firm in your faith.' One of the great tragedies evident in many church circles is that large numbers of Christians do not have their feet shod with the preparation of the gospel of peace. They are slipping and sliding in all directions because they no longer know what to believe or what to hold on to.

Not so long ago I met a few Christians from the area in South Wales where I was brought up, Christians who at one time were on fire for God and had a solid confidence in Scripture. As I talked with them, however, I saw that they no longer thought of the Bible in the way they once did, for their conversation about Christ and his Word was filled with doubts and denials. How sad.

How the devil must rejoice as he sees Christians slipping and sliding in their faith. We see evidence of it not just in ordinary believers but in some of our notable theologians and church leaders.

Do you know what you believe? Do you stand firm on the truths of the gospel? Remember, if you don't stand for anything, then you will fall for anything.

✎ Dear Father, help me to keep close to the words of Scripture, for they take me beyond the words to you, the Living Word. Strengthen me so that I might hold fast to the truths of the gospel, for without them I cannot help but stumble and fall. Amen.

The irreducible minimum

FOR READING AND MEDITATION – 2 CORINTHIANS 1:12–24

'For no matter how many promises God has made,
they are "Yes" in Christ.' (v. 20: NIV)

It is time now to face some very personal and pointed questions.

Do you believe the Bible is the Word of God, divinely and uniquely inspired and reliable in all it affirms?

Do you believe that Jesus Christ is the Son of God, born of a virgin, and the only way to God?

Do you believe that he was crucified for your sins, raised again on the third day and is now sitting on the right hand of God?

These questions are the irreducible minimum of Christianity. These are the basic truths of the gospel. If you don't take your stand on these truths, then you cannot call yourself a Christian.

Do you have your feet shod with the preparation of the gospel of peace – are you ready to stand for the authority of Scripture, the deity of Christ, his substitutionary death, his resurrection from the dead and his return to earth in power and glory?

Are you sure of your spiritual position? How can you fight the enemy if you do not know what you believe? Church leaders need to give a spiritual lead. But many of our leaders do not have a high view of Scripture. How can they give a lead when they don't know where they are going? They don't know where they stand and no one else knows either.

✎ O Father, your Word promises to be a lamp to our feet and a light for our path. Bring those whose feet are slipping and sliding in the faith back to an unshakeable confidence in the gospel. In Jesus' Name I ask it. Amen.

A word to new Christians

The armour of God

FOR READING AND MEDITATION – 2 THESSALONIANS 2:13–27

'. . . stand firm and hold to the teachings we passed on to you . . .' (v.15: NIV)

Permit me to say a word to those who have been in the Christian life for just a short time. Now that you are a Christian, take your stand unflinchingly on the Lord's side. When you meet your old friends, those you used to hang around with in the days before you came to know the Lord, and they propose that you go on doing the things you used to do which you know are not in harmony with God's Word, then be resolute and refuse.

Take a firm stand in the matter and watch that you do not slip or slide toward them. Have your feet shod with the preparation of the gospel of peace.

The first thing that strikes everyone who comes into the Christian life is that it is entirely different from one's former life. You must determine to take your stand with Jesus Christ and when others tempt you, say, 'I cannot betray my Lord. I am bound to him for all eternity. My feet are shod and I am not moving.' You have to know what you believe and be resolute and determined to stand for it come what may.

If I had not done this in the days following my conversion, then I would have forfeited an adventure that has taken me deeper and deeper into God.

❧ O God, how can I have faith in you unless I have faith in the words you have spoken to me in the Bible? Help me stand firm in the faith – today and every day. In Jesus' Name. Amen.

A spiritual adventure

FOR READING AND MEDITATION – JUDGES 7:1–22
'The Lord said to Gideon, "With the three hundred men
that lapped I will save you ..."' (v. 7: NIV)

The armour of God

When the hosts of Midian came against the Israelites, Gideon gathered together an army of 32 000 men. God reduced them to a mere handful of only 300, men whom God saw would stand and never quit. 300 men proceeded to discomfit and rout the Midianites.

God has always done his greatest work in and through a comparatively small number of people. When it comes to spiritual victories, what God wants is men and women who are prepared to 'stand', whose feet are 'shod with the preparation of the gospel of peace'.

Are you standing for God – in your place of work, your home or the environment in which God has put you? Let me put the question another way – are you ready to stand?

You cannot stand until you are prepared to stand. It begins with a firm and resolute attitude, then issues in firm and resolute action.

As in Gideon's day, the Lord is looking for people who will take their stand on his Word, come what may, and commit themselves to doing what he asks even though they may not feel like it or see the sense of it.

Are you such a one? If you are, then I predict that ahead of you is an exciting spiritual adventure.

O God, help me not to miss the highest because of my spiritual unpreparedness. Help me to be ready for all that you have for me – even before I see it. In Jesus' Name I pray. Amen.

Peace that does not go to pieces

FOR READING AND MEDITATION – COLOSSIANS 3:1–17

'...let the peace of God rule in your hearts...' (v. 15: NKJ)

A soldier in battle has to be certain about a number of things c else he will be distracted and become an easy prey for the enem He needs to be certain that he is fighting a just war, under a wis commander, and that he has the constant support of those abov him. It is the same with a Christian soldier.

He too has to be certain about a number of things – his relation ship with God, the truth and reliability of the Bible, the resource that are available to him, and so on. How can his heart be at peac if he is not assured of these things?

It is precisely at this point that we Christians have an advan tage over every other soldier. Not only are we led by the wisest mil itary strategist in the universe, but we have inside information o how the battle against Satan will end – we win! Even in the mids of the hottest conflict, we know that although the devil may wi some of the battles, he will most definitely lose the war.

We would never be able to stand against the 'wiles' of the devi unless we enjoyed peace with God and the peace of God. If you hav peace about the outcome, then you have peace all the way – period

O Father, I see so clearly that if I have doubts about you or about my sa vation, then I will not be able to fight the enemy. But there are no doubts. have peace with you and peace within. I am so thankful. Amen.

The shield of faith

FOR READING AND MEDITATION – 1 JOHN 5:1–12

'This is the victory that has overcome the world, even our faith.' (v. 4: NIV)

bove all,' says the apostle, 'taking the shield of faith with which ou will be able to quench all the fiery darts of the wicked one' Eph. 6:16, NKJ).

Some take *above all* to mean, 'above everything else in impor- nce'. They go on to argue that the last three pieces of armour are ore important than the first three. But the phrase really means 'in ddition to these', and should not be seen as comparing one sec- on of the armour with another. It is a transition phrase, designed introduce us to armour which has a different point and purpose.

The six pieces of armour fall clearly into two groups, the first onsisting of belt, breastplate and shoes; the second of the shield f faith, the helmet of salvation and the sword of the Spirit.

The first three were fixed to the body by a special fastening, nd hence, once put on, immovable whereas the shield, the helmet, e sword of the Spirit could be put on or put down quite easily.

The lesson, quite clearly, is this – the first three pieces of equip- ent should be worn at all times, while the other three are to be ken up when and where necessary.

Gracious Father, I am so thankful for the care and design that has gone to providing for me a sure defence against Satan. I have learned much, yet ee there is still much more to learn. Teach me. Amen.

Having and taking

FOR READING AND MEDITATION – HEBREWS 11:1–16

'But without faith it is impossible to please him . . .' (v. 6: NKJ)

Listen again to this passage: 'Stand therefore, having girded you waist with truth, having put on the breastplate of righteousness, an having shod your feet with the preparation of the gospel of peace.'

Then, in the second section, the word changes: 'Above all, taking the shield of faith … and take the helmet of salvation, and th sword of the Spirit.' The difference between the first three piece and the last three is the difference between *having* and *taking*.

The 'shield' referred to in Ephesians 6 was an extremely larg object, something like four feet in length and about two and a ha feet wide, designed to give as much protection as possible to th front of the body. More important, the front surface was covere with a sheet of fireproof metal so that the fiery darts of the enem would have little or no effect.

Clearly Paul thought that a further defence was needed to pro tect us from the devil's preliminary attacks, in addition to the thre items we have already considered.

When we consider the lengths God has gone to in order to giv us the protection we need against satanic attack, one wonders wh we ever allow ourselves to be defeated by the devil.

O Father, once again I want to record my gratitude for the way in whi you have provided for my defence against satanic attack. Help me to see, how ever, that it will do me no good just to appreciate it; I must use it. In Chris Name I will use it. Amen.

Fiery darts

FOR READING AND MEDITATION – 2 TIMOTHY 4:1–18

'... the Lord stood at my side and gave me strength ...
And I was delivered from the lion's mouth.' (v. 17: NIV)

The main purpose of the shield in Roman times was to protect the soldiers from darts thrown at them. These were covered with inflammable material and set alight immediately before being thrown. Attacked in this way, a soldier would hold up the shield in front, allowing the fiery darts to land on the fireproof metal surface and drop away harmlessly.

Paul says we Christians, too, need a 'shield of faith' – in order to quench all the fiery darts of the wicked one'. Have you ever gone to bed at night feeling perfectly happy and content, only to wake in a sad and melancholy mood? If there was no obvious physical or psychological reason for that, the chances are that you have experienced one of Satan's 'fiery darts'.

Sometimes they come as evil or blasphemous thoughts, which intrude suddenly into our thinking. We may be reading the Bible or kneeling in prayer, when suddenly some filthy thought flashes into our mind. This is a 'fiery dart' from the devil.

They do not come from inside us, but from outside us. They strike us. Some thoughts arise from within our carnal nature. These come from without – from Satan. And we are foolish if we do not recognise this and deal with them in this light.

O Father, help me to recognise the 'fiery darts' of Satan when they are hurled at me. It is only when I recognise them that I can deal effectively with them. Give me insight and understanding. In Jesus' Name. Amen.

The satanic strategy

FOR READING AND MEDITATION – JOHN 13:1–11
'... the devil had already put it into the heart of
Judas Iscariot ... to betray him.' (v.2: RSV)

The 'fiery darts' of the devil are quite different from the thought that are generated by our carnal nature. They come at us, rathe than from within us.

A satanic attack can usually be differentiated from somethin that arises from within by the strength and force with which th thought hits us. Thoughts that arise out of the carnal nature ar unpleasant and offensive, but the thoughts that come as 'fiery dart from the devil burn and sting and inflame.

The other thing one notices about these attacks is that the seem to come in cycles. They are not there permanently but the come at certain times and seasons.

I once counselled a man for one hour a week over a period o a whole year and got him to write down in his diary the times an dates when he felt under satanic attack. When we looked throug his diary together at the end of the year we discovered an amazin thing. Every single attack took place immediately prior to him doin something special for the Lord, like leading a Bible study, conduct ing a service, visiting the sick or giving a public testimony.

I shall never forget the expression on his face as he looked a me and said, 'Who says that Satan isn't a strategist?'

My Father and my God, I realise that even though Satan is a strategist, h is no match for you. You know how to out manoeuvre his every move. Help m to stay close to you that I might experience your strategy and not his. Ame

Blasphemous thoughts

FOR READING AND MEDITATION – 2 CORINTHIANS 2:1–11

'For we are not unaware of his schemes.' (v.11: NIV)

Dr Martyn Lloyd-Jones said, 'The devil has often plagued some of the noblest saints with blasphemous thoughts – blasphemous thoughts about God, blasphemous thoughts about the Lord Jesus Christ and blasphemous thoughts about the Holy Spirit.'

How horrible and terrifying such thoughts can be! Sometimes the devil hurls the most awful words into the mind, but it is important to see that these do not arise from within the heart of the believer – they come from the devil. He is trying to confuse and demoralise you.

How grateful we are to the saints down the ages who have recorded these satanic attacks, for otherwise we would be tempted when experiencing them to believe they had never happened to anyone else. John Bunyan and Martin Luther, masters of the spiritual life, described these in great detail. But how do we deal with this? What action must we take to repel these devilish attacks? There is only one answer – we must take and use the shield of faith.

Faith alone enables you to meet and overcome this particular type of attack. What you must not do is expose your chest and expect the breastplate of righteousness to deal with this problem.

Each piece of the equipment is designed to deal with a particular attack. And the answer here is – faith.

Heavenly Father, I understand the problem – now show me how to apply the answer of faith. How does it work? How can I apply it? Teach me more. In Jesus' Name. Amen.

Prompt action

FOR READING AND MEDITATION – ROMANS 10:1–18

'... faith comes by hearing, and hearing by the word of God.' (v.17: NKJ)

How does faith act as a protective shield? First we must understand what faith is and how the word is being used by Paul in Ephesians 6:16. A little boy, when asked to give a definition of faith, said, 'Faith is believing something you know isn't true.'

Well, that is precisely what faith is not. Faith is believing what you know to be true. But even more – it is *acting* on what you know to be true. Faith is one of the most practical commodities in the Christian faith. 'Faith without works is dead,' says James (Jas. 2:26). There is activity in faith; faith always prompts us to action. 'Faith is the assurance of things hoped for, the conviction of things not seen' (Heb. 11:1, NASB).

Taking the shield of faith, then, is responding to what the devil hurls at us by applying what we believe about God and his Word, the Bible. When Satan sends his 'fiery darts' in our direction, we can stand and lament the fact that we are being attacked.

Or quickly raise the shield of faith and remind ourselves that because we are redeemed by the blood of Christ, he has no legal or moral right to taunt us. Believing that is not enough; it must be acted on – and acted on quickly.

Father, I see that when Satan throws his 'fiery darts' at me I must act, and act quickly. Help my faith to be so strong that it will not need a 'jump start' to get it going. This I ask in Jesus' Name. Amen.

I am your shield

FOR READING AND MEDITATION – GENESIS 14:18–24, 15:1–6

'Abram believed the Lord, and he credited it
to him as righteousness.' (v.6: NIV)

avid said when he stood before Goliath: 'You come to me with a
vord, with a spear, and with a javelin. But I come to you in the name
the Lord of hosts' (1 Sam. 17:45, NKJ). Never forget that God is
uch more powerful than the devil. Hold on to that and quickly
ise your shield whenever you experience an attack of Satan's
ery darts'.

Abraham was tired and exhausted after making a great stand.
have no doubt Satan would have attacked him with thoughts like
is, 'What is the point of all this action of God on your behalf when
u do not have an heir to carry on your line. What is the use of all
ese great promises when you do not have a son? God doesn't seem
have as much power as it would appear.'

Abraham was fearful at this point, until the Lord came to him
d gave him these glorious words: 'Do not be afraid, Abram. I am
ur shield, your exceedingly great reward' (15:1, NKJ). 'I am your
ield.' Hold on to that great truth, my friend, and when under
tack, quickly lift it up and remind the devil that you belong to
e whose power is endless and eternal. His promises are ever sure.
hat is what it means to hold up the shield of faith.

*O God, how grateful I am for the sureness and certainty of your Word.
nce again I feel it entering into the core of my being. Help me to put these
uths into practice the very moment I come under satanic attack. In Jesus'
ame I pray. Amen.*

The helmet of salvation

FOR READING AND MEDITATION – 2 CORINTHIANS 11:1–15

'... I am afraid that just as Eve was deceived by the serpent's cunning,
your minds may somehow be led astray ...' (v.3: NIV)

The helmet worn by a Roman soldier was usually made of bronze or iron with an inside lining of felt or sponge. When a Roman soldier saw an enemy coming, he would take hold of his shield, put on his helmet, take his sword in hand and stand alert and ready to do battle. The helmet immediately suggests that this is something designed to protect the mind, the intelligence, the ability to think and reason. Just as the 'breastplate of righteousness' protects us from emotional distress, so the helmet of salvation protects us from mental distress. It helps us keep our thinking straight, and preserves us from mental confusion and darkness.

Has there ever been a time when we needed something to keep our thinking straight more than we do now? We vacillate and oscillate between despairing pessimism and unrealistic optimism. We face staggering complexities – Aids, violence, nuclear missiles, international tension, economic instability, inner city slums, and so on. The intelligentsia of our day confess to being utterly baffled in dealing with the problems with which human society is confronted.

Where can we turn to ease the pressure on our minds? The only answer is God – and in the helmet of salvation which he provides.

ℵ O Father, I am so grateful that you have provided freedom from the most terrifying of human problems – mental distress. Teach me all I need to know in applying your truth to the important area of my mind. In Jesus' Name. Amen.

The tenses of salvation

FOR READING AND MEDITATION – 1 THESSALONIANS 5:1–11
'. . . let us be self-controlled, putting on faith and love as a breastplate,
and the hope of salvation as a helmet.' (v.8: NIV)

It is important to realise that Paul is not talking here about the salvation of the soul, or salvation as regeneration or conversion. This is the mistake that many make when attempting to interpret this verse. They say, 'Whenever the devil attacks your mind and seeks to oppress it, remind yourself that you have been saved.' Well, there is nothing wrong with that, of course, but this explanation does not go far enough.

The best way to interpret a verse of Scripture is with another verse of Scripture. Thus the text before us today throws a shaft of light on Paul's statement in Ephesians 6:17 for it shows salvation, not just as something in the past but something that is also future. He uses the word in the same way in Romans when he says: 'Our salvation is nearer now than when we first believed' (Rom. 13:11).

In the Bible, the word *salvation* has three distinct tenses – past, present and future.

At conversion, we are saved from the penalty of sin.

Now, day by day, we are being saved from the power of sin.

And one day in the future, we will be saved from the presence of sin. And it is to the future Paul is looking when he invites us to put on the helmet of salvation.

O Father, thank you for reminding me of the tenses of salvation. I see that in order to live effectively, I must view the present tense by the future tense. Help me lay a hold on this. In Jesus' Name. Amen.

An atheist who lost his faith

FOR READING AND MEDITATION – ROMANS 8:18–30

'For we were saved in this hope …' (v.24: NKJ)

Our passage today shows even more clearly what we were discussing yesterday – salvation in the future tense. Paul is talking about when Christ will return, when the kingdom of God will be established and creation delivered from its bondage.

The helmet of salvation, therefore, is the recognition that all human schemes, disorder and chaos will be ended, and when that happens, the universe will see that God has been quietly working out his purposes in and through everything.

That truth, understood and embraced, will enable us to keep our thinking straight in a world that is full of confusion and darkness. The Dean of Melbourne wrote about H.G. Wells, 'He hailed science as a panacea for all ills and the goddess of knowledge and power.' But what were H.G. Wells' conclusions about the world before he died? He wrote, 'The science to which I pinned my faith is bankrupt. Its counsels, which should have established the millennium, led instead directly to the suicide of Europe. I believed them once. In their name I helped destroy the faith of millions of worshippers in the temples of a thousand creeds. And now they look at me and witness the great tragedy of an atheist who has lost his faith.'

There is no protection in the world for the mind.

❧ *Gracious Father, there is just no hope outside of you. If I break with you I break with sanity. Help me to walk closely with you so that your mind becomes my mind. In Jesus' Name. Amen.*

Everything is under control

FOR READING AND MEDITATION – EPHESIANS 1:3–14

'... according to His purpose who works all things
after the counsel of His will.' (v.11: NASB)

The armour of God

The Christian has a hope for the future; he has an understanding that God is working out his purposes in history. We need not be disturbed when human programmes appear to be going wrong.

The Christian expects the world to get worse and worse, for that is what the Bible tells us will happen. He expects false teachings and false philosophies to abound. He expects the world's systems to fail, for anything that is not built on Christ has no guarantee of success.

The Christian knows that wars and international tension are unavoidable, even though every effort is made to avoid them. The world is in such a state and such a condition, that the more attention we give it, the more weary our minds become.

What is a Christian to do in such a world as ours? How are we to react when the devil takes advantage of our sensitivity to world conditions, and focuses our thoughts upon them? Shall we give up? Shall we withdraw from life? No, we put on the helmet of salvation and remind ourselves that in the face of everything that appears contrary, God is working out his eternal plan and purpose.

History is his-story. The Almighty God is at work in the very events that appear to be filled with darkness and confusion.

O God, help me see that although you are apart from the events of history, you are also in the events of history. Ultimately all things are going to glorify you. Thank you, Father. Amen.

Not a private fight

FOR READING AND MEDITATION – 2 CHRONICLES 20:4–26

' "... Do not be afraid or discouraged ...
For the battle is not yours, but God's." ' (v.15: NIV)

We need to have the assurance that a certain, sure salvation is coming and God's plan is being worked out even now, if we are to prevent the devil from bringing us into a state of mental distress.

'History', writes Ray Stedman, 'is not a meaningless jumble but a controlled pattern, and the Lord Jesus Christ is the one who is directing these events.'

Satan says, 'Just look around you at the state of the world. God seems powerless to put things right. He has given lots of promises, but none of those promises has come to pass. Give up this foolish idea that it's all going to work out right.'

If you were to let your mind dwell on that kind of satanic argument, you would soon find yourself in distress. The answer is to put on the helmet, the hope of salvation. Remind yourself that things are not as they appear. The battle is not ours, but the Lord's.

This is not a private fight we are engaged in. We may be individual soldiers fighting in the army of God, but the ultimate cause is sure, and the end is certain. We need not be unduly troubled by what is happening in the world – our commander is not just winning; he has already won.

✎ Lord Jesus, I am grateful that the cross is the guarantee that neither sin nor Satan will ever defeat you. Your victory at Calvary has settled for ever the question of who has the final word in the universe. I am so deeply, deeply thankful. Amen.

We see Jesus

FOR READING AND MEDITATION – HEBREWS 2:1–15

'. . . we do not see everything subject to him.
But we see Jesus . . .' (vv.8–9: NIV)

According to the Bible things are going to get worse; as Jesus said: 'Men's hearts failing them from fear and the expectation of those things which are coming on the earth' (Luke 21:26, NKJ).

How are Christians going to stand when the darkness deepens and things get very much worse? It is the hope of salvation, and this alone, which enables believers to live out their lives free from mental distress.

Our newspapers are filled with murder, violence, economic distress, rape, abortion and child abuse. And our conscience, which through conversion has been sensitised to the moral laws of God, begins to reverberate as it comes up against the reports of things we know are contrary to the divine principles.

Satan, seeing our concern, attempts to exploit it to his own ends. 'Things are getting worse, aren't they?' he says. 'Why don't you just admit that God has lost control of his world?'

If we do not have the helmet of salvation to put on at such a moment, we would finish up with the same attitude as H.G. Wells, who, after the World War II, wrote, 'The spectacle of evil in the world has come near to breaking my spirit.' Again I say, there is no protection in the world for the mind.

My Father and my God, where would I be if I could not cling to a text such as that in my reading for today? My spirit too would be near to breaking. I am so thankful that in you there is hope – hope with a capital H. Amen.

The way to an undisturbed mind

FOR READING AND MEDITATION – COLOSSIANS 1:9–28
'. . . Christ in you, the hope of glory.' (v.27: NKJ)

We preach the gospel in our churches and still enjoy freedom of speech. But there are areas of the world where this is not possible, where Satan is openly worshipped and faith is not expressed openly.

What do these Christians do to prevent themselves from becoming wearied by their adverse circumstances? They put on the helmet of the hope of salvation. This, more than anything, keeps their thinking straight. But no matter where we live, those of us who have enlisted in the army of God must do the same. We must not succumb to the popular delusion that the working out of all human problems lies just around the corner, through the application of humanistic ideas and philosophies.

How long has the world chased this futile dream? Almost from the dawn of history, men and women have been grasping the elusive hope that something can be worked out here.

But God never said that. Consistently throughout the Scriptures he has said that man, in his fallen condition, is totally unable to work out his problems. We do know, however, that he has reserved a day of salvation when all wrongs will be righted.

It is in the strength of the hope of that day of salvation only that our hearts and minds can be kept undisturbed.

✎ O Father, how can I ever be grateful enough that I am caught up in an eternal purpose. I live in the present, yet I draw also from the certainties of the future. Nourish this hope within me until it drives out every fear. In Jesus' Name. Amen.

The sword of the Spirit

FOR READING AND MEDITATION – JAMES 4:1–10
'... Resist the devil – stand firm against him –
and he will flee from you.' (v.7: AMPLIFIED)

John Stott points out that 'of all the six pieces of armour or weapon-ry listed, the sword is the only one which can clearly be used for attack as well as defence'. And the kind of attack envisaged here is one that involves a close encounter, for the word used for sword is *machaira*, meaning a short sword or dagger.

There is more to spiritual warfare than standing up to the devil. Here we have the potential to make the devil 'flee'. The word *flee* is a very strong word in the original Greek. Not a strategic with-drawal; it means beating a swift and hasty retreat. What an amaz-ing truth! It is possible for a Christian so to resist the devil that he races away as fast as he can.

This truth must not be seen in any way as limiting the devil's power, for he is a strong and determined foe. It means a Christian able to wield the sword of the Spirit can ensure that he is overpower-ed and discomfited.

We are right to develop a healthy respect for the devil's wiles and ingenuity, but we are wrong to allow him to terrorise us. We have the assurance that to engage in conflict with the devil is not a hope-less task.

✣ *O Father, the thought that I, a sinner saved by grace, am able to send Satan into retreat almost overwhelms me. Yet I must believe it for your Word tells me so. Help me understand even more clearly the authority I have in Christ. In his Name I ask it. Amen.*

The power of precise Scripture

FOR READING AND MEDITATION – MATTHEW 4:1–11

' "… It is written … It is written again …" ' (vv.4, 7: NKJ)

The sword of the Spirit is the Word of God, the Bible, the inspired Scriptures.

In the passage before us is a perfect illustration of how Jesus used the sword of the Spirit when rebutting the temptations of the devil. Notice how, prior to the temptation, Jesus was anointed by the Holy Spirit (Matt. 3:13–17). Jesus was 'led up by the Spirit into the wilderness to be tempted by the devil' (v.1, NKJ). During the temptation our Lord, filled with the Spirit, resisted every one of the devil's statements – by using the precise words of Scripture.

Follow me closely, for this is extremely important: Christ did not utter a newly formed statement or something that came to him on the spur of the moment. He quoted a text which had already been given by God and written down. The weapon used by our Lord was the Word of God, the Scriptures.

Can you see the point I am making? Satan is not rebuffed by clever phrases that may sound theologically sophisticated and refined; he is defeated only when we quote to him the precise words of Scripture. If this was the strategy Jesus had to use, then how much more you and I. Nothing defeats Satan more thoroughly and effectively than the sword of the Spirit, which is the Word of God.

 ✒ *O God, open my eyes that I might see more clearly than ever the power and authority that lies in your sacred Word, the Bible. Help me to know it better. For your own dear Name's sake. Amen.*

The Bible – an inspired book

FOR READING AND MEDITATION – JOHN 16:1–15

'"... when he, the Spirit of truth, has come,
he will guide you into all truth ..."' (v.13: NKJ)

Why are the Scriptures described as a sword provided by the Holy Spirit? Quite simply, he gave them to us. It was the Holy Spirit who inspired men to write the Scriptures: 'Men spoke from God as they were carried along by the Holy Spirit' (2 Pet. 1:21). Again in 2 Timothy 3:16 we read: 'All Scripture is God-breathed.'

The Bible is not a mere human document, the product of the mind of man. The Holy Spirit breathed into men and inspired them, not to write mechanically as someone would talk into a tape recorder, but giving them an additional ability to write without error.

It is vital, if you are to win the battle against Satan, that you not only see this, but also believe it. Considering how powerful Satan is, we need something that is even more powerful. And the Bible, the inspired Word of God, is our strength.

We must, however, go one step further – only the Holy Spirit can enable us truly to understand God's Word: 'We have received, not the spirit of the world, but the Spirit who is from God, that we might know the things that have been freely given to us by God' (1 Cor. 2:12, NKJ). Without the Holy Spirit, we would be no more able to understand the Scriptures than a blind man could judge a beauty contest.

❧ *Gracious Holy Spirit, just as you breathed into the Bible to give it its life and power, breathe also into my heart today so that I might know and understand its truth. I ask this in Jesus' Name. Amen.*

Divide and conquer

FOR READING AND MEDITATION – 1 CORINTHIANS 2:1–16

'... the things of the Spirit of God ... are spiritually discerned.' (v.14: NKJ)

Only the Holy Spirit can help us to understand and properly interpret the Word of God. A man may have a fine mind, a good seminary training, a theological degree, but as our text tells us, truth is 'spiritually discerned'.

We need to understand – only the Holy Spirit can show us how to use the word aright. Doubtless this was the consideration in the mind of the apostle when he penned the statement we are considering, 'the sword of the Spirit, which is the word of God'.

It is one thing to know the contents of Scripture; it is another thing to know how to use those contents, in a way that defeats and overcomes the devil. Only the Holy Spirit can enable us to do this.

The relationship between the Holy Spirit and the Word of God is an important one. We cannot put the emphasis on one side or the other. The moment we separate the Spirit and the Word, we are in trouble.

Donald Gee said, 'All Spirit and no Word, you blow up. All Word and no Spirit, you dry up. Word and Spirit – you grow up.' Without the Spirit, the Word is a dead letter; with the Spirit, it is a living and powerful force. The devil will 'divide and conquer' if he can.

❧ My Father, when I separate the Spirit from the Word and the Word from the Spirit, I am in trouble. Help me to be as open to the Spirit as I am to the Bible, and as open to the Bible as I am to the Spirit. In Jesus' Name. Amen.

The divine design

FOR READING AND MEDITATION – JOHN 14:15–27

' "… the Helper, the Holy Spirit … will teach you all things, and bring
to your remembrance all that I said to you." ' (v.26: NASB)

How does the Holy Spirit enable us to use Scripture in practice?
When we come to God's Word, depending entirely on the Holy Spirit
to reveal its truth to us, the Holy Spirit can impress the truth of the
Scriptures into our innermost being, thus building the Word of God
into our spirits.

It takes root within us, and whenever we stand in need of a
word with which to rebut the devil, the Holy Spirit brings it to our
remembrance.

And here's the most wonderful thing – the word of God on our
lips will have the same effect upon the devil as if he was hearing it
from the lips of Jesus himself!

Approaching the Bible in this way, said the late J.B. Phillips, 'is
like rewiring a house where the electricity has not been turned off'.
You touch something that lets you know there is a current of power
flowing through its pages that was not put there by any man.

The Holy Spirit has gone into it, so is it any wonder that the
Holy Spirit comes out of it?

*My Father and my God, I know the Spirit dwells in your Word. I come
now to ask that he might dwell also in me, to open up my whole being to the
truth and power that lies in its inspired pages. In Jesus' Name I ask it. Amen.*

The coal miner and the Ph.D

FOR READING AND MEDITATION – HEBREWS 4:1–13
'For the word of God is living and active and sharper
than any two-edged sword . . .' (v.12: NASB)

I remember being present some years ago in a church in South Wales when a debate was held between a university professor and an ordinary coal miner. The subject was: 'Is the Bible true?'

The university professor presented his arguments *against* in a clear and cogent fashion, and I remember feeling quite sorry for the miner as I envisaged some of the difficulties he might have when making his reply. After the professor had finished, the miner stood to his feet and for over an hour I witnessed one of the most amazing demonstrations of the Holy Spirit at work that I have ever seen in my life.

The miner began by asking everyone to bow their heads as he prayed a prayer that went something like this: 'Lord, I have not had much education, but you know that I love your Word and have spent my life searching its pages. Help me now to say something that will convince my friends here that your Word is true.'

He then proceeded to demolish the arguments of the professor simply by quoting appropriate Scriptures without making even a simple comment. When he finished, there was thunderous applause. The professor's intellectual arguments had been torn to pieces by the sword of the Spirit – by that, and by that alone.

O Father, the more I hear, the more I want to hear. For I was created by your Word, designed according to your Word, and I can never remain content until I am indwelt with your Word. Teach me even more. In Jesus' Name. Amen.

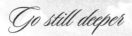
Go still deeper

FOR READING AND MEDITATION – JOHN 17:1–19

'. . . Your word is truth.' (v.17: NKJ)

Christians who do not accept the authority of the Scriptures undermine the very foundation they need to stand on. Without an authoritative Bible, we have no effective weapon against Satan. If you are not certain that the Bible is the Word of God, you are like a soldier with a broken sword in his hand.

To use the sword of the Spirit effectively, we need to have as wide a knowledge of the Bible as possible.

When Satan advanced in the wilderness of temptation, Jesus knew exactly what Scriptures to use.

There were three different temptations and Jesus selected three different parts of Scripture. He knew exactly the right words to select to rebut each temptation of the devil.

If we are to conquer Satan in the same way that Jesus conquered him, then we must know the Bible.

It is no good saying to the devil, 'The verse I want to use against you is somewhere in the Bible.' Quote it to him and quote it precisely.

You need a deep and intensive programme of study if you are to become proficient in the use of the Scriptures against Satan. Commit yourself to exploring the Bible more deeply and thoroughly than you have ever done before.

O Father, I see that the more I know of your Word, the more effective I will be in resisting Satan. Show me how to go more deeply into the Scriptures than I have ever done before. In Jesus' Name I pray. Amen.

A final exhortation

'Praying always with all prayer and supplication in the Spirit, being watchful to this end with all perseverance and supplication for all the saints' (Eph. 6:18, NKJ).

What is the meaning of this further and final exhortation?

It is not, as one commentator writes, 'Paul is giving us in this verse the final piece of armour for the Christian who is in conflict with the devil: "Praying always with all prayer …" '

This surely cannot be so, for Paul's reference to 'praying always with all prayer', although closely related to the six pieces of armour, is quite different from it and does not fall within the bounds of the careful and close analogy that he has been making.

What then does he mean when he includes this further intriguing statement? He is saying, I believe, that 'praying in the Spirit' is something that ought to pervade all our spiritual warfare. It is something we have to do, and keep on doing, if we are to win the battle against Satan and his forces.

Paul is saying, 'Put on the whole armour of God, every single piece, and in the proper order; but in addition to that, at all times and in all places, keep on praying.' In other words, the armour provided for us by God cannot be used effectively unless it is worn by a praying Christian.

✎ *O Father, thank you for inspiring your servant Paul to give us this insight, for we see that without it we would be defeated by the devil. Help me become a watchful and praying Christian. In Jesus' Name. Amen.*

Not a postscript

FOR READING AND MEDITATION – COLOSSIANS 1:1–12

'We give thanks to the God and Father of our Lord Jesus Christ,
praying always for you.' (v.3: NKJ)

If we were to stop when Paul finishes his description of the Christian's armour, we would miss the whole meaning of the apostle's thought, for the six pieces of armour provide us with adequate defence against the devil only when worn by a praying Christian. Ephesians 6:18 is a culmination of all that Paul has been saying before. 'Stand praying', cries the great apostle, 'always with all prayer and supplication in the Spirit.'

The danger is that we feel, once we have our spiritual armour on, that we can relax, that the armour will protect us. That is foolish, and something Satan would want us to believe. The armour of God must always be thought of in terms of our relationship with God. If there is no communion with him, the six pieces of armour will be ineffective. The armour of God is not something that is magical or mechanical; it functions as a spiritual defence only when worn with prayer. The following hymn expresses it beautifully:

> *To keep your armour bright*
> *attend with constant care*
> *still walking in our Captain's sight*
> *and watching unto prayer.*

Father, I see that with all I have learned about defending myself against the devil, I must still go a step further. Help me to understand this step, for it is vital that I am not just protected against Satan, but fully protected. Amen.

And yet ...

FOR READING AND MEDITATION – 1 THESSALONIANS 5:11–24

'Be unceasing in prayer – praying perseveringly.' (v.17: AMPLIFIED)

John Stott, in his commentary on Ephesians, says, 'Equipping ourselves with God's armour is not a mechanical operation; it is in itself an expression of our dependence upon God.'

Some Christians like to begin each day by going through the motions of dressing themselves in the armour of God. In their minds they put on the belt of truth, the breastplate of righteousness, the shoes of the preparation of the gospel of peace and so on. I have no objection to this myself, but do not look just to the armour to protect you and think that nothing more needs to be done.

Let me remind you again – every single piece of armour, excellent and valuable though it is in itself, will not work unless always, and at all times, we are in a close, prayerful relationship with God.

Go over the six pieces of the Christian soldier's equipment once again: the belt of truth, the breastplate of righteousness, the shoes of peace, the shield of faith, the helmet of salvation and the sword of the Spirit. Strong protection.

And yet, having all this great and wonderful equipment available, we can still suffer defeat if we do not stand in the strength and power God provides. And that power can flow only along the channel of fervent, believing prayer.

Father, day by day it is becoming increasingly clear that unless I am continually linked to your resources through believing prayer, the armour you have provided for me gives me only a limited defence. Help me never to forget this. Amen.

Standard operating procedure

FOR READING AND MEDITATION – 1 TIMOTHY 2:1–10
'I want men everywhere to lift up holy hands in prayer,
without anger or disputing.' (v.8: NIV)

Dr Martyn Lloyd-Jones says, 'I have known Christians who have been well acquainted with the theology of the Bible and known it in an extraordinary manner, but who did not believe in prayer meetings, who did not seem to see the utter and absolute necessity of "praying always" in the way that is indicated here by the apostle.'

You cannot defeat the devil if you know nothing of a vital, day by day relationship with God through prayer.

I know people, and I am sure you do too, who have a wonderful understanding of Scripture, experts at pointing out other people's errors, but because they do not have a close relationship with God in prayer, they fall easy prey to the devil.

A whole church or community of Christian people can experience the same problem; they can have a good, sound knowledge of the Bible, yet know nothing of a strong corporate ministry of prayer in their midst. Such a church can easily be paralysed by the devil.

It may seem that I am labouring the point, but it is absolutely imperative we understand that our effectiveness in spiritual warfare depends not on the armour alone, but on our ability to maintain a close and intimate relationship with God through prayer.

Father, I think I have it now – no prayer, and everything else fails to work the way you designed it to. Drive this truth so deeply into my spirit that for the rest of my life, it will be standard operating procedure. Amen.

The four 'alls'

FOR READING AND MEDITATION – MATTHEW 14:22–23

'... he went up on a mountainside by himself to pray.' (v.23: NIV)

So, what can we do to make our prayer lives more contributive?

The place given to prayer in both the Old and New Testaments is remarkable. All the great saints of the Old Testament knew how to pray – Abraham, David, Daniel, Jeremiah, Isaiah, to mention just a few. The same prowess in prayer can be seen also in the New-Testament saints. But of course the greatest prayer warrior was none other than our Lord Jesus Christ.

Although he possessed great knowledge and wisdom, he found it essential to turn aside time and time again to pray. On certain occasions he would spend whole nights in prayer or rise long before dawn in order to pray and maintain his communion with God.

Is it surprising, therefore, that being so dependent on prayer, he should have told his disciples: 'Men ought always to pray, and not to faint' (Luke 18:1, AV). Praying is the only alternative to fainting – we must pray or else we faint. Paul's teaching with regard to prayer in Ephesians 6:18 revolves around four 'alls'. We are to pray at all times, with all prayer, with all perseverance and for all the saints.

Most Christians, however, pray at some times, with some prayer, and some degree of perseverance for some of God's saints. When we replace *some* by *all* in these expressions, we are on our way to effective praying.

✎ *My Father and my God, I see that through prayer, you offer me the most breath-taking power. Help me humbly to take it and use it wisely. In Jesus Name I pray. Amen.*

The various forms of prayer

FOR READING AND MEDITATION – COLOSSIANS 4:1–12

'Continue earnestly in prayer, being vigilant
in it with thanksgiving.' (v.2: NKJ)

What does it mean to 'pray always with all prayer and supplication'? Paul means, I believe, that we should pray with all forms or kinds of prayer. You see, there are many different forms of prayer that are available to us. Firstly, there is verbal prayer, when we present our prayer to God in carefully chosen words and phrases. Secondly, there is silent prayer, when no words cross our lips but prayer flows directly from our hearts. Thirdly, there is ejaculatory prayer, when we express sounds rather than words, as when we sigh or groan in prayer. Then there is public prayer, common prayer or 'praying together' – or, as some prefer to call it, 'praying in concert'. We are to be at it always, and in endless ways.

But there is a certain form of prayer that Paul refers to which deserves closer examination – the prayer of supplication. This is that aspect of prayer sometimes described as 'petition', when we pray with regard to special requests and needs.

We must not overlook this, for it is so easy to be caught up in adoration and praise that we neglect to focus our prayers on the various needs that arise from time to time, not only in our own lives, but also in the lives of others.

Father, help me to see the senselessness of trying to muddle through life in my own strength when you have made your power and resources available to me through prayer. Help me grow in prayer. In Jesus' Name. Amen.

Praying in the Spirit

FOR READING AND MEDITATION – ROMANS 8:18–30

'... we do not know what prayer to offer nor how to offer it worthily ...
but the Spirit Himself ... pleads in our behalf ...' (v.26: AMPLIFIED)

What does it mean to pray 'in the Spirit'? Some claim the word *in the Spirit* mean praying with the emotions – or feeling greatly moved as one prays. There are times when one feels deeply affected emotionally as one prays, but this is not the meaning of the phrase 'praying in the Spirit'.

It has no relationship to the emotions that we feel in prayer. I am not saying that feelings are unimportant in prayer; I am simply saying that I do not believe this is what Paul had in mind when he used the phrase 'praying in the Spirit'.

The 'spirit' spoken of here is not the human spirit, but the Holy Spirit. Some believe that 'praying in the Spirit' is when we pray in other tongues. I believe it is much more than that.

Prayer that is 'in the Spirit' is prayer that is prompted and guided by the Spirit. Dr Martyn Lloyd-Jones calls praying in the Spirit 'the secret of true prayer' and goes on to say, 'If we do not pray in the Spirit, we do not really pray.'

I would hesitate to make such a sweeping statement myself, but I would go so far as to say that if we do not know what it means to pray in the Spirit, our prayers will have little impact upon Satan and his forces.

✎ *Dear Father, I have so much to learn about prayer that unless you take my hand and guide me, I can soon lose my way. Teach me how to enter the deeper levels of prayer. In Jesus' Name. Amen.*

Spirit-aided praying

FOR READING AND MEDITATION – JOHN 6:56–69

' "It is the Spirit who gives life …" ' (v.63: NKJ)

Many Christians seem to be content to recite prayers, knowing nothing of the thrill of entering a dimension of prayer in which the Holy Spirit has full control. There is nothing wrong with liturgical or written prayers – they can be a wonderful primer for one's spiritual pump. Many people tell me that the prayers I frame at the bottom of each page have sometimes helped them more than the actual notes I have written. Using written prayers can be helpful, but we must heed the apostle's exhortation to move on into that dimension which he calls 'praying in the Spirit'.

The best description of 'praying in the Spirit' I have heard is that given by some of the old Welsh preachers, like Daniel Rowlands, Christmas Evans, and others. They describe it as 'praying with unusual liberty and freedom'.

There is hardly anything more wonderful in the Christian life than to experience liberty and freedom in prayer. I can remember the minister and elders of the church in which I was converted in South Wales saying after a prayer meeting in which there had been great liberty and power, 'Tonight we have prayed in the Spirit.'

Have you not experienced moments when, after struggling in prayer, you were suddenly taken out of yourself and words just poured out of you? At that moment, you were 'praying in the Spirit'.

O Father, forgive me that I try to do so much in my own strength instead of learning how to let you do it in me. Teach me how to let go and let you take over in everything – particularly my praying. In Jesus' Name. Amen.

First principles

' "Launch out into the deep …" ' (v.4: NKJ)

There are times when I struggle in prayer and find it difficult to concentrate, only to discover that suddenly I am taken out of myself and given a fluency and freedom that transforms my prayer time from that point on. When that happens, I know I have been praying in the Spirit. This is what Paul talks of in Ephesians 6:18.

Formal prayer is fine and has its place, but oh, how we need to experience more and more times of praying in the Spirit.

But how do we attain these times? Is it the Spirit's responsibility to bring us there, or do we have some responsibility in the matter too? I believe we can learn to pray in the Spirit.

Come to God in an attitude of dependence. This means recognising that your greatest need in prayer is not an ability to put words together or form fine phrases, but the Holy Spirit's empowerment.

Yield yourself totally to the Spirit for him to guide and direct your praying. Be continually aware that he wants to have the bigger part in your prayer life.

Start with these two principles, and learn to depend less and less on your own experience or ability, and more and more on the Spirit's enabling. Once you experience what it means to 'pray in the Spirit', you will long to experience it more and more.

O Father, my appetite is being whetted. Help me 'launch out into the deep' and give myself to you in the way that you are willing to give yourself to me. In Christ's Name I ask it. Amen.

Not some ... but all

FOR READING AND MEDITATION – EPHESIANS 4:17–32

'... for we are members of one another.' (v.25: NKJ)

'Keep alert with all perseverance' reminds us never to allow ourselves to become lethargic in relation to the matter of prayer, but always ready to make our requests and petitions known to him. But what is the purpose of this spiritual alertness and watchfulness? This question brings us to the second phrase: 'Making supplication for all the saints' (Eph. 6:18, RSV). Our watchfulness and concern must not be only on our own behalf, but on behalf of all other Christians also.

Why does Paul exhort us to pray for all rather than some Christians? The answer is that all Christians need praying for. Every believer is under attack; no one is exempted.

The letter of Jude tells us that we are partakers of a 'common salvation'. But not only do we enjoy a common salvation: we are fighting a common enemy. In our encounter with this common enemy we experience common difficulties – hence the need to be intensely aware of each other's needs.

We cannot, of course, take the armour of God and put it on another Christian, but we can pray for one another and thus call in spiritual reinforcements. We can pray that their eyes might be opened to the danger they are in and that they might be able to equip themselves to stand against Satan and his powerful forces.

O Father, forgive me, I pray, that sometimes I am so taken up with my own spiritual struggles that I forget my brothers and sisters face the same difficulties also. Save me from my self-centredness, dear Lord. In Jesus' Name I pray. Amen.

Satan's pincer movement

FOR READING AND MEDITATION – LUKE 22:24–34

"'... I have prayed for you, Simon, that your faith may not fail.'" (v.32: NIV)

Another reason Paul bids us pray for one another is because the failure of any one of us is going to have some effect upon the spiritual campaign which, through the church, God is waging against the devil.

The battle line between the forces of God and the forces of Satan is the church – and that means you and me. What is Satan's best tactic in attempting to bring about the church's spiritual defeat? He probes at every point he can, looking for the weakest part.

When he finds a weak Christian (or a group of weak Christians), he calls for reinforcements and in what military strategists call 'a pincer movement', he attempts to break through at that point. And when one Christian fails, all of us to some extent are affected, for we are all part of the one line of defence.

How the devil rejoices when an individual Christian falls – especially a church leader; he will make sure there is a newspaper reporter around to pick up on the story.

We are called to a ministry of prayer, not just for ourselves but for one another also, that we might stand perfect and complete in the will of God and that our faith will not fail when under attack by the devil.

Father, I am encouraged as I think that today millions of Christians around the world will be praying for me. Help me never to fail in my responsibility to pray for them. In Christ's peerless and precious Name. Amen.

Pray for me that ...

FOR READING AND MEDITATION – ROMANS 12:1–13

'... be transformed by the renewing of your mind, that you may prove
what is that good and acceptable and perfect will of God.' (v.2: NKJ)

The apostle ends his section on spiritual warfare (Eph. 6:10–20) on
the following personal note: 'Pray on my behalf' (vv.19–20, NASB).

Paul knew full well the power that was against him, and he does
not hesitate to ask for the prayers of his brothers and sisters in the
church in Ephesus. Imagine this great apostle, probably the most
powerful and effective disciple of Christ, asking his friends to pray
for him. And why not? The greater a Christian is, the more he realises his dependence on the prayers of others.

Notice that his request for prayer is clear and specific: 'that utter-
ance may be given to me in the opening of my mouth, to make
known with boldness the mystery of the gospel.'

Whenever you ask someone to pray for you, be equally specific.
Don't just say 'Pray for me', but 'Pray for me that ...'. Note, too, that
Paul's request was not that he might be delivered from prison, but
that through his testimony in prison the gospel of Christ might be
advanced.

He knew that the most important thing at the moment was not
to triumph over prison, but to triumph in it. He knew he was where
God wanted him for that time, and he would allow no self-interest
to interfere with the divine schedule.

*O Father, teach me, as you taught your servant Paul, to know your will
and purpose so clearly that I might know just how and what to pray for. I ask
this in and through the strong and mighty Name of Jesus. Amen.*

The final word

'To the intent that now the manifold wisdom of God might be made known by the church to the principalities and powers . . .' (v.10: NKJ)

God has given us firstly the belt of truth – a willingness to let God's truth govern every part of our lives. Secondly, the breastplate of righteousness – seeing clearly that we are saved only by Christ's righteousness. Thirdly, the shoes of the preparation of the gospel of peace – our determination to stand firmly in the faith.

Fourthly, we must raise the shield of faith – the quick action by which we act upon God's truth and refuse Satan's lies. Fifthly, we must put on the helmet of salvation – the glorious hope that, one day, God will right all wrongs and establish his eternal kingdom. And sixthly, we must take up the sword of the Spirit, the Word of God, and wield the written Scriptures in the same way that our Lord did in his wilderness temptations.

Yet having done all this, it is still possible to be defeated by the devil, unless we know how to pray in the power of the Spirit. And we must pray, not just now and again, not simply when we are in trouble, not only when things go wrong, but continuously, fervently, powerfully and perseveringly.

Our prayers must catch alight and burst into flame. Against such praying, the principalities and powers are helpless.

My Father, now that I have seen the resources that are available to me in Christ, I realise that my responsibility to avail myself of those resources is greater than ever. Help me to put everything I have learned into action. For your own dear Name's sake. Amen.

The great design

FOR READING AND MEDITATION – REVELATION 19:1–10

' "Let us rejoice and be glad ... For the wedding of the Lamb has come,
and his bride has made herself ready." ' (v.7: NIV)

What is the central purpose behind the creation of the world? Is there
a single major purpose running through history, or are there several different designs – all equal in importance?

The answer of Scripture is this: the one outstanding objective
God had when he set out to create the world was the selection of a
bride for his Son. Here is the key to history.

Scripture after Scripture shows that there is a romantic purpose
in the universe, and that from all eternity God desired to provide his
Son with an eternal companion, described by John in the book of
Revelation as 'the bride, the wife of the Lamb' (Rev. 21:9).

This alone unfolds the meaning behind all of history and makes
it comprehensible. It is difficult to comprehend a cosmology that
has a love story at its core. Yet such is the case – the bride purposed
for God's Son is the central object of history.

From the opening act of creation, this has been the goal on which
the Almighty has set his heart. Indeed, as we unravel the facts of
history and place them alongside Scripture, we find that lying at
the heart of the universe is a love story of immense magnitude.
Amazing grace! How sweet the sound!

*Gracious Father, as I begin to see the wonders of your great design throughout the universe, I am filled with awe that I should be chosen to be part of
your glorious family. Help me to be worthy. For Jesus' sake. Amen.*

History – his-story

FOR READING AND MEDITATION – PSALM 74:12–17

'God is my King from ages past ...' (v.12: TLB)

Secular historians can systematise the characters and events comprising history's raw material, but they are unable, without reference to God's design in Scripture, to interpret its true significance.

The psalmist recognises a truth that chroniclers fail to, namely, that God is the Architect of history and without him, the march of the ages fails to make sense.

The ancient Greeks regarded history as a complete circle, going nowhere in particular and never reaching an identifiable goal. The historian G.N. Clarke, in an inaugural address given at Cambridge, said, 'There is no secret and no plan in history to be discovered.'

Andre Maurois, the French biographer, is on record as saying, 'The universe is indifferent. Who created it? Why are we here on this puny mud heap spinning in infinite space? I have not the slightest idea, and I am quite convinced no one has.'

How sad! To most historians, history is one senseless crisis after another, and they are unable to explain where we have come from or where we are going. The Christian, however, holding in his hand the authoritative word of God, stands fast, for he knows that there is a loving purpose running throughout all of history. There is no such thing as secular history: history is his-story.

O Father, thank you for reminding me that history is your story. It began with you, and it will end with you. Help me to see that nothing can interfere with your eternal design – nothing. I am so relieved. Thank you, Father. Amen.

According to plan

FOR READING AND MEDITATION – ACTS 17:22–31
' "From one man he made every nation of men . . .
and he determined the times set for them . . ." ' (v.26: NIV)

The proposition that the events of history contribute to God's ultimate purpose of finding a bride for his Son is given added weight by these words from Paul's sermon on Mars Hill: '(God) created all the people of the world from one man, Adam, and scattered the nations across the face of the earth. He decided beforehand which should rise and fall, and when . . .' (v. 26, TLB)

According to the great apostle, the rise and fall of such mighty empires as Assyria, Greece and Rome were in direct line with God's predetermined purposes and plans. The raising up of men like Pharaoh, Darius, Nebuchadnezzar and Belshazzar was the backdrop to a stage on which God would play out his eternal purposes.

Henry Halley, in his *Bible Handbook*, says, 'The Old Testament is the account of a nation (Israel). The New Testament is the account of a Man (Christ Jesus). The nation was founded and nurtured by God in order that the Man might come into the world.'

Although many do not see the deep import, one day the whole universe will know that the events which have taken place have been ordered, directed and supervised by God with one glorious goal in mind – the wooing and winning of a bride for his eternal Son.

O God , how can I worry and fret when your hand is so evidently at work in the world? Help me to see today that in your plans and purposes for the universe, you have included me. My gratitude knows no bounds. Amen.

The cross – inherent and integral

FOR READING AND MEDITATION – REVELATION 13:1–8

'...the Lamb slain from the foundation of the world.' (v.8: AV)

The selection of a bride for his own beloved Son: some might be saying to themselves, 'This sounds a romantic theme to select– but how realistic is it? Can it be supported from Scripture?'

It can. God had the plan of redemption in mind when he created the universe; I refer, of course, to the cross.

Christian teachers have always insisted that because the Scripture says that Christ was once offered for sins (Heb. 9:28), the cross is a finished fact of history. As far as men are concerned, the actual physical event of Christ's crucifixion took place on a hill outside Jerusalem somewhere around AD 33.

As far as God was concerned, it took place prior to the creation of the world. There can be no disagreement with this, of course, providing we see that the cross is not something that was imposed on history, but something that came out of it. Our text today tells us that Christ is the Lamb slain from the foundation of the world.

What does this mean? It means that the cross is not something that merely happened at Calvary, but the outward expression of something that was on God's heart from all eternity.

The cross is not a part of history – it is all of it. It is integral to the framework of the universe. Christ is the Lamb slain from the foundation of the world.

O Father, I see now why the cross cannot be what so many think it is – an incongruity. It is integral and inherent in life – life's foundation. I am so grateful. Amen.

The ground plan of the universe

FOR READING AND MEDITATION – EPHESIANS 1:3–14
'For he chose us in him before the creation of the world
to be holy and blameless in his sight . . .' (v.4: NIV)

The cross is the axis of the universe. Whenever we see the cross up-lifted in history, we must realise that we are seeing, at a point of time, something that is really timeless. We sometimes refer to the cross as being the point at which history divides, but really it is the point at which it begins. The universe began with an act of self-sacrifice when God, in anticipation of mankind's rebellion, offered up his life in the person of his Son. One writer puts it this way, 'The cross is the ground plan of the universe.' It is.

A missionary tells how, during the days when the Japanese Christians were persecuted for their faith, they would use a mirror with the form of a cross invisibly etched into it. When the Christians gathered together, placed the mirror on a table and allowed the sunlight to fall upon it, a reflection of the cross would then appear on the ceiling, quite distinct and very plain. The Christians would sit and worship with the cross before them, and if anyone not known to be a believer entered the house, the mirror was quietly taken out of the sun's rays, whereupon the cross would disappear.

We sit and gaze at a complex universe, and if we have eyes to see, out of its heart appears a cross. The cross in time is but a reflection of the cross in eternity.

O Lord Jesus, help me to see your Cross in a way I have never seen it before – not as something that is just timely, but as something that is timeless. For your own dear Name's sake I pray. Amen.

The scarlet thread of existence

FOR READING AND MEDITATION – HEBREWS 9:19–28

'... without the shedding of blood there is no forgiveness of sins.' (v.22: RSV)

If the cross is 'the ground plan of the universe', would we not expect to find intimations of it wherever we looked? For those who have eyes to see, it is reflected in all parts of God's universe. The seed dies that the plant may live. Mountains are barren that the valleys might be fertile.

In olden times, the foundations of houses and cities were often laid in drops of blood taken from the firstborn.

Is there something written in people's hearts that says 'without the shedding of blood there is no forgiveness of sins'? John Wesley had two simple tests for any teaching he gave, and he expected the tests to corroborate each other.

'Is it in the Bible?' he asked first. And then, 'Is it in experience?'

The cross is a scarlet thread that runs through the garment of existence.

Dr W.E. Sangster tells how he once took a little boy into a cathedral. The boy looked up and said, 'There's a cross up there.' Sangster pointed to the floor and said, 'There's a cross down here.' Of course – because the cathedral was a cruciform building. You stand at Calvary and say, 'There is a cross up there.' I point you to the earth and say, 'There is a cross down here.' It is not an incongruity – it is inherent in life. Indeed, it is life's foundation.

Father, I am filled with wonder and amazement that you should build your creation around a cross. All the time you planned the universe, you had the meeting between me and your Son in mind. Thank you, blessed Father. Amen.

The Church of the Lamb

FOR READING AND MEDITATION – JOHN 1:19–29

'"... Look, the Lamb of God, who takes away the sin of the world!"' (v.29: NIV)

God planned our redemption even before he created the universe. Christ is the Lamb slain from the foundation of the world. God had a Lamb before he had a man. What a mystery! How shall we pierce into the heart of this?

Somewhere in Switzerland there is a church that bears the title *The Church of the Lamb*. It got this title from a most intriguing incident. As the building was nearing completion, a workman standing on the topmost part of the roof suddenly slipped and fell. It took him just a few seconds to fall from the top of the building to the stony ground below, and had it not been for a strange coincidence, he would have met certain death. A farmer taking a flock of lambs to market happened to be passing at the moment of his fall. Instead of the man falling on the stony ground, he fell on top of one of the lambs. The lamb, of course, was instantly killed, but the man miraculously survived with no serious consequences.

A similar story unfolds as we attempt to build up a picture of the origins of the universe. High on top of his creation, God placed a man made in his own image, but in a moment of rebellion he fell to what would have been eternal ruin. However, God prepared a Lamb to break his fall.

O Father, how grateful I am that you had prepared the Lamb before you prepared a man. I stand in utter amazement at such love that anticipated our rebellion and prepared an answer even before sin began. Thank you, Father. Amen.

The world's first wedding

FOR READING AND MEDITATION – GENESIS 2:15–24

'Then the Lord God made a woman from the rib he had taken out of
the man, and he brought her to the man.' (v.22: NIV)

A golden thread seems to bind all things together and form one
single purpose – the selection of a bride for God's Son. God anticipated the entrance of sin into the world and laid down, in the broad
beams of creation, a cross. In this act, the Almighty took the pre-
caution of ensuring that the future goal of finding a bride for his Son
would not be frustrated by satanic interference or human failure.

The romantic purpose lying at the heart of the universe is seen
clearly in the creation of Adam and Eve. The creation of the first
human pair can be adequately explained only when it is set against
the backdrop of the theme we are pursuing – The romance of redemption. First, Adam is created and given the position of care-
taker of the earthly Paradise. Some time later Adam is put to sleep,
a rib is taken from his side, and God builds a woman. The woman
is then brought to the man and the world's first wedding takes place
with God as the officiating minister and paradise as the sanctuary.

And here's the truth we must grasp: we shall never truly understand the ways of God in the creation of Adam and Eve unless we
see it as the dress rehearsal for the plan of eternal redemption.

❧ O Father, my heart is full of eager anticipation as I wait to see another
glimpse of your purpose in the creation of Adam and Eve. Teach me more
dear Lord. For Jesus' sake. Amen.

Two in one

FOR READING AND MEDITATION – GENESIS 5:1–5

'He created them male and female, and He blessed them and
named them Adam in the day when they were created.' (v.2: NASB)

We ended yesterday by saying that the way God went about the
creation of Adam and Eve was a divine rehearsal for the plan of
redemption. Is this just a fanciful theory – or is it rooted in the
Scriptures? I believe that the more we examine the Bible, the more
evident it becomes that the goal toward which the universe is moving, and for which it waits in eager anticipation, is the final wedding of the ages when Christ will be eternally joined to his church
(Rom. 8:23; Rev. 19:67). Let's see in what ways Adam and Eve's
creation prefigures the truth of eternal redemption.

Many Bible scholars believe that when God created Adam, he
made him with a complex nature, which was later divided, and returned to him in the form of a woman. Some, of course, regard this
as pure fiction, but before dismissing it, pause for a moment to
consider the text which is our spiritual focus for today: 'He blessed
them and named them (plural) Adam (singular) in the day when
they (plural) were created.' Some interpret these words as meaning
that on the day Adam was created, God placed the embryo of the
woman (Eve) deep within him. Adam was not just one, but two in
one – hence the explanation: 'God named them – Adam.'

✎ Father, I feel that you are taking me down into the depths today and my
feet are not able to touch the bottom. Unlock the mysteries of your Word to
me, so that I shall not miss one aspect of your great and glorious purposes.
In Jesus' Name I pray. Amen.

Why did God create a woman?

FOR READING AND MEDITATION – 1 CORINTHIANS 11:7–12

'...neither was man created for woman, but woman for man.' (v.9: NIV)

We continue meditating on Adam's creation.

One commentator says, 'Eve had an embryonic existence in Adam before she actually appeared in the flesh; she was in Adam from the very moment of his creation.' Some believe that Adam prior to Eve's creation, contained within himself the qualities of both maleness and femaleness. This, they say, explains why Adam, although observing that every one of the animal creation had a mate, seemed perfectly content to be alone.

Further evidence for this is drawn from the fact that it was not Adam who said, 'It is not good for the man to be alone' (Gen. 2:18) – but God. We have a picture of Adam as a man complete in himself, containing both maleness and femaleness, and feeling no need or desire for human companionship.

Why, then, did God create a woman? One answer to this question is that for human nature to experience true wholeness and completeness, it must obey one of the deepest laws of the universe, namely 'whoever wants to save his life will lose it, but whoever loses his life ... will find it' (Matt. 16:25). For Adam to grow and develop in his humanity, he needed to have someone to whom he could give himself – hence one reason for the necessity of Eve's creation.

⮑ O Father, I am concerned that I do not miss one single brush stroke in this fascinating picture which is daily developing before my gaze. Deepen my understanding of your ways and your Word. For Jesus' sake. Amen.

God obeys his own laws

FOR READING AND MEDITATION – HEBREWS 2:5–15
'But we see Jesus … crowned with glory and honour
because he suffered death …' (v.9: NIV)

For Adam to enjoy wholeness and completeness, it was necessary for him to obey the law which states 'whoever wants to save his life will lose it, but whoever loses his life … will find it'.

The law of 'saving our life by losing it' is not something God designed for the regulation of his subjects, but is something which he obeys himself. If God should violate it then he would cease to be God, and if man violates it then he ceases to be man. God obeys every law he demands of us, and by giving himself to Adam in the act of creation – and later to the whole human race in the act of redemption – he especially obeys and illustrates the law of finding life by losing it.

This law is not based on God's whim, nor even upon his will – it is based on God's character. Is it any wonder then, that when he made a man in his own image, he copied into him this selfsame principle? If Adam had not been provided with someone to whom he could give himself then he would never have developed as a person. Thus in providing Adam with someone with whom he could share himself, God established the pattern that the way to wholeness in human relationships is to be a giver, before one is a receiver.

Lord God, I am overwhelmed to realise that you not only draw up the laws that guide and govern your universe, but you obey them too. And you especially obeyed this law of finding your life by losing it. I am so thankful. Amen.

At last!

FOR READING AND MEDITATION – SONGS OF SONGS 2:1–13

'He has taken me to the banquet hall,
and his banner over me is love.' (v.4: NIV)

If Adam contained the qualities of both maleness and femaleness, why did God make a woman? For one reason, that in order to experience true wholeness, man needed to have someone, of equal status to himself, to whom he could give himself.

In God's universe, giving is more important than receiving – if we do not give, then we just do not get. Adam needed someone outside of himself, someone to whom he could give himself and in the giving, experience growth. God separated the female side of his nature and gave it a new identity in the form of another human being – Eve. She was then brought to him so that he might love, protect and minister to her. In that mysterious but beautiful act, God made it clear that the wholeness and completeness Adam had previously enjoyed, independent of another human being, had now changed. He must find completeness, not only in his relationship with God, but in Eve his wife.

When Adam discovered his newly created wife, in the words of the *Revised Standard Version*, he blurted out in surprise and joy: 'At last!' What did he mean? Let me share with you my own speculations. I believe Adam sensed, in that moment, the joy that his completeness could be found in another, and it was this that excited him.

✑ *O Father, you have wrought love and the necessity of love into the very fibre of everything, within us and without. We are made by love and for love. And when we find love – we find everything. I am so thankful. Amen.*

A cameo of redemption

FOR READING AND MEDITATION – COLOSSIANS 1:13–23

'He has ... transferred us to the kingdom of his beloved Son,
in whom we have redemption ...' (vv.13–14: RSV)

The question has often been raised: why did God place the woman in the man, then take her out of him and later bring her back to him so that they could be 'one flesh'? Why didn't God create them simultaneously from the dust of the earth?

Out of the many answers that could be given to this question, one stands out above them all. We saw earlier how God's eternal purpose, that a bride should be found for his Son, broke into the act of creation when he laid down the cross in the foundation of the universe – and a similar situation can be seen in the manner in which God went about the creation of Adam and Eve. God, it seems, is unable to wait to unfold the romantic purpose that lies upon his heart and gives a hint of it in the way he makes the first human pair. The woman being placed in the man, then taken out of him and later being joined to him, is really a cameo of the whole story of redemption. For what is redemption all about? Is it not that, long before we ever appeared in time, we were predestined in Christ, came out of his side at Calvary, and are now being prepared for the day when we shall become his eternal bride?

꙳ O Father, I am so thrilled. Can it be that the excitement in my heart is but the reflection of your own at the anticipation of the wedding that will one day take place in the skies? Amen.

Redemption – prefigured

FOR READING AND MEDITATION – REVELATION 5:6–14

' "... You are worthy ... because you were slain, and with your blood
you purchased men for God from every ... nation." ' (v.9: NIV)

The creation of Adam and Eve in the Garden of Eden, so moving
and so beautiful in itself, derives real glory from what it prefigures
– the selecting of a bride for God's Son. What you have been watching is God's great heart of love spilling over into a romantic rehearsal of the truth that spans the ages.

What is that truth? That the bride who was conceived in Adam,
created from his rib, then brought to him for their union to be consummated, is a picture in time of what is really going on in eternity.
The Bible teaches that when God looked at Christ in eternity, he saw
the redeemed in him. Before we appeared in time, we existed in the
mind and purposes of God. Paul puts this glorious fact thus: '...cho-
sen ... in him before the foundation of the world' (Eph. 1:4, AV).

If we were in him, when did we come out of him? At Calvary,
when the blood which became the foundation for our salvation
came forth from Christ's side. Paul says: 'Christ loved the church
and gave himself up for her' (Eph. 5:25). The church (or bride) was
conceived in Christ, and created from his side – but how is the consummation to take place? Ah – we have a little way to go before we
are ready for that!

*O Father, how can I cease to be grateful for the love, the care and the pre-
cision that has gone into the planning and the procuring of my salvation?
Help me to be as joyful in my salvation as you are. For your own dear Name's
sake. Amen.*

The enemy of God's purposes

FOR READING AND MEDITATION – 1 PETER 5:1–11

'Your enemy the devil prowls around like a roaring lion . . .' (v.8: NIV)

Now appears the archenemy of all God's plans and purposes – Satan. If it is true that the divine purpose of history is the wooing and winning of a bride for God's Son, then it is also true that Satan's supreme purpose is to frustrate the divine intention and bring about its failure.

Before we can understand the strategy which Satan employs in trying to achieve this aim, we must ask ourselves: who exactly is this mysterious personality whom the Bible variously addresses as the Devil, Satan, Lucifer, Tempter, Destroyer, Beelzebub and Prince?

Many modern-day theologians have stopped believing in a personal devil, and explain the presence of evil in the world as simply the result of negative forces. Let me assure you of one thing – even if you don't believe in the devil – he certainly believes in you. And most of his strategy and cunning is focused on hindering you from becoming part of God's eternal purposes.

Satan is more than an evil influence – he is an evil intelligence. The more he can encourage doubt about his existence, the better he likes it. Were he better understood he would be more hated, more resisted and more defeated. It suits Satan well for Christians to slumber in the bland assurance that he does not exist.

O Father, help me to recognise that the adversary is not merely an influence, but an evil intelligence. Give me, I pray, a deep spiritual understanding of how he operates and how I can conquer and overcome him. This I ask in Jesus' Name. Amen.

If there is no devil...?

FOR READING AND MEDITATION – REVELATION 12:9–12

'...that ancient serpent called the devil or Satan,
who leads the whole world astray...' (v.9: NIV)

As we have said before, Satan wants us to doubt his existence.
Michael Green, in his book *I Believe in Satan's Downfall*, says, 'Like
any general who can persuade the opposition to underestimate him,
Satan (supposing him to exist) must be enchanted at the present
state of affairs which leaves him free to operate with the maximum
of ease and efficiency, confident that nobody takes him seriously.'

A poem I came across some years ago puts it most effectively:

> *Men don't believe in the devil now*
> *like their fathers used to do;*
> *they reject one creed because it's old,*
> *for another because it's new.*
> *But who dogs the steps of the toiling saints,*
> *who spreads the net for his feet,*
> *who sows the tares in the world's broad fields,*
> *where the Saviour sows his wheat?*
> *They may say the devil has never lived;*
> *they may say the devil has gone,*
> *but simple people would like to know –*
> *who carries his business on?*

❧ *Father, I see so clearly that the chaos and disruption in the universe
points to an outside enemy. Help me to know the wiles of Satan so that I might
stand invincibly against him. For your own dear Name's sake. Amen.*

A glimpse of Satan's origin

FOR READING AND MEDITATION – LUKE 10:1–20

'He replied, "I saw Satan fall like lightning from heaven."' (v.18: NIV)

One of the questions I am often asked, especially by young Christians, is this: Why did God create the devil? What possible purpose could the Almighty have had in bringing into existence such a vile, ugly, psychopathic creature as Satan?

The simple answer, of course, is that God did not create the devil; he created an angel of immense beauty and intelligence who, by pride and self-centredness, chose to rebel against God and became the personality we now describe as the devil. What did Jesus mean when he said, 'I saw Satan fall like lightning from heaven.' We cannot be fully certain what was in Jesus' mind when he uttered these words, but several things are clear, not only from what he said, but from the context. Jesus had sent out the seventy to go ahead of him as messengers of the kingdom, and they returned, triumphant, telling how demons were subject to them in Christ's Name. Then comes this great exclamation which, in context, spells out for us several important facts. It indicates Satan's home was once in heaven with God, that he fell from that blissful state, that Christ's disciples have power over the enemy and that their names are written in the very heaven from whence he fell.

Father, I see that much hangs on the judgment I make about the devil. Help me to see this whole subject in its proper perspective. Satan may be powerful, but he is not all-powerful. That attribute is yours – and yours alone. I am so thankful. Amen.

The king of tyre

FOR READING AND MEDITATION – EZEKIEL 28:1–19

"'... I drove you in disgrace from the mount of God, and I expelled you,
O guardian cherub, from among the fiery stones.'" (v.16: NIV)

Poetic and mysterious, this verse is considered by evangelical scholars to have reference to the fall of Satan.

S.D. Cordon says that the first ten verses of Ezekiel 28 contain a message to the prince of Tyre, while the next nine verses are a lamentation over the king of Tyre. The language used of the prince is appropriate to a man – indeed he is addressed as 'a man' – but the language used of the king is highly inappropriate to a man: indeed, it could hardly be used of any human being.

Gordon points out that the same spirit dominates both the prince and the king. The parallels are quite obvious. Both have tremendous beauty, wisdom and power, and both defy and rebel against the living God. Both are charming, proud, prosperous, intelligent and in a position of great prominence. See how the language in the second portion unfolds the rise and fall of Satan. He is pictured as dwelling in close intimacy with God, blameless in all his ways, full of wisdom, skillful in operation and perfect in beauty. But then he became proud and was cast out of heaven: 'your heart became proud'; 'you corrupted your wisdom'; 'I threw you to the earth'. Designated as the king of Tyre, scholars believe he is really the Prince of Darkness.

Father, I am so grateful that although your Word may not give me all the answers I would like to know, it gives me all the answers I need to know. Thank you for what you are showing me about the origins of my adversary. Amen.

High treason

FOR READING AND MEDITATION – ISAIAH 14:1–15

'How you have fallen from heaven, O morning star, son of the dawn!
You have been cast down to the earth...' (v.12: NIV)

Here Isaiah taunts the king of Babylon. The proud monarch will be laid low and his power will be broken. It seems at first that he is addressing the king of Babylon but, as with Ezekiel's king of Tyre, another figure is seen behind the words.

Dr Martyn Lloyd Jones says, 'These descriptions, although primarily meant to apply to Tyre and Babylon, are generally agreed to have a much wider meaning. That is quite customary in prophecy. You start with the immediate, but it is also a foreshadowing of something bigger which is to come. They are also symbols, as it were, of the power of the devil and his forces.'

Most certainly the words of the passage can hardly be applied to a man. Listen: 'How you have fallen from heaven, O morning star ... You said in your heart, "I will ascend to heaven ... I will make myself like the Most High"' (vv.12–14). And to this fivefold 'I will' of Satan, God gives his response: 'But you are brought down to the grave' (v.15). It is clear that Satan desired to be God. The archetypal spirit turned from good to evil, and from God to self through self-centredness and pride.

✎ O Father, when I see that it was pride that turned an angel into a devil, I fall in contrition at your feet and pray that self-centredness shall never find a place in me. Root out any pride in me so that I will be your loyal and obedient subject. For Jesus' sake. Amen.

If I were God...

FOR READING AND MEDITATION – PSALM 73:1–28
'You guide me with your counsel, and afterwards
you will take me into glory.' (v.24: NIV)

If God is almighty and all-powerful, why did he not annihilate Satan when he first rebelled against him?

I often thought if I were in charge I would run the universe a lot differently from the way God does. I would make sure, for example, that every person sat down to at least one square meal a day, and I would show scientists how to prevent the ills that surround the universe.

The more thought I gave to the issue of 'If I were God', however, the more I realised that it must be the easiest thing in the world for God to follow the examples I have given. The fact that he doesn't must mean that there are factors he has in mind of which I know nothing at all. These factors contribute to the way that he seems to contradict, from the human point or view at least, a commonsense approach. The truth is, of course, that in God there is not just power, but purpose, and this means that he only allows that which he sees will work out for the ultimate achievement of his plans.

𝒩 *Gracious Father, I am so grateful for this conclusion. Help me to put my feet firmly on the fact that because you are a God of purpose and not just power, you will never allow anything to happen unless you can ultimately redeem it. Thank you, Father. Amen.*

God's eternal greatness

FOR READING AND MEDITATION – ISAIAH 45:15–25

' "... there is no God apart from me, a righteous God and a Saviour;
there is none but me." ' (v.21: NIV)

Why did God not annihilate Satan when he first rebelled against him? Any misunderstanding here will prevent us from comprehending the great design that runs throughout the universe. The truth is, of course, that God never allows anything to take place in his universe unless it accords with his eternal purpose. Things may seem to have little purpose when we look at them from a temporal point of view, but when viewed against the backdrop of eternity, they take on a completely different perspective.

The philosopher Alfred Whitehead put it succinctly, 'I hazard a prophecy that the religion which will conquer the world is that which can render clear to popular understanding some eternal greatness in the passage of temporal fact.'

If we give ourselves only to purposes that are bounded by time, then we have nothing left when time ends. 'The eternal greatness incarnate in the passage of temporal fact' is precisely what God has spelt out in the Bible. The loving purposes of an all-wise God stretch, not only back into the eternal past, but also into the eternal future. I make the point again: God never allows anything to take place in his universe unless it accords with his eternal purpose.

O Father, you who have the secret of making all things work your way – even Satan and sin – work again today in my life to turn every opposition into an opportunity, and every problem into a possibility. In Jesus' Name I ask it. Amen.

The satanic strategy

'"... I will build my church, and the gates of Hades will not overcome it."'
(v.18: NIV)

Did Satan know from the beginning that it was God's ultimate intention to one day provide a bride for his Son?

Welsh theologian, Cynddylan Jones, suggests one of the reasons which led Satan into the sin of anarchy was his knowledge that the bride would occupy a position on the throne far higher than his own. This knowledge he suggests, provoked in Satan a jealousy which he could not contain, and led him to attempt to usurp God's authority and gain the throne for himself.

Cynddylan Jones goes on to say, 'Ever since Satan was turned out of heaven for attempting to grasp the throne for himself, it has been one of his main objectives to do everything he can to frustrate, and if possible, prevent the arrival of Christ's bride on the throne which God shares with his Son. This is why he has taken up the position of the "prince of the power of the air".'

We have no way of knowing, of course, whether Cynddylan Jones' theory is correct, but we do know from such passages as the one before us today, and also from experience, that one of Satan's prime targets is the Christian church – that blood-washed host who, one day, will be his glorious bride.

My Master and my God, day by day the conviction is deepening within me that I am part of a purpose which did not begin at my birth – nor will end at my death. I am destined for a throne – and nothing can stop that destiny. I am so grateful. Thank you, Father. Amen.

Two favourite approaches

FOR READING AND MEDITATION – REVELATION 12:1–6, 17:1–6

'Then another sign appeared in heaven: an enormous red dragon ...' (12:3, NIV)

'... a woman sitting on a scarlet beast ...' (17:3, NIV)

Although Satan is bent on attacking every person on the face of the earth, he does not need to bother about those who are already safely in his control. Those, however, who have committed themselves to Jesus Christ, his archenemy, become a prime target. Someone said, 'Before you became a Christian Satan knew exactly where you lived, but the moment you committed yourself to Christ, he underlined your address in red ink.'

Why did temptation seem to increase when you became a Christian? It did increase; you passed from security into the firing line. There are many ways in which Satan attacks the people of God, but two of his favourite strategies are opposition and seduction. The first passage (Revelation 12) gives us a graphic image of the bloodthirsty dragon, waging war against the offspring of the woman: 'those who obey God's commandments and hold to the testimony of Jesus' (v.17). The other is a picture of the seductive prostitute: 'a woman sitting on a scarlet beast ... drunk with the blood of the saints' (Rev. 17:3, 6). The pictures are complicated and variously interpreted, but in both cases, Satan's strategy is crystal clear – the liquidation of the people of God.

O Father, how can I sufficiently thank you that I have come into a new world, and a new world has come into me. Help me to so live that I will be a disappointment to the devil, but a delight to you. For your own dear Name's sake. Amen.

The archetypal temptation

FOR READING AND MEDITATION –
GENESIS 3:1; 2 CORINTHIANS 11:3, 14
'Now the serpent was more crafty than any of
the wild animals the Lord God had made.' (Gen. 3:1, NIV)

No examination of Satan's strategy could ignore the archetypal temptation in the Garden of Eden, for it provides some illuminating insights into how the Tempter works. Satan is greatly concerned to divert attention from the third chapter of Genesis. How he laughs when exponents of Scripture say the first few chapters of Genesis are not historical but allegorical. No undercover agent likes anyone to expose his methods – and Genesis 3 does just that!

Before we examine in detail Adam and Eve's temptation, let's look at some general characteristics. When Satan approached Eve in Eden, he came in the form of a beautiful serpent – a subtle disguise. He relied, as he always does, on cunning, craftiness and guile. His temptation caught Eve by surprise. This method – approaching from an unexpected direction – is something Satan still delights to use. His aim is to encourage disobedience against God and get men and women under his control. This severs their relationship with God just as surely as his own is severed. Devoid of creativity, he can only spoil what God creates. 'Satan has to row his boat down God's waterways: he has none of his own.'

✎ O Father, now that I am beginning to see, and see clearly, the strategies which Satan employs, I pray that what I am learning may stay with me for the rest of my life. I cannot fumble the business of living for you. Time is too short and life too serious. In Jesus' Name I pray. Amen.

Hungry? Then – watch out!

FOR READING AND MEDITATION – GENESIS 2:8–17, 3:2–3

'"... You are free to eat from any tree in the garden; but you must not
eat from the tree of the knowledge of good and evil ..."' (2:16–17, NIV)

The way Satan came to Eve demonstrates how he approaches us
through the natural channels of our God-given faculties. Satan's
temptation of Eve was a three pronged attack, firstly to her bodily
desires, secondly to her mind and thirdly to her ambition.

Satan said to Eve: 'Did God really say, "You must not eat from
any tree in the garden"?' (Gen. 3:1) How subtle! Everyone has a natural desire for food, but unless we are careful, this can become a
target for Satan's temptation. Eve allowed the temptation to get the
better of her, and took the first step on the road to ruin.

The amount of evil that comes into the world through the misuse of perfectly natural bodily functions, such as hunger, sex, sleep
is quite enormous. A contemporary writing on this point says, 'Most
of the time, it is unnecessary for Satan to be very sophisticated in
his approach; he can reach us very effectively through basic physical functions. The strategy which Satan used in the Garden is a
device he employs to great effect today'. Many present-day Christians are lying around achieving nothing for God because they have
given way to Satan's temptation to indulge their appetites rather
than curb them. They are servants still – but to the wrong master.

✍ *My Lord and my God, help me to harness all my desires and drive them
in your purposes, lest Satan take advantage over me and use them to drive
me. For your honour and glory I ask it. Amen.*

The second temptation

FOR READING AND MEDITATION – GENESIS 3:1–5; 1 TIMOTHY 2:14

'... Adam was not the one deceived; it was the woman who
was deceived and became a sinner.' (v.2:14, NIV)

Satan uses doubt in the battle for the mind.

Firstly, he gets Eve to doubt God's goodness: 'Did God really say,
"You must not eat"?' This was not only a misrepresentation of what
God had said, but it carried the subtle suggestion that God did not
really love her and was out to deprive her of a legitimate pleasure. It
is satanic propaganda used to great advantage even today.

Secondly, he gets her to doubt God's word. 'Did God really say?'
The suggestion is that God is not dependable, and most likely has
not revealed to Eve his full purposes and intentions. Have you ever
faced this kind of temptation? I'm sure you have. You can hardly be
a Christian without hearing Satan say something like, 'That's an
outdated idea which was all right in the past but can't be followed
today.' Or, 'There are exceptions to every rule; this one doesn't apply
to you.'

Thirdly, he gets her to doubt God's holiness. 'You will not surely
die,' he says. 'Your eyes will be opened, and you will be like God ...'
(vv. 4–5). See what he is suggesting? God will not follow through on
his threats. All will turn out well in the end – however disobedient
you may be.

✎ *O Father, help me to realise that I, too, like Eve, have to face the subtleties
and strategies of Satan. Keep me ever dependent on you – for if I have to
fight him myself, I'm sunk. In Jesus' Name I pray. Amen.*

The third temptation

FOR READING AND MEDITATION – GENESIS 3:5; 1 JOHN 5:18–21

'We know that we are children of God, and that the whole world is
under the control of the evil one.' (v.19: NIV)

Satan's third attack on Eve – was to appeal to her ambition. Naturally Eve was attracted by the delectable fruit that hung from the tree of the knowledge of good and evil, just as she was by the prospect of further knowledge. Satan's master stroke, however, was to instil within her the desire to be as God: 'When you eat of it your eyes will be opened, and you will be like God.'

This desire 'to be as God' turned Satan into the kind of being he is. He was created a creature of immense power, beauty and intelligence. Such gifts ought to have produced in him a spirit of dependence, humility and gratitude, but Satan saw them as the basis of his power, and a springboard to even greater things.

'All power tends to corrupt, and absolute power corrupts absolutely.' Satan's god was no longer the Lord – but himself. And Satan has succeeded. Our age is filled with people striving to be as God – so driven by ambition and a desire for knowledge for knowledge's sake that they seem to have little concern whether the pursuit of it will eventually destroy mankind.

There is little doubt, in my mind at least, that the strategy devised by Satan at the dawn of history is the same strategy he uses today.

꩜ O Father, I tremble inwardly lest I, too, use my gifts and talents as a basis for greatness rather than a basis for gratitude. Help me to be great in humility, for then I shall never need to be afraid of being great in resources. For Jesus' sake. Amen.

The consequences of disobedience

'. . . she took of its fruit and ate; and she also gave to her husband with her,
and he ate. Then the eyes of both of him were opened . . .' (vv.6–7: NKJ)

Look now at the consequences of Eve's disobedience. The first of these was sin. Eve sided with the Tempter, yielded to his suggestions, ate of the fruit and became the first human being to disobey God.

A second was that she involved Adam in her disobedience. Sin is always like that. Sin usually has an effect on or implicates another. A third consequence of Adam and Eve's sin was that they felt dirty and defiled. Prior to the Fall they had been naked without feeling ashamed, but now they became embarrassed by the natural state.

Fourthly, they hid from God. His presence, which was once a joy, now became a threat. Remember, it was not God who made the break – but them. As the wayside poster says, 'If God seems far away, guess who moved?' Sin distances us from God.

A fifth consequence was the rise of fear in their personalities. 'I was afraid,' said Adam (v.10). Sin cuts off the only force greater than fear, namely love. A sixth consequence was spiritual death. 'You will surely die' (Gen. 2:17). In the death of their spiritual sensitivities, they were dead while they lived. Lastly, their sin resulted in judgment. They were expelled from the Garden of Eden. They had chosen to be separate from God, so separated they must be.

❦ *Gracious God and Father, help me to see that sin is always followed by consequences. Help me and strengthen me to rebut every one of Satan's temptations. In Jesus' Name I pray. Amen.*

What does God do now?

FOR READING AND MEDITATION – HEBREWS 8:1–13

' "This is the covenant I will make . . . I will put my laws
in their minds and write them on their hearts . . ." ' (v.10: NIV)

If God's major goal in creating the universe was the selection of a bride for his Son, then how would he proceed with those purposes once the first human pair had failed him?

Adam and Eve were expelled from Eden – a punishment that most certainly fitted the crime. But look, God came and made garments of skins for the rebel pair. He clothed them, undeserving though they were. So far from being unloving as suggested, he is unbelievably large-hearted and magnanimous. Later, when Eve gave birth to her firstborn child, she said: 'With the help of the Lord I have brought forth a man' (Gen. 4:1). Yes – with the help of the Lord! God had expelled them from the Garden of Eden – but he had not abandoned them.

From the moment the first human pair were sent from the Garden of Eden, God began to spell out through the types, figures, shadows and pictures of the Old Testament the truth that, despite their failure, he was determined to redeem what had been lost, and find a new humanity fit to be a bride for his Son. So what did temptation and sin accomplish in the conflict which took place in Eden? It served to show God in his true colours – and Satan in his.

Father, how I long to be like you – indomitable, reconciling, inspiring and victorious. Copy into my character the lineaments of your own nature so that when I am confronted by difficulties, I don't break up – but break out. For Jesus' sake. Amen.

Human rights – forfeited

FOR READING AND MEDITATION – ROMANS 5:12–21

'For if the many died by the trespass of the one man, how much more
did God's grace ... overflow to the many!' (v.15: NIV)

In some parts of the Bible, the sin that took place in the Garden of
Eden is attributed not so much to Eve as to Adam. This is not done
to excuse Eve, but to draw attention to the fact that Adam, being
the first human being in the universe, was ultimately responsible
and is what theologians call 'the federal head'. Eve is recognised by
Scripture as being under her husband's covering, so that the final
responsibility rests upon him.

When Adam sinned, he lost legal rights to the dominion God
gave him and became a slave to Satan. Paul draws our attention to
this in Romans 6: 'Don't you know that when you offer yourselves to
someone to obey him as slaves, you are slaves to the one whom you
obey?' (v.16). The legal rights of dominion God gave Adam at his
creation were forfeited when he sinned, and the position of rulership passed into Satan's hands. It became obvious that if Satan's
dominion was to be revoked, then a way must be found to return
to God the legal rights surrendered by Adam, without violating the
principles of justice on which the universe had been founded. Could
God find such a way? Blessed be his Name – he did!

✎ O God my Father, impress deep within me yet again today the fact that
because I am your child, I share with you the ability to overcome all obstacles.
Give me the resilience of spirit that finds a way around everything. For Jesus
sake. Amen.

God comes to our rescue

FOR READING AND MEDITATION – 2 CORINTHIANS 5:14–21

'All this is from God, who reconciled us to himself
through Christ . . .' (v.18: NIV)

Since Satan now possessed the legal rights which had been given into Adam's hands, God, being bound by his own moral laws, could not legally annul that arrangement.

Charles Finney, the great revivalist and also a lawyer, says, 'If God acted contrary to the laws which he himself has devised, then the universe would crumble and fall apart. God is as much bound by the rules of his universe as you and I. He could not do anything else – and still be God.'

In attempting to unravel this great problem, God could not call upon an angel to try to recover humanity's rights, for the nature of man and the nature of angels is so vastly different. Someone had to be found who was a member of the human race – yet without sin. Anyone who contained within himself the least shadow of sin would be instantly disqualified. And why? Because it would mean that he would immediately come under Satan's legal control. As the dominion of the earth had been legally given to a man, and lost by a man, it could only be properly recovered by a man. How could such a redemptive remedy be found? No angel could have helped us. God came himself – in the person of his own eternal Son.

✗ O Father, how like you it is not to stand on the rim of the universe surveying our plight, but to plunge in to our rescue. What unspeakable love, what limitless compassion, what amazing grace! I am deeply grateful. Thank you, Father. Amen.

The biggest little word in history

FOR READING AND MEDITATION – GALATIANS 4:1–7

'…when the time had fully come, God sent his Son … to redeem
those under law, that we might receive the full rights of sons.' (vv.4–5, NIV)

G.M. Trevelyan once said, 'The case against God was so mountainous
and watertight, that unless one believes in the Incarnation, and that
God himself came into the muddle of the world to redeem it, then
there is quite simply no adequate solution to the problem of sin.'

God came to us in the person of his Son; he came in order to
redeem us. What other religion has a message like this?

The Hebrew religion says, 'God is outside his world – looking
on.' The Buddhist religion says, 'God is apart from the world – but
still interested in our welfare.' The non-religionist says, 'God is above
all things and has little time for the human race, which must be a
big disappointment to him.' The Christian says, 'Yes, it is true that
God is outside of his world, but it is also true that by virtue of his
Incarnation, he has come into it.'

God came and involved himself in our plight. He lifted us up –
from underneath. This is why the word *Incarnation*, although not
to be found in Scripture, is one of the greatest words in the Christian
faith. Notice, the word is 'in-carnate' – not excarnate, or even super-
carnate. And that 'in' is the biggest little word in history.

✎ *Almighty God, the idea of you becoming a human being completely
astounds me. You went further than I could have ever dreamed of – and now
I'm going further into you than I ever dreamed. I feel within me the tingle of
your destiny beckoning me onward, and I follow with all my heart. Amen.*

The beginning of the end

FOR READING AND MEDITATION – MATTHEW 2:7–23

'... Herod ... was furious, and he gave orders to kill all the boys
in Bethlehem ... who were two years old and under.' (v.16: NIV)

When Jesus Christ entered our world as an authentic member of humanity by way of the Incarnation, the thin end of the wedge was introduced between Satan and Adam's race. Realising this, Satan set out to do all he could to stop the birth of Christ taking place, and failing that, to prevent him from offering himself as a substitute for sin on Calvary's cross.

The striking picture of Satan anticipating the birth of the 'male child' in Revelation 12, says, 'The dragon stood in front of the woman who was about to give birth, so that he might devour her child the moment it was born. She gave birth to a son, a male child, who will rule all the nations with an iron sceptre. And her child was snatched up to God and to his throne' (vv.4–5). Whether or not we interpret this passage as having reference to Herod's attempt to have Jesus killed, it is evident from other Scriptures that Satan did everything he could to prevent Christ from coming into the world and hinder him from achieving his God-ordained mission. The flurry of demonic activity in the gospels is to be expected, for if Jesus came to destroy the works of the devil, then it is not surprising that Satan should be stirred to great wrath.

My gracious Father, why do I worry and fret when your ability to outmanoeuvre Satan is so clear and obvious? Help me to rest in the knowledge that as long as I am in you, then his attempts to defeat me will be brought to nothing. Thank you, dear Father. Amen.

The wilderness battle

FOR READING AND MEDITATION – MATTHEW 4:1–11

'Then Jesus was led by the Spirit into the desert
to be tempted by the devil.' (v.1: NIV)

We saw yesterday that Jesus' life was under attack by Satan right from the start. The most dramatic of Christ's temptations is often described as 'the wilderness battle'. Here the temptations are brought together in an initial onslaught. If Jesus could be made to fail at the commencement of his ministry, then the whole redemption plan would have been foiled.

The timing of this period of temptation is interesting – it came immediately after Jesus had been baptised. It was a moment of great elation. He had seen the Holy Spirit descend in the form of a dove, heard the voice of God speak from the sky, and received heaven's highest commendation: 'This is my Son, whom I love; with him I am well pleased' (Matt. 3:17).

The setting of the temptation was equally significant. Jesus was to have no privileged position. The first Adam had faced Satan's temptations surrounded by a lush garden. Jesus, the Last Adam, faced Satan's temptations in the burning heat of an empty and arid wilderness. Mark tells us also that he was among the wild animals (Mk. 1:13) – another hint that the last Adam succeeded where the first Adam failed. Adam had named them all in those early days in Eden. Now, in their company, Jesus set out to win where Adam had lost.

⊰ Matchless and beautiful Son of God, your coming to me was at awful cost. Help me to respond to you without regard to what it costs me. For your own dear Name's sake I ask it. Amen.

The lessons of the wilderness

FOR READING AND MEDITATION – LUKE 4:1–14

'When the devil had finished all this tempting, he left him ...
Jesus returned to Galilee in the power of the Spirit ...' (vv.13–14: NIV)

The first temptation in that initial confrontation came through the body: 'If you are the Son of God, tell this stone to become bread.' Christ had not eaten for 40 days – food must have been appealing.

The second temptation came through the mind. On the pinnacle of the temple, Satan says: 'If you are the Son of God, throw yourself down from here. For it is written: "He will command his angels concerning you"' (vv. 9–10). See how Satan quotes – but misinterprets – the Word of God.

The third temptation assailed Christ's ambition: 'I will give you all their authority and splendour ... if you worship me' (vv. 6–7). This must have been particularly interesting to Satan, for it was through ambition that he himself fell. The whole purpose of Jesus coming into the world was to reverse the situation into which Adam had fallen. He was intending, through obedience and trust, to repair the breach that Adam had made. If Satan was to succeed, he had to break down that trust and obedience. The plan worked in Eden, but not here. Jesus gave it short shrift. No playing with temptation, but a firm rebuke. He did not ask Satan to go – he told him to go. At a firm rebuttal, backed by the Word, Satan always flees.

Blessed Lord Jesus, help me to focus on the principles you used against Satan, and build them into my daily experience – trusting obedience, no toying with temptation and a firm rebuttal backed by Scripture. For your own Name's sake. Amen.

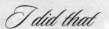

I did that

FOR READING AND MEDITATION – LUKE 23:32–38

'When they came to the place called the Skull,
there they crucified him . . .' (v.33: NIV)

It seems appropriate to remind ourselves of the fact that Christ died not only for our sins, but by our sins. Many believe that Jesus Christ was done to death by a few wicked monsters of iniquity, such as Herod, the priests and the Roman soldiers. There is much more to the Cross, however – Jesus Christ was done to death by an accumulation of ordinary sins, the sins that you and I have committed, or are committing still.

What kind of sins put Christ on the cross? There was the bigotry of the Pharisees. Have you ever been bigoted? There was the self-seeking of the Sadducees. Have you ever been self-seeking? There was the rationalisation of Pilate. Have you ever pretended to be interested in someone else, while all the time you are only interested in yourself? Then there were the cheap taunts of the unreflecting crowd. Have you ever joined others in censorious judgment on someone you did not know? These were the sins that nailed Christ to the tree – and we committed those very sins. One of the purposes of the cross is to make us see plainly what is normally hidden – the foulness and deadly nature of ordinary sins. As you look at the cross – pause – and think – and say, 'I did that.'

Blessed Lord Jesus, I confess I never realised what sin could do until I saw its dreadful consequences in your Cross. I see afresh that you not only died for my sins, but by my sins. I am grateful more than these humble words can convey. Thank you, Lord. Amen.

Obedient to death

FOR READING AND MEDITATION – PHILIPPIANS 2:1–11

'... he humbled himself and became obedient to death –
even death on a cross!' (v.8: NIV)

What really happened at Calvary? How did Jesus win the great battle with Satan? What we know is profoundly wonderful. Christ won the battle over Satan by the continued obedience of his earthly life, begun the moment he was born and continued until the moment he died. That had never been done before – or indeed since.

Christ had, of course, been obedient to his Father's will in eternity, but now that he had become flesh, obedience was demanded that had never before been seen in human nature. Not one single person, Adam included, has lived a perfect life without flaw or failure. Christ's obedience broke the hold that Satan had over the human race and snapped the entail of disobedience that was an integral part of our Adamic nature.

How beautifully Paul says: 'Who, though he [Jesus] was in the form of God, did not count equality with God a thing to be grasped, but emptied himself ...' (vv. 6–7, RSV). Satan, instead of humbling himself, regarded his status as something to be grasped. He became the embodiment of disobedience. Adam, too, rejected the form of a servant. He grasped at a status. But where the first Adam failed, the last Adam won. What a Saviour!

Blessed Lord Jesus, I see so clearly that if it were not for your perfect life of obedience, you could never have offered yourself as a sacrifice for the sins of the world. Deepen my understanding of this as I ponder it throughout this day. For your own dear Name's sake. Amen.

Death could not keep its prey

FOR READING AND MEDITATION – 1 CORINTHIANS 15:1–20
'But Christ has indeed been raised from the dead,
the firstfruits of those who have fallen asleep.' (v.20: NIV)

He is risen! What a word to begin a day. Jesus has won the battle over sin by reason of the fact that he has, as one quaint Welsh preacher put it, 'taken on death and squeezed the life out of it'. Human life is bounded by death. The warning God gave in the beginning that 'when you eat of it you will surely die' (Gen. 2:17) has come true at a number of levels. Disobedience produced spiritual death and also physical death. Paul speaks of death being 'the last enemy' (v.26), and it was this that Christ overcame at Calvary.

The truth of the resurrection is being dimmed in some parts of Christendom – and with it an infinite sadness has come over us. Let us make up our minds not to dim the resurrection but to declare it – and declare it as the most amazing and transformative fact of history.

We need to remember, too, that it is resurrection we are talking about, not resuscitation. Lazarus was raised to life, but he died again – that was resuscitation. Jesus was raised to life and will never die again – that is resurrection. And here's the exciting thing. Because he lives for ever, so shall we. No wonder Christians see death as simply moving from one house into another!

Blessed Lord Jesus, there are just no words to express my gratitude for the victory you accomplished by your rising from the dead. And now that victory is mine. I may die physically, but I shall never die spiritually. I am one with you – forever. Hallelujah! Amen.

The ransom payment

FOR READING AND MEDITATION – ISAIAH 53:1–12

'. . . the Lord has laid on him the iniquity of us all.' (v.6: NIV)

Jesus conquered by taking upon himself the sins of the world.

Even a casual reader of the New Testament will notice its writers struggle to find words to express their gratitude. Christ has paid the corresponding price, or ransom, for their sins. On the cross, Jesus took upon himself all the guilt and failure of a world that had turned away from God. Paul goes further and states the curse for breaking God's law – rightly belonging to us – fell upon Christ as he hung upon the cross, for 'anyone who is hung on a tree is under God's curse' (Deut. 21:23; Gal. 3:10).

Paul says that God 'made him [Christ] who had no sin to be sin for us, so that in him we might become the righteousness of God' (2 Cor. 5:21). Jesus not only exposed sin, but also accepted God's righteous judgment, sacrificed himself in willing acceptance of the price and, in some mysterious way, bore the consequence on our behalf. Sin demands payment and punishment in any righteous world, and God in Christ bears the dreadful cost. It was no pathetic beaten figure who cried out from the cross: 'It is finished.' It was God's own Son – royal, priestly and sovereign. He alone did it! Hallelujah!

O Lord Jesus – what a mystery! My debt of sin was so great that no earthly currency could pay it. You transformed yourself into the image of a man, took my sins on yourself, carried them to Calvary and bore them all away. Blessed be your matchless Name for ever! Amen.

Sin's back is broken

FOR READING AND MEDITATION – ROMANS 6:1–14

'... our old self was crucified with him so that the body of sin might be done away with, that we should no longer be slaves to sin ...' (v.6: NIV)

Christ on Calvary freed us from the power of sin. The apostle John tells us that 'everyone who sins is a slave to sin' (John 8:34). This means that every human being, in a moral sense at least, is a slave – for who amongst us can stand up and say we have never committed sin?

Rousseau begins his famous book, *The Social Contract*, with the blunt assertion that 'Man is born free yet everywhere he is in chains'. The great mass of humanity, although enjoying physical freedom, is nevertheless in moral and spiritual chains. Iron fetters of evil habits hang upon their souls: stout fetters, forged in hell, hold them in the most terrible bondage. They are prisoners to sin. No one can commit sin and be its master; sin eventually masters everyone. And continuance in sin is slavery. Outwardly people may appear to be free, but inwardly they are in the most galling bondage.

How was slavery broken in the British Empire? Not by the slaves organising a revolt. It only happened when William Wilberforce, whose heart burned with a passion to set men and women free, broke the grip of slavery upon our nation. That is what Christ did on the cross. He took hold of sin and devitalised it, making it possible for us – if we wish – to be free of its soul-destroying power.

✎ *Father help me to understand all the implications of what I have read today. If sin's back is broken, then I need no longer be its slave. Help me to walk this day – and every day – in the realisation of that fact. For Jesus' sake. Amen.*

The harrowing of hell

FOR READING AND MEDITATION – 1 PETER 3:18–22

'...He was...made alive by the Spirit, through whom also he went
and preached to the spirits in prison ...' (vv.18–19, NIV)

Christ actually went down into hell and ravaged the inmost dungeons of Hades, described as 'the harrowing of hell'.

The passage before us is notoriously difficult to interpret, but let me share what I believe it to mean. Genesis 6:1–4 refers to sinners in the days of Noah, the fruit of the illicit union between the 'sons of God' and the 'daughters of men'. The strange beings that resulted from this union – the Nephilim – were giants in disobedience. They are described by one theologian as 'archetypal sinners', and await their judgment in the deepest hell. What I think Peter is saying here is that Christ's death was of such tremendous power and significance that it pierced the deepest dungeons of hell – even to the place where the Nephilim were incarcerated.

We must be careful not to draw from this passage the conclusion that some have come to – namely, that one day all those who are locked up in hell will be released and finally converted. He did not preach the Good News in the sense of giving the spirits an opportunity to be saved, but rather to herald his victory over the powers of hell.

O Lord Jesus – what a victory! You have neutralised the poison of death, defeated the powers of hell and left word with them that whatever power they have will one day be finally removed. I await that day with joyful anticipation. Thank you, Lord. Amen.

Mortally wounded

FOR READING AND MEDITATION – 1 CORINTHIANS 2:1–10
'Yet among the mature we do impart wisdom,
although it is not a wisdom of this age or of the rulers of this age,
who are doomed to pass away.' (v.6: RSV)

Satan has been inflicted with a mortal wound. Although he is still able to exercise a tremendous amount of power, whenever he is reminded of the Cross, he is forced to cower in terror. *Moffatt* translates this text: 'We do discuss "wisdom" with those who are mature; only it is not the wisdom of this world or of the dethroned Powers who rule this world.' Doesn't that put the situation in a nutshell? Satan and his forces still rule – but they are dethroned, and are bound to admit defeat. Satan's position, as a result of Christ's victory on the cross, has been described by one writer in these words: 'He is like a thirty-foot conger eel with its throat cut which continues for hours thrashing about in a fishing boat, refusing to lie down and die.'

Naturally, now that Satan knows he has received a mortal blow, he has become extremely active and belligerent. But it is all to no avail – the end is inescapable. A great bottomless pit is reserved for the devil and his angels, as is also the lake of fire. This is the logical and inevitable outcome of the solid achievements obtained at Bethlehem, Calvary and the first Easter Day.

✒ *0 Father, now that I am seeing afresh what the cross and the resurrection are all about, I long that they will not remain just a theory, but become solid fact in my life. Help me to live victoriously over sin and Satan – today and every day. For Jesus' sake. Amen.*

The birth of the church

FOR READING AND MEDITATION – ACTS 6:5–15

'So they stirred up the people and the elders and the teachers of the law.
They seized Stephen . . .' (v.12: NIV)

From the struggle between Good Friday and Easter Day, our Saviour emerged with the keys of death and hell, exclaiming: 'I am the Living One; I was dead, and behold I am alive for ever and ever!' (Rev. 1:18). After Christ had risen from the dead, however, he was faced with the task of continuing his ministry against Satan and his forces. Although undeniably defeated, they still maintained a stubborn resistance to the divine will. How would he accomplish it?

At Pentecost the divine purpose became clear when, through the power and presence of the Holy Spirit, the church was born. When Christ had been here on earth, he had worked through a human body to accomplish the downfall of Satan and to bring salvation, but now that he had returned to heaven, he needed a mystical body in order for the benefits of redemption to be made known to all people everywhere. When the church came into being, it is not surprising to find, once again, the same flurry of demonic activity that we saw in the gospels and around the cross. Satan recognised in the birth of the church – as he did at the creation of Adam – a singularly important part of God's eternal purpose in bringing about his eternal downfall and defeat.

Gracious Father, the more I follow the trail of your purposes as laid down in your Word, the more I am filled with amazement. What an incredible story it is. And to think I am part of your eternal purposes. There's just no way I can put my thanks into words. Amen.

Satan loses a choice servant

FOR READING AND MEDITATION – ACTS 9:1–19
'But the Lord said to Ananias, "Go! This man is my chosen instrument
to carry my name before the Gentiles . . ." ' (v.15: NIV)

What a setback Satan must have received when one of his most zealous ambassadors, Saul of Tarsus, became both a follower of Christ and one of the most skilful strategists in the matter of spiritual warfare. No other man, save Jesus of Nazareth, has left such an impression upon the ages.

What actually happened to him? Men have tried to explain him away by saying that he was an 'epileptic visionary'. My response to that is to say that this 'epileptic visionary' has brought more sanity and wholeness to more people than any man who ever lived, save only his Master. Paul's conversion, I believe, began with Stephen, who with the face of an angel, prayed for his enemies amid a shower of stones. As his murderers laid their garments at the feet of Paul, then known as Saul, something happened – that face, that prayer! Both haunted him night and day. Angry with himself, he became angry with others: 'Meanwhile, Saul was still breathing out murderous threats against the Lord's disciples' (v.1). How Satan must have delighted in that. Yet in a blinding moment on the Damascus Road, all was changed. He who had laid others low was himself laid low. The disciple of Satan became a disciple of Christ.

✎ *Gracious Father, I am grateful for the stamp of authenticity that is upon the life and letters of your servant Paul. His conversion still converts. If Paul was insane, Lord, then I would like more of his kind of insanity. Amen.*

Are your ears red?

FOR READING AND MEDITATION – EPHESIANS 3:1–12

'His intent was that now, through the church, the manifold wisdom of God should be made known to the rulers . . . in the heavenly realms.' (v.10: NIV)

The church drew to itself the anger and outrage of Satan and his forces. 'In Christ,' says one writer, 'we not only inherit the love of God, but also the hatred of the devil, for it is Christ in the Christian, and the Christian in Christ whom Satan would love to destroy.' Another reason for this anger, of course, is that out of the church flows the wisdom and power of God, which enables God's people to bring Satan's cunning stratagems to nothing.

How true is the modern-day church to this ideal? Not very true, I am afraid. Listen to what Michael Green, Rector of St Algates, Oxford, says, 'The church . . . seems to be preoccupied with its own survival, its petty concerns, its tradition, its canons and its revised worship books – or else coming out with dicta about many of the contemporary problems of our society, without getting to the heart of the matter. It scratches at the spots caused by measles, without getting down to the disease itself.'

What is that disease? It is sin and Satan. But generally speaking, we do not hear much about these in the contemporary Christian church. If the church lived up to the ideal set for it by our Lord, then the devil would have a lot to contend with.

O God, help us to stand before you this day with an open face, an open mind and an open being. Don't let us wriggle or rationalise our failures, and thus slip past your redemptions. We are cornered – and we know it. For Jesus' sake. Amen.

There's a war on

FOR READING AND MEDITATION – EPHESIANS 4:1–16

'... he ... gave some ... to prepare God's people for works of service, so that the body of Christ may be built up ...' (vv.11–12, NIV)

How true is the church to the ideal Christ has set for it? As I travel to different churches and speak at various meetings, I am somewhat saddened that there is so little emphasis on prayer, the power of the Holy Spirit, and the need to resist the subtle pressures of a world that is hostile to the truths of Holy Scripture. But what saddens me even more is the fact that the church seems to be ignorant of the fact that there's a war on. For many, 'church' is a place to go to once a week, where they sing a few songs, listen to a sermon and then return to the normal business of daily living. Few, it seems, see the church as a training centre in which they can receive instruction in the art of spiritual warfare.

The church is more than a training ground, of course, but it seems to me that we need to bring about a proper balance between work and worship. The early church had no illusions about their part and place in this spiritual battle. They believed in a devil who was like a wounded lion, a soldier in armour, a formidable wrestler, and an angel of light. Is this how you see him? If you don't, then believe me – that suits him admirably.

✎ Father, one thing is clear – it's time we, as your people, pulled ourselves together and realised that there's a war on. What must you think of us when instead of fighting the devil, we spend so much time fighting each other? Help us, dear Lord – and forgive us. In Jesus' Name. Amen.

A call to arms

FOR READING AND MEDITATION – EPHESIANS 6:10–20

'For our struggle is not against flesh and blood, but against ...
the spiritual forces of evil in the heavenly realms.' (v.12: NIV)

How ready are we Christians to take up this responsibility of 'mopping up' operations while waging war against Satan? We who once were bound by Satan now have the task of binding him! Far too many Christians have established a peaceful co-existence pact with the devil, and say, 'If you won't trouble me, then I won't trouble you.' Let me make it clear –there is no room for spiritual pacifists in the kingdom of God. Every Christian, once enlisted in the Lord's army, is expected to train in the strategy of both offensive and defensive warfare. As God's people we are called to arms in a battle that, at times, demands fierce hand-to-hand combat with the forces of darkness. When reading Ephesians 6:12, the word *against* occurs five times? It indicates that when a Christian comes over on to the side of Jesus Christ, he becomes identified as being for God and against the devil.

Today, therefore, I want to issue a 'call to arms' to everyone who is reading these lines, and ask you to join with me in mobilising the forces of prayer for an all-out attack on our adversary, Satan. I beg you, make a fresh commitment to God right now and let him know that you are not only for him, but against the devil.

❧ *Father, I sense this is a challenging moment, not only for me, but for the thousands who will be reading these lines today. Help us all to respond to this 'call to arms', and stand up to Satan and his forces with the power that you have given us. I commit myself to that task now – in Jesus' Name. Amen.*

Stand your ground

It's time that we, as God's people, got our priorities right and recog nise that there's a war on. And this 'war', we ought to remember, is not a cold war, where we eye each other from a distance, but a red hot, hand-to-hand conflict with the forces of darkness.

Listen carefully: no one who is a true Christian and not engaging in deliberate sin need ever be afraid of the devil. If you only knew it – the devil is afraid of you. Satan is a bluffer – he will try to persuade you that he has power over you, but the truth is that on the Cross his grip on humanity was broken. Maintain a prayerful contact with God, nourish yourself in his word, and break with all known sin, then you have more power over the devil than he has over you.

Do not try to overcome him in the energy of the flesh (Acts 19:13–17). Both Satan and the forces of darkness are willing to admit defeat only when faced with the Name of Jesus Christ – the cruci fied, risen, ascended and glorified Lord. He alone is their conqueror and they are vulnerable only when approached on the grounds of his victory.

O God, I see how foolish I have been in failing to see that my fear of Satan comes from Satan himself. No more will I allow him to bully and dominate me. In your Name I command him to stand back from my life and release every hold he has upon me. In the mighty Name of Jesus. Amen.

Satan is a squatter

FOR READING AND MEDITATION – LUKE 13:10–17

' "Then should not this . . . daughter of Abraham, whom Satan
has kept bound for eighteen long years, be set free . . . ?" ' (v.16: NIV)

God has entrusted to the church the responsibility for conducting
the 'mopping up' operations following his conquest of Satan on the
cross of Calvary. Just how effective are we in carrying out the designs
and desires of our Lord? Unfortunately, many of us are terrified of
facing Satan.

The truth is that he ought to be terrified of facing us. Hopefully,
however, the truths and Scriptures we have examined will help us understand our legal rights and responsibilities in relation to the devil.
I once heard a preacher describe Satan as a squatter, someone who
takes up residence on someone else's property and refuses to leave.
He camps on ground to which he is not entitled, and refuses to leave
unless presented with a legal eviction order drawn up in the courts of
heaven and executed by God's authorised representatives on earth.

Write this down somewhere in your Bible so that you come
across it time and time again: every true believer has the legal right
and authority to evict Satan from God's property. The eviction order
has been handed down to you and I at Calvary's cross and, providing
we are truly born again, we have the power to evict Satan from every
place we find him.

*O God, is it possible that you are being balked in this 'mopping up' process
you have handed over to your church? Have you accomplished so much on
Calvary only to see it nullified by your people? It must not be. Help us, dear
Father. Help me. In Jesus' Name I pray. Amen.*

Preparing for government

FOR READING AND MEDITATION – ROMANS 8:15–25

'The creation waits in eager expectation for
the sons of God to be revealed.' (v.19: NIV)

God still allows the devil to be active because it furthers his purposes. At this stage in her history, the church is being made ready for the task of reigning with Christ on the eternal throne. The whole of history has been moving toward Christ coming for the church, his bride, and joining himself to her in a union that will last throughout all eternity. The bride will have many tasks to perform in eternity – not the least, that of universal government. How better to prepare us for government than by exercising our God-given authority in the world at present?

The purpose of God for his church is to teach her the art of reigning, by allowing us to confront the hostile forces of Satan. This forces us to align ourselves with the Scriptural fact that we are more than conquerors in Christ. If there were no hostile forces to be faced, then the truth of our authority in Christ would be academic – something to believe, but which makes no great difference. The reason, then why God permits Satan to have a continued fling is because he sees that through learning to overcome him, his church can be prepared for government.

◁ *Gracious Father, I have often wondered why you didn't consign Satan to hell immediately after his defeat on the cross. Now I see why – you are using him to keep me spiritually alert, and to prepare me for rulership. What can I say, dear Lord, except thank you. Amen.*

Keep looking down

FOR READING AND MEDITATION – EPHESIANS 1:15–2:10

'. . . God raised us up with Christ and seated us with him
in the heavenly realms . . .' (v.2:6, NIV)

Although it is our future destiny, there is a sense in which we are
already with Christ on the throne. Our thoughts have been occu-
pied with the way Christ came to this earth and identified himself
with us through his birth, baptism, temptation, crucifixion, resurrection and ascension. We learned that when Christ went to the
cross, he went as the representative of the human race. Because he
was without sin, death and the grave could have no claim on him
– hence he arose. When he returned from the grave, he made it
possible for all those who believe in him to be part of his victory.
The same applies to his exaltation and ascension. When Christ took
his seat in the heavenlies, we who believe were similarly identified
with him there.

What does this mean in practical terms? It means that, position-
ally at least, we are not standing on the earth looking up, but sitting
on the throne looking down. A Christian walked into a friend's office
one day and saw a plaque on his desk that read, 'Keep looking down.'
'Haven't you got that wrong?' he said. 'Shouldn't it read, "Keep looking up"?' 'Oh no,' said the friend. 'I am already "up" – this is to remind me that the world and Satan are below me – in fact, where they
truly belong – under my feet!'

*O Father, I see how this truth, if I get hold of it, can influence and deter-
mine my attitudes to many things. Help me to live in the 'heavenlies' – but yet
not be so heavenly-minded that I am of no earthly use. For Jesus' sake. Amen.*

The balance of power

FOR READING AND MEDITATION – 2 CORINTHIANS 10:1–5
'The weapons we fight with ... have divine power
to demolish strongholds.' (v.4: NIV)

One of God's purposes in allowing Satan to confront the church is to give us 'hands-on' training in the art of overcoming. Because the crown is only given to the conqueror, the church must learn the art of overcoming in preparation for her position of rulership when she occupies the throne in eternity. In order to learn the techniques of overcoming, God has given us many powerful weapons. They make a long list, but let me name some: the cross, the Word of God, the Name of Jesus, the blood of Jesus, the Holy Spirit, obedience, watchfulness, resistance, spiritual gifts, faith and persevering prayer. I shall pick one from this list and focus on that, with the hope that some thoughts and conclusions will spark concerning the others. The one I have selected is – persevering prayer.

Through prayer the church has the opportunity of disorganising the wiles of Satan, and working with God toward the control of the hostile forces that circulate in the universe. Who holds the balance of spiritual power in this mad, sinful world? The scientists? No. The politicians? No. The law-enforcers? No. It is we Christians who hold the balance of power in the universe. If we don't use it, then evil will hold unhindered sway.

✎ *O Father, if it is true that, through prayer, we can release greater spiritual power into the universe, then I have to ask myself: why am I not praying more? Help me not just to pray more, but to pray with more power. For Jesus' sake. Amen.*

Prayer – a restraining influence

FOR READING AND MEDITATION – JAMES 5:13–20

'...Tremendous power is made available through
a good man's earnest prayer.' (v.16: J.B. PHILLIPS)

Through persevering prayer, the church is able to exercise a powerful influence in the affairs of the world. It is my conviction that if the church got down to the work of real intercession, there would be released into the universe such tremendous spiritual power that it would minimise many of the problems we are witnessing in our day and age. Satan delights to see the world in a mess. He actively engages in producing misunderstanding between employees and employers, between students and teachers, and between one race and another. Daily on our television screens are scenes of hatred and violence. How Satan must laugh at that.

The church, I believe, could provide a greater restraining and calming influence in many of the world's affairs if it would get down on its knees and pray. Thank God for those who know the value of prayer and are actively involved in this ministry. If Satan was not opposed by the millions who come against him every day in prayer, then the balance of power would swing to the side of evil, and the world would enter a time of unimaginable chaos and disaster. It is through prayer that the church releases into the world a restraining and moderating influence in the affairs of men.

Gracious Father, when I see the responsibility you have placed upon your church, I tremble. But when I see the power you have made available to us, I rejoice. Make me an expert in the art of spiritual warfare I pray. For Jesus' sake. Amen.

Priority number one

FOR READING AND MEDITATION – ACTS 4:23–31
'After they prayed, the place where
they were meeting was shaken ...' (v.31: NIV)

'The greatest thing we can do for our country,' said a minister, 'is to pray earnestly, regularly, persistently for those in the corridors of power, whether in government, the media or education.'

When Peter and John were released from prison, the church celebrated with a prayer meeting. They planned no social or political action, but ascribed glory to God. No wonder the place where they were praying was shaken. Daniel was placed by God in a situation absolutely in the grip of principalities and powers. What did he regard as his priority? To draw up a petition? No. To organise a demonstration? No. His priority was prayer – three times a day. And he didn't care who knew about it (Dan. 6:10).

Many preachers point out that intercessory prayer is an intense spiritual battle in which we do not struggle against flesh and blood, but against principalities and powers of darkness. We often take the statement, 'our struggle is not against flesh and blood' to mean, 'our struggle is *not only* against flesh and blood', but the apostle does not use the word *only*. The truth he wants us to understand is this – we do not struggle against flesh and blood at all. It is through prayer that principalities and powers are defeated.

✎ *O Father, daily you pile up the arguments to convince me that I am part of your cosmic purposes and plans. How can I remain unconvinced? Train me, dear Lord, to become a military strategist in bringing about the downfall of principalities and powers. In Jesus' Name I ask it. Amen.*

He loves – we love

FOR READING AND MEDITATION – 1 JOHN 4:7–21
'We love because he first loved us.' (v.19: NIV)

'God does nothing in the world redemptively – except by prayer.'
John Wesley meant that when God seeks to bring about changes in
the world, he first sets his people praying. Prayer is the ramp over
which God's redemptive purposes flow into the universe.

Why should God choose to enter the universe in this way? Arch-
bishop William Temple made a statement which brought a flood of
spiritual illumination into my life. He said, 'God does not wish to
go over the head of his church in bringing about any redemptive
purpose in the world, for that would be contrary to his intention of
making her co-equal with his Son.'

What an incredible thought! God is so committed to the church
that if she will not cooperate with him in bringing about his redemptive purposes, those purposes will simply remain unfulfilled. You
may think that God has taken a great risk in committing himself to
his church in this way, but in actual fact this is not so. Why? Because
when God pours his love into the church it creates in our hearts a
deepening desire to do his will. It is one of the greatest mysteries
of the universe – the mystery of love creating a desired response.

*O Father, now I see why I love to do the things you want me to do. Your love
flows into my heart, and instantly my love flames in a glad and joyous response. Teach me how to love, dear Lord – not to get a response, but just for
the joy of giving. For your own dear Name's sake. Amen.*

What an honour!

FOR READING AND MEDITATION – PSALM 149:1–9
'To execute upon them the judgment written:
this honour have all his saints ...' (v.9: AV)

God is preparing us for our role by inviting us to cooperate with him in ruling and reigning in the world now through persistent, believing prayer. Despite all her shortcomings, her weaknesses and her failures, the church is still the greatest force for good in the world today. The church contests Satan's rule in human hearts, and opposes the devil by the prayers of God's people. A traveller in central Africa came across a tribe of moon worshippers, and after spending some time with them, he expressed his surprise that they should worship the moon rather than the sun. 'The sun is much bigger and brighter,' he said. 'I would have thought that it would be a much more attractive object of worship.' They replied, 'The sun foolishly shines in the daytime when there is plenty of light. The moon is much wiser – it only shines at night when it is dark.'

What would people of this world say if told them that the reason things are not worse is because the church is restraining Satan's influence? No doubt they would think us mad. Nevertheless, it is true that if the church did not wield the power it has been given in prayer, a floodtide of demonic activity would break through and the world would become a madhouse.

Gracious Father, the responsibility you have given your church to combat principalities and powers through prevailing prayer is clearer to me than ever before. Help me, and the rest of your church, not to duck this challenge but to rise to it – today and every day. For Jesus' sake. Amen.

Marriage and redemption

FOR READING AND MEDITATION – MATTHEW 25:1–13

' "At that time the kingdom of heaven will be like ten virgins who ...
went out to meet the bridegroom." ' (v.1: NIV)

The romance of redemption – the assumption that there is one single major purpose running throughout history – the selection of a bride for God's Son. Have we proved that assumption? I am more convinced than ever that this is the great design holding together the whole universe. Nothing has contributed more to deepening my conviction on this matter than a study I examined some years ago, which claimed that God designed marriage to illustrate the romantic purpose lying behind redemption. In order to see the parallels between marriage and redemption, we must examine the way in which a wedding ceremony was conducted in the days of Christ. I shall focus on the different aspects of a Jewish wedding, taking each point in turn, and drawing from it a spiritual parallel.

Watch how beautifully it all adds up to the fact that God designed marriage to illustrate his plans and purposes for the redemption of mankind. We shall start on these parallels tomorrow, but I urge you to refrain from turning to the next page, and concentrate instead on acquainting yourself with every detail of the Scripture passage before you. The more time you spend with this, the more you will be ready for the *denouement* that is to follow.

✎ *O gracious God, my heart beats a little faster, and my whole being tingles at the prospect of discovering the purposes of redemption in a Jewish marriage ceremony. Prepare me spiritually for what is to come in these final few days. For Jesus' sake. Amen.*

What a price!

FOR READING AND MEDITATION – 1 PETER 1:13–25

'... it was not with perishable things such as silver or gold that you
were redeemed ... but with the precious blood of Christ ...' (vv.18–19, NIV)

The first step in the Jewish wedding ceremony was for the prospective bridegroom to travel from his father's house to the home of the prospective bride. Christ, too, left his Father's house, and came to this earth to woo and win a bride for himself (Eph. 5:25–27).

Next the father of the bride negotiated the price to be paid to purchase his daughter. This payment, according to the *Universal Jewish Encyclopedia*, was always part of the groom's financial responsibility. Christ, too, had to pay a price for the purchase of his bride – not silver or gold, but his own precious blood (1 Cor. 6:19–20). After the payment of the purchase price came the establishing of the marriage covenant. At betrothal the man and woman were deemed already to be husband and wife, even though no physical union had taken place. As believers, we too have been declared to be sanctified or set apart for Christ, and are awaiting the day when we shall be joined to him forever (Eph. 5:25–27). After betrothal, the groom and bride drank from a cup over which a benediction had been pronounced. A covenant relationship had been established. Christ, our heavenly Bridegroom, symbolised his betrothal to us in a similar way – through communion or the Last Supper (1 Cor. 11:25).

✎ *O Lord Jesus, how can I ever get over the wonder of your relentless love, that brought you from eternity to live and die on this earth for me. Help me to be as relentless in my love for others, as you are in your love for me. In your Name I ask it. Amen.*

The waiting time

FOR READING AND MEDITATION – ACTS 1:1–11

'After he said this, he was taken up before their very eyes,
and a cloud hid him from their sight.' (v.9: NIV)

After the marriage covenant, the groom left the bride's home and remained at his father's house, usually for twelve months. Christ, too, returned to his Father's house after paying the purchase price.

During the period of separation, the bride gathered her wardrobe and prepared for her future life with her bridegroom. The groom prepared the living accommodation for his bride in, or near, his father's house. Christ, our heavenly Bridegroom, is also preparing a place for his bride, and has appointed ministries to prepare and perfect the bride for the coming wedding (John 14:2; Eph. 4:11–13).

After this period of separation, at a predetermined time, the groom, best man and other male escorts left the house of the groom's father, usually at night, and conducted a torchlight procession to the house of the bride. Christ, too, will come at an appointed time from his Father's house in heaven, accompanied by a great angelic host (John 14:3). The bride, expecting her groom to come, knew only the approximate time of arrival – thus, the groom's arrival was preceded by a shout. Christ's return, too, will be preceded by a shout – the voice of an archangel and the trumpet call of God (1 Thess. 4:16). We expect our Saviour to return, but we do not know the day or the hour of his coming.

✎ Blessed Lord Jesus, every thought of you causes my heart to dance and sing! You came into my life and have set joy within my heart. Am I grateful? Look into my heart, Father, and see! Amen.

The world's last wedding

FOR READING AND MEDITATION – JUDE VERSES 17–25

'To him who is able to keep you from falling and to present you before
his glorious presence without fault and with great joy...' (v.24: NIV)

The groom received the bride with her female attendants and returned with her to his father's house. Scripture teaches that Christ's
bride will be caught up with the Lord to be with him in his Father's
house (1 Thess. 4:14–17).

The bride and groom then entered the bridal chamber, and in
the privacy of that place, entered into a physical union, consum-
mating the marriage. Christ's union with the church will not be a
sexual one, but it will be a physical one. In a way that the human
mind cannot understand – Paul calls it a 'mystery' (Eph. 5:32) –
the church which is his bride will be joined to Christ and be one
with him forever. In Genesis, we affirmed God was so excited about
his plan to prepare a bride for his Son, that he had to illustrate it in
the way in which he created the first man and woman. We, who
were predestined in Christ before the foundation of the world, and
who were created from his side through his shed blood, will one
day be joined to him in a glorious act of consummation. The staggering truth is that the redeemed will not just be close to Christ, or
even spend a long time with him; we shall be one with him – for
ever and ever and ever.

❧ *Father, I stand in dumb adoration before the wonder of your eternal
plans and purposes. I am discovering more than my mind can take in. Help
me understand it, for the more I understand it, the more I shall stand upon
it. Thank you, Father. Amen.*

We stoop to conquer

FOR READING AND MEDITATION – REVELATION 21:9–27
'... he ... showed me the holy city Jerusalem coming down out of
of heaven from God, having the glory of God ...' (vv.10–11, NIV)

A single romantic purpose runs through the universe. This purpose
was laid down in creation, when God built a cross into the very
foundation of the universe. When Satan rebelled, even this could
not interfere with God's purposes, for he had anticipated it and provided a way of redemption. When Satan appeared to win an important victory over the first human pair, God allowed it, knowing
the situation would yield even greater glory for himself. If Adam
and Eve had not failed, doubtless they would have procreated a
race of sinless beings living in a close relationship with the Trinity.

In procuring their downfall, however, Satan overreached himself. He thought he had spoiled the plan for sinless beings to come
into a close relationship with their creator. Instead he saw sinful
beings – who are, of course, washed and redeemed – becoming one
with their creator. When Satan eventually sees Christ's bride ascend
the throne in eternity, he will finally realise, that the rulership he
tried to grasp for himself is not his. It is given, not to those who
strive but to those who submit. In the eternal scheme of things, the
way up is the way down. We stoop to conquer. Sinners throw themselves at Christ's feet, and finish up with him on a throne. Hallelujah!

*O Father, there are just no words to express my gratitude that you have
chosen me – a deep-dyed sinner – to be part of Jesus' spotless Bride. Let the
wonder of this stay with me, not just today, but every day for the rest of my
life. In Jesus' Name. Amen.*

Shut up – to write

FOR READING AND MEDITATION – COLOSSIANS 1:1

'Paul, an apostle of Christ Jesus by the will of God ...' (v.1: NIV)

Paul's letter to the Colossians is one of his finest pieces of correspondence, written or dictated by him during his imprisonment in Rome in AD 62.

The letter seems to have been prompted by Paul's discovery that the Colossian Christians were experiencing a threat to their faith. Bishop Handley Moule described it as an 'error that cast a cloud over the glory of the Lord Jesus Christ, dethroning him and emptying him of his divinity, thus making him one of a multitude of mediators...instead of the only mediator.' Paul, always ready to defend his Saviour, writes to correct that error and show that Christ is first and foremost in everything. Believers are rooted in him, alive in him, hidden in him, complete in him, and so are equipped to make Christ first in every area of their lives.

Paul begins his letter by laying down his credentials: 'an apostle of Christ Jesus by the will of God'. But although being shut up in prison prevents him from travelling, his spirit is free to reach out through his pen and bless the world. Think of it like this: had he not been imprisoned we might never have had his New-Testament letters. From prison his influence extended to the ends of the earth and throughout the ages. He was shut up to write – immortally.

✎ O Father, help me understand that to a Christian there is no bondage but sin. Physical restrictions may hinder me bodily but my spirit is always free to soar. Circumstances do not have the last word in my life – you do. Amen.

Grace and peace

FOR READING AND MEDITATION – COLOSSIANS 1:2

'To the holy and faithful brothers in Christ at Colosse:
Grace and peace to you from God our Father.' (v.2: NIV)

'When Paul wrote his letters to the churches of the New Testament,'
says Dr William Barclay, 'he wrote in exactly and precisely the way
ordinary everyday people wrote ordinary everyday letters in the ancient world.' First a greeting, then a word of thanksgiving, the special contents, a closing greeting and sometimes an autographic conclusion. Paul greets the Colossians with, 'holy and faithful brothers
in Christ'. The faith of the Colossian Christians may have been under
attack, but they had not succumbed to error. I doubt whether Paul
would have called the Colossian believers – 'stalwart followers of
Christ' as Eugene Peterson words verse 2 in *The Message* – if they
had been moved from their true spiritual centre in Christ.

Paul continues: 'Grace and peace to you from God our Father.'
Can grace and peace come from other sources? Of course. Insur-
ance companies talk about periods of 'grace'; politicians talk about
negotiating 'peace' between countries or troubled groups. But what
a difference between human grace and peace, and the grace and
peace which comes from the heart of the Father. One is temporal,
the other eternal; one limited, the other unlimited. The best of men
and women are only men and women at best. But what comes from
God is always perfect. Perfect peace, perfect grace.

*Father, when you are the source of the peace and grace that flow into my
life then I need never be impoverished. Your heart is always open to give;
may my heart always be open to receive. In Jesus' Name. Amen.*

Scripture's Siamese twins

FOR READING AND MEDITATION – COLOSSIANS 1:3–4

'We always thank God ... because we have heard of your faith ...
and of the love you have ...' (vv.3–4: NIV)

Paul had heard good things about the Colossians from Epaphras, and he gave thanks to God for their faith in Christ and their love for all the saints.

Two important qualities: faith and love. The New Testament often joins these two together; sometimes they are even called 'Scripture's Siamese twins'. If you are to have love for others you must first of all have faith in God. Without a vertical relationship with God, love for others can soon run out of energy.

I read of an African government agency which invested a large sum of money to improve the lifestyle of a tribe living in grass huts on a hillside. To replace these flimsy dwellings the government built brick houses at the foot of the hill, but the people felt uncomfortable in their new houses and, after just a few days, moved back into their old huts. An exasperated official said to the missionaries who lived among them, 'These ungrateful people need a lot of loving. I'm afraid the best we can do is to lift them; we leave it to you to love them.' Love that is not linked to God soon runs out of impetus. Governments can lift people but they can't love them. Only when we have faith in God can we go on loving the unlovely and the unresponsive.

✎ O God my Father, teach me the secret of faith and love, the alternate beats of the Christian heart. My faith draws love from you, and my love expresses that faith in love to everybody. Thank you, Father. Amen.

A spring in our step

FOR READING AND MEDITATION – COLOSSIANS 1:5A

'...the faith and love that spring from the hope that
is stored up for you in heaven...' (v.5: NIV)

Where are the origins of faith and love? From the hope that is stored
up for us in heaven. It is important to remember that the Christian
experience is characterised by hope, as much as by faith and love.
The concept of hope was something the ancients regarded as dubi-
ous and uncertain. But Christian hope is as certain as tomorrow's
dawn. It is the assurance that whatever we enjoy of God's presence
and blessings here will be multiplied in heaven. Heaven is the beginning of things beyond the power of our imagination to conceive.

How powerfully does the prospect of heaven influence your daily
walk with Christ? We must be careful, of course, that we do not become so heavenly-minded that we are no earthly good. However,
we ought to live in the light of heaven's coming glory. What we have
here 'in Christ' is just a foretaste of what is to come. Some of our
present spiritual experiences may seem like heaven, but really they
are just a little bit of heaven to go to heaven in.

Hope is not a consequence of faith and love, but its origin.
Faith and love spring from hope. When we hold before us the sure
and certain hope of our accommodation in heaven, then out of
that hope spring faith and love. They don't just saunter into our
lives – they spring!

*O God, there is so much emphasis on the now that I am apt to forget the
truth of what I have been reading about today. Help me keep heaven ever
before me. Then I know faith and love will 'spring'. Amen.*

That's the truth

FOR READING AND MEDITATION – COLOSSIANS 1:5B–6

'All over the world this gospel is bearing fruit and growing ...' (v.6: NIV)

The reason Paul tells the Colossians they had heard the true gospel was to hold up before them a standard by which all other gospels could be evaluated. This was Paul's reassurance that what they had learned through him was the word of truth.

How we need to lay hold of what Francis Schaeffer described as 'true truth'. The 'true truth' is the truth contained in the gospel of Jesus Christ. It is the final truth. Nothing can be added to it nor subtracted from it. It is the truth, the whole truth and nothing but the truth. Sometimes when I talk to a person about Christ (especially young intellectuals) their attitude is, 'Well, that may be true for you, but I have a different truth.' The truth of the gospel, however, is not relative. It is absolute and therefore universal – the same truth for all.

Paul reinforces this by telling the Colossians that they had received the same gospel that was being received all over the world – and was bearing fruit. The gospel of Christ does not need to be 'enriched' with new ideas; it is well able to sprout and bring forth life of itself. The gospel is 'the grace of God in truth'. Nothing must be added to it and nothing must be taken away.

Father, how grateful I am for the simplicity of the gospel. I can add nothing to it to make it more effective and if I take anything away, it becomes ineffective. May I never be moved from its simplicity. Amen.

High praise indeed

The all-sufficient Christ

FOR READING AND MEDITATION – COLOSSIANS 1:7–8

'You learned it from Epaphras, our dear fellow-servant,
who is a faithful minister of Christ …' (v.7: NIV)

The Bible, among other things, is a book of biographies. Some are moderately complete, others are short and terse. We have enough information on Epaphras, the leader of the church at Colosse to put together a picture of the kind of man he was: '… our dear fellow-servant, who is a faithful minister'. This is high praise indeed.

The worth of praise is always determined by the one giving the praise. I wonder what Paul had in mind when he called Epaphras a fellow-servant. Did he mean that Epaphras was easy to work with? Probably so. The final test of an individual's work is not only to ask 'What has he or she done?' but also 'Could other people work with him or her?' Epaphras was a good colleague. Yet in addition he was a 'faithful minister'. He wasn't merely loyal to his fellow workers in the ministry; he was devoted to the needs of his flock.

Epaphras would have been well aware of the faults of the Colossian Christians, but was ready to notice and commend the virtues of his people. What a compliment, 'You never heard him say an unkind word against anyone.' No greater eulogy, I believe, could be given than that we were good colleagues, faithful in our work and service for Christ, and swift to see and ready to speak of the good in others.

O God, may I so live before you that at my passing people may also say of me that I was easy to work with, devoted to Jesus Christ, and saw the good in others more quickly than the bad. In Jesus' Name. Amen.

There's more

FOR READING AND MEDITATION – COLOSSIANS 1:9–10

'… we have not stopped praying for you and asking God to
fill you with the knowledge of his will …' (v.9: NIV)

Paul was not only a great preacher; he was also great in prayer. And
his prayers always bore down on particular matters. Those who
seem to have great prowess in prayer lose no time in getting to spe-
cifics. They don't indulge themselves in flowery phrases like, 'O thou
that gildest the heavens and settest the stars in space' but quickly get
down to details. After telling the Colossian Christians that he had
prayed ceaselessly for them since the day he had heard about them,
Paul makes the first of his petitions. He asks God to fill them with
knowledge of his will. The word *fill* suggests that however much
the Colossians had received, there was still room for more. You see,
no one can ever rest and say, 'I am now completely Christian.' For the
definition of a Christian grows the more we see of Christ and the
more we know of him. Rabindranath Tagore, the Indian poet, said,
'The eternal cry is – more.'

Also significant is the phrase 'bearing fruit in every good work'.
Paul prayed that the life of God might flow through the Colossian
Christians and produce substantial spiritual fruit: not fruitless suck-
ers, but fruit that the Master can enjoy – on the lowest branches
the low-hanging fruit of humility and on the highest branches the
knowledge of God.

✎ *O God, the days of my life go by at tremendous speed, but you are still
pouring, and there is always room in my heart for more. And the more of you
I receive the more of you I want. I love you Father. Amen.*

You'll get through

FOR READING AND MEDITATION – COLOSSIANS 1:11–12

'... being strengthened with all power ... so that you may have
great endurance and patience ...' (v.11: NIV)

One of the current buzz words is the word *power*. I hear it everywhere I go. People say, 'We need more power to witness, to work miracles, to make the world sit up and take notice.' I agree. My personal
burden and prayer has been to see the power of God moving mightily on masses of people in true revival. But what Paul had in mind as
he prayed for power to be seen in the lives of the Colossian Christians was power to joyfully endure all trials.

You need a full supply of God's power if you are to continue
steadfastly despite opposition, setbacks and frustrations. Paul, writing to the Corinthians, said that through endurance the servants of
God commend themselves (2 Cor. 6:4). Today many contend with
fierce antagonism, bitter disappointment, rejection from friends or
family, a marriage failure, loss of friendship, a financial reversal or
something similar. But listen carefully to me: you will get through.
And the reason you will get through is that God's power is at work
in your life. You may be shaken but you will not be shattered, knocked
down but not knocked out. What is more, you will come through the
experience with thanksgiving. You will be thankful because through
your difficulties you will be brought closer to God himself.

✎ *My Father and my God, you do not promise to keep me from difficulties,
but you do promise me that you will bring me through. On that I can rely.
And that is enough. Thank you, Father. Amen.*

Gone! Gone!

FOR READING AND MEDITATION – COLOSSIANS 1:12B–14

'... the Father ... has qualified you to share in
the inheritance of the saints ...' (v.12: NIV)

Probably Paul's prayer ends with the phrase 'joyfully giving thanks to the Father' (v.12a) because next he talks about blessings that were already theirs. When he reminds the Colossians they are qualified, he means all the conditions necessary for becoming an heir of God and a joint heir with Christ had been met by their acceptance of Christ, and they were now full members of God's new society. But more: they had been 'rescued ... from the dominion of darkness and brought ... into the kingdom of the Son he loves'. Never forget that salvation is a rescue mission – a deliverance. We don't climb out of the darkness; we are delivered from it. That's why the Son gets all the glory, for the glory always goes to the one who saves, not to the one who is saved.

'... in whom we have redemption, the forgiveness of sins' – the Christian faith begins at the point of redemption. We need redemption from our sins and forgiveness for our sins. Both are provided in Jesus Christ. I know of nothing more wonderful than redemption and forgiveness. The slate is wiped clean. Once I ask for forgiveness from Christ then I am, as far as God is concerned, a person without a past history. I am just like a newborn baby; I have a future but no past. How amazing!

✎ O Father, forgive me if the wonder of redemption and forgiveness does not hit my soul with the force and power it ought. Help me open my heart to the thrilling fact that all my sins are gone. Gone! Hallelujah!

The right way for everything

FOR READING AND MEDITATION – COLOSSIANS 1:15–16

'He is the image of the invisible God, the firstborn over all creation.' (v.15: NIV)

Paul plunges into reminding the Colossian Christians of the supremacy and sufficiency of Christ. He knows that once they grasp this, it will be more than enough to protect them from error. Jesus is the image of the invisible God and takes the place of idols in their lives. 'He is the firstborn over all creation.' This does not mean that Christ is the first created being.

But pause to consider these amazing words: '…all things were created by him and for him'. This is an important Scripture. If everything is created by him and for him, then creation is designed to work his way. When it does it works effectively; when it follows some other way it works towards its ruin. The way of Christ is written not only into the texts of Scripture, but into the texture of the whole of creation. He is inescapable. Just as you cannot jump out of your skin, so you cannot escape Christ, for his stamp is upon the whole of his creation. Like the watermark in paper, Christ is written into the structure of our beings. This means that the Christian way is the right way to do everything. The non-Christian way is the wrong way to do everything. Everything.

✎ *Father, I look around and see that the world is finding out how not to live. And finding out painfully – through inner conflicts, guilt and fears. Oh why don't people turn to you? Father, I am so thankful I know you. Amen.*

Christ – a centripetal force

FOR READING AND MEDITATION – COLOSSIANS 1:17–18

'He is before all things, and in him all things hold together.' (v.17: NIV)

One commentator says, 'Everything in him is centripetal; everything outside of him is centrifugal.' Everything in Christ is bound together in perfect harmony, not simply by power, but by love. In the same epistle we find: 'And over all these virtues put on love, which binds them all together in perfect unity' (Col. 3:14).

A man, disinherited by his family because he became a Christian, continued to relate to his family even through their reluctance. Slowly his love for them won through. He held the family together because he was held together within – by being in Christ.

Some years ago now, a nuclear scientist shut himself in his office for hours refusing to take any calls. The fact had hit him as never before that what held all creation together was not a force but a Person – Christ.

On one occasion our Lord said: 'He who is not with me is against me, and he who does not gather with me scatters' (Matt. 12:30). Everything outside of Christ scatters. Get among any group of Christians, talk about Christ and you are together. Talk about our 'church customs' and you are apart. Let this simple but solemn truth grip your soul with new force today: in him all things hold together, out of him all things fly apart.

☙ O Father, I am so grateful that your Son is my centre. In him I am held together, never to fly apart. Let this truth be more than something I hold; may it be something that holds me. In Jesus' Name. Amen.

The order of the resurrection

FOR READING AND MEDITATION – COLOSSIANS 1:18

'And he is the head of the body, the church …' (v.18: NIV)

Colossians and Ephesians have similar themes, from different perspectives. Ephesians portrays the church of Christ, whereas Colossians depicts the Christ of the church. Ephesians focuses on the body; Colossians focuses on the head. Paul shows us here Christ is not only the head of creation; he is also the head of the church.

The formation of the church is undoubtedly the greatest project God has ever undertaken. Tom Rees described it as 'The divine masterpiece'. Nothing in heaven or earth can ever eclipse it.

Those of us who count ourselves as part of Christ's body, the church, should remember, as Dick Lucas writes, 'If a body does not hold fast to its head it can hardly hope to survive!' The head will never lose contact with the body, but the body often loses contact with the head, and loses co-ordination and direction. Christ's pre-eminence is not acknowledged if the church refuses to go in the direction which the head desires and dictates.

What does Paul mean when he says Christ 'is the beginning and the firstborn from among the dead'? He is referring to our Lord's resurrection. Christ's rising from the dead marked the beginning of a new order – *The order of the resurrection*. Others who were physically raised from the dead were raised only to die again. Those who die in Christ will be raised never to die again.

Father, how glad I am that I belong to The order of the resurrection. *I can think of nothing more secure. All honour and glory be to your matchless Name. Amen.*

Christ – the pleasure of God

FOR READING AND MEDITATION – COLOSSIANS 1:19–20

'For God was pleased to have all his fulness dwell in him ...' (v.19: NIV)

This passage bursts with meaning. Paul tells us: 'God was pleased to have all his fulness dwell in him.' *Pleased* – note that.

'God dwells in every Christian,' said E. Stanley Jones, 'but he dwells sufferingly. We give him a great deal of pain. He stays, but not without some degree of travail.' The one Person in whom God dwells without any pain or suffering is Jesus. As one commentator said, 'God is at home in Jesus.' The same commentator said, 'The attempt to impose divine qualities upon the framework of human nature has always resulted in a monstrosity – always except in the case of Jesus.' Jesus' divinity was part of his very nature. In him the supernatural was natural. All his virtues were balanced by opposite virtues. When I consider the sinless life of Jesus it comes as no surprise to find that at the River Jordan, God opened the heavens above him and said: 'This is my Son, whom I love; with him I am well pleased' (Matt. 3:17). No wonder, for he is a wonderful Son.

Paul also reminds us that Jesus is the centre of reconciliation for everything, and that through the cross peace will be established in every corner of the universe. He restores to the universe the principle of harmony which sin so brutally disturbed.

✎ *Father, how I long that by dwelling in your Son I too might become a centre of reconciliation. Through Christ's work in me may I bring peace and harmony to my world today. Amen.*

Three life positions

FOR READING AND MEDITATION – COLOSSIANS 1:21–23

'Once you were alienated from God and were enemies in your minds …' (v.21: NIV)

In one of the most beautiful sections of the New Testament, Paul reminds the Colossians of what Christ has done. The central dynamic of the Christian life is not what we do for Christ but what he has done for us. Dick Lucas analyses these verses as follows: what you once were, where you now stand and how you must go on.

And what were we? 'Enemies,' says Paul. Many are unwilling to apply this term to themselves in their unconverted state. They say, 'I was never at enmity with God, just apathetic to him.' But dig deep into every human heart and you find antagonism. We don't like the idea of God telling us what to do, and act rebelliously. Yet where are we now through grace? Reconciled. The enmity is over and peace has come to our hearts. We stand in God's presence: 'holy … without blemish and free from accusation'.

And how do we go on? We are to 'continue in [the] faith, established and firm, not moved from the hope held out in the gospel' (v.23). If we are to continue in the faith then we must remain content with the gospel that brought us to Christ and not try to change it. Those who seek to add or take away from the gospel do not continue in the faith; they contaminate it.

Father, grant that I might never move from the gospel that challenged me and changed me. May my song ever be, 'On Christ the solid Rock I stand, all other ground is sinking sand.' In Jesus' Name I pray. Amen.

The continuing cross

FOR READING AND MEDITATION – COLOSSIANS 1:24

'… I fill up in my flesh what is still lacking in regard to
Christ's afflictions …' (v.24: NIV)

This verse has perplexed many and we must approach it with care.
When Paul says he must fill up in his flesh 'what is still lacking in
regard to Christ's afflictions' is he suggesting there was some defi-
ciency in Christ's atonement? No, the meaning of the verse is this:
Christ had suffered on the cross for the sins of the world and now
Paul 'filled up Christ's afflictions by experiencing the added sufferings necessary to carry this good news to a lost world' (NIV Study
Bible). J.B. Phillips puts it in a slightly different light: 'I am suffering on behalf of you who have heard the gospel, yet I am far from
sorry about it. Indeed, I am glad, because it gives me a chance to
complete in my own sufferings something of the untold pains
which Christ suffers on behalf of his body, the church.'

We rightly make much of the sufferings of Christ on the cross,
but what about the continuous suffering he undergoes from those
who bear his Name, yet do such ugly things? Churches split over
the question of Holy Communion, whether to use one cup for all or
individual cups. Communion is a time of blessedness, but it is turned
into a time of bitterness. Next time you have a cross to bear because of some people in the church, remember Christ has a cross
to bear for all the people in the church.

✎ O Father, I accept that because I am in Christ I am involved in his sufferings also. Help me to regard this as a real privilege, and not a problem, as
a blessing, not a burden. In Jesus' Name. Amen.

Saying goodbye to a text

FOR READING AND MEDITATION – COLOSSIANS 1:25

'I have become its servant by the commission God gave me to
present to you the word of God in its fulness ...' (v.25: NIV)

Having the heart of a servant constitutes a God-given ministry. I
like this definition of servanthood, 'becoming excited about making
other people successful'. True servanthood involves a desire to make
the Word of God fully known and Christians fully mature. Paul says:
'to present to you the Word of God in its fulness'. How do we make
known the Word of God in its fullness? By following closely the principles of exposition. A crying need of the contemporary church,
generally speaking, is for systematic Bible teaching, and by that I
mean the verse-by-verse exposition of the Scriptures. There is a
tendency to devise clever talks on current events commencing with
a Biblical text but making no further reference to it. A man said to
me recently, 'Our pastor always begins with a text from the Bible...
then immediately says goodbye to it.' Though there is a place for
topical preaching, the church needs a regular system of presenting
a verse-by-verse exposition of the Scriptures so the Word of God
will be fully known.

I am sure you have heard, 'A text taken out of its context quickly becomes a pretext.' No one can know Christ better, without
knowing the Scriptures better. There is no better way of knowing
the Scriptures than by going through them verse by verse.

*Father, I see that only through systematic study of your Word can it be
fully understood, and only through the Word can Christ be fully known. Help
all your servants handle the Word of God well – myself included. Amen.*

A Christ not in us ...

'... the glorious riches of this mystery, which is Christ in you,
the hope of glory.' (v.27: NIV)

Paul refers to this great truth: 'Christ in you, the hope of glory' as a mystery which, though kept hidden for generations, had now been made known. 'The mystery ... now disclosed' refers, of course, to the fact that Christ indwells Gentiles as well as Jews and welcomes them into his church on equal terms with Israel (see Ephesians 3:2–6).

There are many who hold to the fact that Christ is for them, but they have no experience of Christ being in them. They may be ready to assert with the rest of us that we have an advocate with the Father, Jesus Christ, the Righteous (1 John 2:1), but they do not know him as a power within them. Paul is saying the secret of maturity is having Christ within, thinking, willing and feeling in the heart of his consenting servant.

'Christ in you, the hope of glory.' What a phrase. But is it only a hope – a possibility? The word *hope* in Scripture means a sure and certain expectation with no shadow of doubt, no trace of dubiety. To have Christ near to us is not enough. He must be in us, subduing the deep selfishness of our nature, ridding us of our moral rottenness. And as William Law said, 'A Christ not in us is ... a Christ not ours.'

O Father, what a thought: Christ is not just near to me or around me but living in me, his conquering life overcoming my inward death. How wonderful. All honour and glory be to your precious Name. Amen.

Beyond small talk

FOR READING AND MEDITATION – COLOSSIANS 1:28

'We proclaim him, admonishing and teaching
everyone with all wisdom …' (v.28: NIV)

This verse gives us a penetrating insight into the heart and mind
of the great apostle. Paul was thinking here not primarily of his
public ministry, but of his personal relationships with believers.
Maturity is not for a spiritual elite – it is for everyone.

How did Paul go about the task of helping people become mature? By 'admonishing and teaching everyone with all wisdom'. To
admonish is to warn or correct them – to teach is to educate, to
lead people into deeper truths and a richer understanding of the
things of God. Does this mean that we ought to be seeking to correct and teach each other? Of course not. I am sure Paul enjoyed
'small talk' in the same way that we do, but I am also sure that when
an occasion arose in which he saw a need to correct, encourage or
exhort, he would immediately seek to do so. Paul concentrated on
the goal of bringing others to maturity, and I can imagine him asking, 'How is your prayer life going? What's your relationship with
the Lord like? Are you having any struggles that you might want
me to pray about or help you with?' How different relationships
would be in the body of Christ if, when talking with our Christian
brothers and sisters, we would be as interested in their spiritual
health as we are in their physical health.

*Heavenly Father, I know that to be mature in Christ is to be mature indeed.
Help me become excited about making others spiritually successful. I yield my
all to be mature and to help others become mature. In Jesus' Name. Amen.*

Mightily enkindled

FOR READING AND MEDITATION – COLOSSIANS 1:29

'To this end I labour, struggling with all his energy,
which so powerfully works in me.' (v.29: NIV)

The words 'To this end I labour' sound strained and tense until we come to 'struggling with all his energy, which so powerfully works in me'. The *Amplified Bible* expresses it: 'For this I labour, striving with all the superhuman energy which He so mightily enkindles and works within me.' Paul's labour did not depend on human energy but the power that came from Christ. He lived by the energy which Christ mightily enkindled and generated within him.

Dr Larry Crabb asked counsellors, 'How often when you interact with people in counselling are you aware of an energy flowing through you that doesn't come from you but from Christ?' Few hands were raised. Permit me to ask you a similar question now: how aware are you when you go about your service for Jesus Christ of a superhuman energy flowing through you and out of you? If you were to ask that question of me I would say, 'Much too infrequently.'

Paul, however, threw his heart and soul into everything he did and found the energy of Christ matching every effort. When he said 'I labour' he was using the Greek term *kopiao*, signifying labouring to the point of weariness. He poured out what was poured in with all the energy Christ generated within him. Too often our experience begins and ends in these words, 'To this end I labour, struggling.'

O God, forgive me that so much of my life can be expressed in those words: 'I labour ... struggling.' Help me experience the energy of Christ working in me and through me. In his Name I pray. Amen.

One heart and one mind

FOR READING AND MEDITATION – COLOSSIANS 2:1–2
'My purpose is that they may be encouraged in heart
and united in love …' (v.2: NIV)

Here Paul really opens up his heart and speaks of his great concern for them, a concern that grew no doubt out of the news from Epaphras that a serious error was circulating among them. The *Amplified Bible* uses these words: '…that your hearts may be encouraged as they are knit together in love'. Nothing is more encouraging to believers than knowing their hearts are united in love. However, the opposite is also true: nothing can be more discouraging than knowing their hearts are not united in love.

But love is not enough. Lasting unity depends on truth as well as love. The believers at Colosse must be of one mind as well as one heart. The errorists in Colosse believed that revelation could be received outside of the Saviour, but here Paul lays down that all essential truth is found in Christ. Just as in New-Testament times, so today men and women claim to have insight and revelation beyond that which Scripture unfolds. The unity of believers is at risk when the people of God are not of one mind on the essential things. A common mind about the truths of the Bible and the supremacy of Christ is the only possible basis for Christian unity. If there is no common mind there can be no common heart.

✎ *O Father, help your children everywhere to have not only a common heart but also a common mind. And help us, too, not to sacrifice truth in the interests of unity. In Jesus' Name we pray. Amen.*

An exciting treasure hunt

FOR READING AND MEDITATION – COLOSSIANS 2:3

'... in whom are hidden all the treasures of
wisdom and knowledge.' (v.3: NIV)

The point Paul has been making is that no essential truths are withheld from anyone who belongs to Christ. 'All the treasures of wisdom and knowledge' are hidden in him. But it is hidden truth. That means our Lord conceals as well as reveals. You know and you don't know; you see and you don't see. But what you don't know and don't see spurs you on to continuous discovery.

This perpetual discovery has kept me on my toes for over 50 years. Every day there is some new surprise to be found. Daily I come to the Bible, and I am beside myself with excitement as I see something I had never seen before. I fail to understand how Christians can exist without delving into the treasures of wisdom and knowledge found in Christ and revealed to us in the Scriptures.

'This unfolding revelation of Christ,' says one writer, 'puts a surprise around every corner, makes life pop with novelty and discovery, makes life well worth the living.' The Christian life is dynamic, not static. The more you know, the more you know you don't know, and what you know sets you on fire to know more. We will never go beyond him. Never.

✎ O Father, I am so glad that what I know of you and your Son impels me to find out more and more. I am on the most exciting treasure hunt in the world – set to discover the treasures hidden in Christ. Amen.

In good order

FOR READING AND MEDITATION – COLOSSIANS 2:4–5

'I tell you this so that no-one may deceive you
by fine-sounding arguments.' (v.4: NIV)

Paul, as Eugene Peterson puts it in *The Message*, didn't 'want any-one leading them off on some wild-goose chase after other so-called mysteries or secrets'. They must not allow themselves to be deceived.

Had Eve checked Satan's words against the Word given her by God, and held to that, then she would not have been deceived. If all Christians carefully examined what they read and heard and checked it against the infallible Scriptures, error would have little freedom to circulate. We do well to examine everything we hear for the truthfulness of its content, and not allow ourselves to be taken in by the attractiveness of its packaging.

Though error was threatening the churches at Colosse and Lao-dicea, it is obvious from Paul's next words that things were not all that bad. 'I … delight to see how orderly you are and how firm your faith in Christ is.' They were standing firm in an orderly and un-broken fashion. These two go together – orderliness and a firm faith in Christ. It works the other way also: where there is no firmness of faith in Christ there is no order; instead there is disorder. Firmness of faith in Christ and good order are root and fruit. Loss of faith in Christ and disorder are also root and fruit. In him we are in good order; out of him we are in dis-order.

❧ *My Father and my God, I am so thankful that life holds together at the centre when we are firmly fixed in your Son. We stay in good order when we are under your orders. Amen.*

Give, take, build

FOR READING AND MEDITATION – COLOSSIANS 2:6–7

'... just as you received Christ Jesus as Lord, continue to live in him ...' (v.6: NIV)

No better definition of the Christian life could be given than this: '... as you received Christ Jesus as Lord, continue to live in him'. These two requirements – receiving and continuing – ought to be made clear to every new Christian. Some think receiving Christ is the end, but it is only the beginning.

How did we receive Christ? By surrender and receptivity. We give to him and take from him. Give and take – this is relationship reduced to its simplest terms. Our giving involves giving the one and only thing we own – ourselves. When he has that, he has all. And part of the purpose of giving is so that we may receive. God asks that we give our all in order that he may give his all. Paul says: 'As you received Christ Jesus as Lord'. He is 'Lord', remember, not merely an example or teacher. Lord! And you cannot call him Saviour unless you call him Lord. He saves those he owns – no others.

Rooted in Christ we grow in him. We hardly bury a seed to see the last of it. Established in him we are built up in him. And the final test is how thankful you are. If you do not give thanks regularly for the fact that you are favoured of God then you ought to question whether you are indeed a Christian.

✎ *Dear Father, I would give, give, give, take, take, take, build, build, build. Let all I take from you fit me to give more. I would be the best person I can be. And above all, thank you for saving me. In Jesus' Name. Amen.*

Godless philosophies

FOR READING AND MEDITATION – COLOSSIANS 2:8
'See to it that no one takes you captive through hollow and
deceptive philosophy …' (v.8: NIV)

Paul now challenges the Colossians with a sharp and clear warning:
don't go near false teachers; they will take you captive. J.B. Phillips
words Paul's cautionary message like this: 'Be careful that nobody
spoils your faith through intellectualism or high-sounding nonsense. Such stuff is at best founded on men's ideas of the nature of
the world and disregards Christ!'

Philosophy is defined as 'seeking after wisdom or knowledge,
especially that which deals with ultimate reality'. Yet any philosophy not true to Scripture leads nowhere. Philosophical theories may
sound fascinating, but they contain no real answers to the mysteries
of the universe. The truth is found only in Christ. 'Any philosophy
that leaves out God,' said someone, 'is like a blind man in a dark
room looking for a black cat that isn't there.' It is likely that Paul
had the error of the Gnostics in mind. Gnosticism purported to
offer mature Christians a better way, whereby they could outgrow
the simplicities of the apostles' teaching and move on through secret
knowledge, and their faith in Christ, to more enlightening things.
Many fell for it in the days of the early church. If something is not
Christocentric it will surely end up being eccentric – off centre. Our
Lord is the truth, as well as the way and the life.

*Gracious and loving heavenly Father, how glad I am that my faith has
come to rest not in a combination of Christ and secret knowledge, but in him
and in him alone. Protect my soul from entertaining error, dear Lord. Amen.*

Music vaster than before

FOR READING AND MEDITATION – COLOSSIANS 2:9

'For in Christ all the fulness of the Deity lives in bodily form…' (v.9: NIV)

God came into matter at the Incarnation and made it the vehicle of divine revelation. Nothing could be more important for our existence on earth, environed as we are with matter. The material is not alien; it is an ally.

The spiritual world manifests itself through the material, in material form and material relationships. Listen to these words: '…a body you prepared for me … I have come to do your will, O God' (Heb. 10:5, 7). God's will for Christ was to be done in and through a body. The Gnostics taught that matter was evil. Hindus believe matter is illusion. Christians, however, say matter is God-made ('God saw that it was good' – Genesis 1) and can be used to good purposes. The kingdom of God, remember, is to come on earth.

There is nothing in God that isn't in Jesus. Jesus is God accommodated to human form, for now and always. Christ's body was taken up into Deity and will probably bear the marks of the nail prints through all eternity. His humanity is not something he takes off like a wrap. Christ is both human and divine – forever. In our Lord body and spirit were reconciled, and because of that, as one poet put it, 'There beats out music vaster than before.'

O Lord Jesus Christ, the meeting place of God and man, matter and spirit, and the reconciling place of all, grant that I may witness to the Word who became flesh. In Jesus' Name I ask it. Amen.

Fullness of life in him

FOR READING AND MEDITATION – COLOSSIANS 2:10

'… and you have been given fullness in Christ,
who is the head over every power and authority.' (v.10: NIV)

The Gnostics bypassed the Incarnation saying it was beneath God's dignity to touch matter, let alone enter into it. Instead, they taught, you could attain fullness of life by knowing God directly. In reality, as E.Stanley Jones wrote, 'Apart from Jesus we know little or nothing about God, and what we do know is often wrong.' Let me pick up Jesus' famous statement once again: 'I am the way and the truth and the life' (John 14:6).

Nowadays some Christians, in order to accommodate other religions, take 'Christ and'…: Christ and Mohammed, Christ and Buddha, Christ and Jung. By adding to him they reduce universality, for he is universal. To be in him, is to be in everything that is of reality in the universe. But there's more: the believer also shares his victory – he is head over every power and authority. We need fear no longer the prince of darkness. Christ is in control of everything and everyone. Dick Lucas says that this verse unfolds two themes: one, the fact that because we have the fullness of God's presence with us here then we have all we can have this side of heaven, and two, with regard to heaven's victory over powers and principalities we share with Christ all that he has won. To this I say a hearty 'Amen'.

O God, help me to make this my affirmation: fullness of life is in Christ; emptiness of life outside of him. This is my verdict. May I live by it every day of my life. In Jesus' Name. Amen.

Complete in him

FOR READING AND MEDITATION – COLOSSIANS 2:11–12

'In him you were also circumcised, in the putting off
of the sinful nature …' (v.11: NIV)

It is unlikely that these verses are intended to combat the same error that had caused controversy in the Galatian church, namely that Gentiles should be circumcised just like Jews. More probably false teachers were persuading Christians that they needed to combine their faith in Christ not just with secret knowledge, but with man-made regulations such as circumcision, adherence to dietary rules, observance of religious festivals, and so on.

It may have been also that Gnostics were convincing believers to accept the idea that circumcision was an act of dedication and consecration, a second initiation subsequent to baptism. Paul counters the argument by saying circumcision is unnecessary because they already possess a purification of which Christ is the source. At conversion a circumcision not done by hands takes place – that of being forgiven sins and cleansed from unrighteousness.

They had died with Christ in baptism, so now it followed that as he was raised from the dead, so they too were raised with him. We need not add to what Christ has done. God can do nothing great-er for us than he has done in Christ. Paul says that we are complete in Christ only when we acknowledge his completeness. 'It takes a complete Christ,' said D.L. Moody, 'to make a complete Christian.'

✎ O Father, I see the importance of trusting only in you and in the atoning merits of your Son. I need nothing for my salvation other than my trust in him. Thank you, my Father. Amen.

Our cancelled IOU's

FOR READING AND MEDITATION – COLOSSIANS 2:13–14

'He forgave us all our sins, having cancelled
the written code … nailing it to the cross.' (vv.13–14, NIV)

God has made us alive with Christ, and when his life pulses through
our souls then freedom from sin is possible. Paul now launches into
a graphic description of salvation. God has not only made us alive
with Christ but he has cancelled the written code that was against
us, nailing it to his cross. What beautiful word pictures.

Take the first: *Written code* means a handwritten note. It is the
Greek term for an IOU – an acknowledgement of a debt and recognition that payment is obligatory, with certain penalties being required if payment is not made. The word *cancelled* in the Greek
(*exaleipho*) means 'to sponge or wipe off'. This is what Christ has
done with our sins. The written code that condemned us has been
sponged off by the blood of Christ. It is as if it had never been.

But Paul uses one more word picture: 'He took it away, nailing it
to the cross'. In ancient times the record of a paid debt would sometimes be nailed to a public notice board so that everyone could see
the matter was settled. Our Lord nailed the debt we owed to the most
public place in the universe – the cross. When Christ cried: 'It is finished' he meant that the work of our redemption was complete.
The cancelled note hangs on the cross for all to see.

*Father, when the hosts of hell try to tell me that my sins are not forgiven
I shall point them to the cross and show them the cancelled note. I am eternally grateful. Amen.*

Stripped of sham authority

FOR READING AND MEDITATION – COLOSSIANS 2:15

'And having disarmed the powers and authorities,
he made a public spectacle of them…' (v.15: NIV)

This is exciting stuff. J.B. Phillips translates: 'And then, having drawn the sting of all the powers ranged against us, he exposed them, shattered, empty and defeated, in his final glorious triumphant act!' Now that of Eugene Peterson: 'He stripped all the spiritual tyrants in the universe of their sham authority at the cross and marched them naked through the streets' (THE MESSAGE).

Paul saw the triumphal procession that customarily took place after a great conquest in Roman times. Hundreds of weary prisoners of war would be tied to chariots and dragged through the streets so that everyone could witness their discomfiture and shame. For the citizens it was a wonderful sight, but a sad experience for the conquered. This is a striking illustration of the conquest our Lord achieved at Calvary. Just as the Roman citizens could see that they had nothing to fear from the once proud soldiers being paraded before them, so we no longer need to fear Satan and his minions. If Satan and his forces have any power over us it is only because we let them. They attempt to masquerade as conquerors, but it is all a sham. They have been ignominiously defeated. Satan thought he would have a great victory at the cross but the tables have been turned. It is Christ's victory the cross proclaims.

O Father, I see that Christ's victory on the cross is my victory too. He won it by fighting; I enter into it by just trusting. It sounds too good to be true. But also too good not to be true. Amen.

Shadow-lands

FOR READING AND MEDITATION – COLOSSIANS 2:16–17
'Therefore do not let anyone judge you by what you eat or drink,
or with regard to a religious festival...' (v.16: NIV)

In the light of the Christ's triumph, Paul encourages the Colossian believers to celebrate a life free from unnecessary rituals.

Clearly an attempt was being made in the church at Colosse to persuade the believers to worry about diet and keeping religious festivals. This was calculated to make people believe Christ's sacrifice was not enough to achieve holiness; matters such as rituals were essential. Paul dismisses the idea in no uncertain terms. Eugene Peterson paraphrases the opening statement of verse 16: 'So don't put up with anyone pressuring you in details of diet, worship services or holy days.' Strong words – and words most definitely needed if they were to maintain their life of freedom in Christ. Paul goes on to say: 'These are a shadow of the things that were to come; the reality, however, is found in Christ.' The shadow-land referred to here is the law found in the Old Testament. The rituals it prescribed were to be kept, but they were just shadows of what was to come. Their true value lay not in what they were, but what they pointed to. Christ is the fulfilment of all that the Old Testament prefigured, and in him is found all spiritual reality. Those who depend on rituals and ceremonies for their salvation are living in the shadows. Christ is all that is needed. All.

Father, how glad I am that I am in Christ and that he is in me. What need have I of standing in the shadows when I can stand in the sunshine of your love as shown to me in Christ? Amen.

Pride must die…

FOR READING AND MEDITATION – COLOSSIANS 2:18
'Do not let anyone who delights in false humility and
the worship of angels disqualify you for the prize.' (v.18: NIV)

J.B. Phillips translates this verse: 'Don't let any man cheat you of your joy in Christ by persuading you to make yourselves "humble" and fall down and worship angels.' Some commentators believe one aspect of the error threatening the church at Colossse was the insistence on the veneration of angels, as mediators in addition to Christ. If this was so then it was Gnosticism in another guise. Paul characterises the individuals concerned in this way: 'Such a person goes into great detail about what he has seen [in visions], and his unspiritual mind puffs him up with idle notions.' Here we see the root of the trouble: they were puffed up with pride. They claimed to have inside knowledge but really they had found a 'spiritual' way (so called) of drawing attention to themselves and a new device for inflating their self-importance.

When counselling Christians with strange ideas about the faith I have found that often the underlying motivation is to be different. They have little or no sense of identity, and as aligning themselves with others is not enough of a boost for them, they turn round and go in the other direction. Thus they are different. The root of all this is, as Paul discerned, pride. William Law put it well when he said, 'Pride must die in us or Christ cannot live in us.'

≪ *Father, help me to remember that it was pride that turned an angel into a devil and brought havoc to this fair universe. May I be so secure in you that I will find my identity in that, not in being different. In Jesus' Name. Amen.*

Keep connected

FOR READING AND MEDITATION – COLOSSIANS 2:19

'He has lost connection with the Head,
from whom the whole body ... grows ...' (v.19: NIV)

The all-sufficient Christ

The type of person causing trouble in the Colossian church had lost connection with the head. Apparently they were still Christians, but had not held fast to Christ, the head of the church.

A similar situation occurred when a group of Christians in the church in Pergamum followed the erroneous teachings of Balaam and the Nicolaitans (see Revelation 2:12–17). They were still members of the congregation. Christ called them to repentance because it is impossible to remain true to him, and at the same time toy with an error that robs him of his supremacy and sufficiency.

When we drift away from Christ we drift away from each other. Show me a church where the members have lost connection with the head, and I will show you a church whose members have lost connection with each other. That church may have exciting social activities, a wonderful musical programme and clever debates, but if its members are not united with Christ then it no longer functions as a church; it becomes a club. What contributes to the spiritual life and health of a church is the head. Its ministers, teachers, musicians all have a place, but as Paul explains: 'the whole body ... grows as God causes it to grow.' This is an astonishing statement. Growth comes not from men but only from God.

Father, save me from thinking that because a church increases in numbers it is growing. I see that growth comes only when we, your people, are connected to the head. Help us stay connected, dear Father. Amen.

Rules versus relationships

FOR READING AND MEDITATION – COLOSSIANS 2:20–22

'Since you died with Christ to the basic principles of this world,
why ... do you submit to its rules ... ?' (v.20: NIV)

It seemed some Colossian converts had already succumbed to the false teaching circulating in the church. How can we reconcile this with Paul's commendation of their faith in chapter 1? I think the answer must be that a small number were in danger of being swayed by this error, and it is to those he now issues his warning. In these final verses of Chapter 2 Paul is at his most trenchant. Why do you live, he asks, as if you still belonged to this world? Why do you submit to its rules? By asking this he is equating the theories of the errorists with the religion of the world.

It is obvious that the world cannot do without religion. Humanity, made in God's image, has an inbuilt desire to worship. If it rejects Christ as the only way to God it has to find the elements of its religious structure elsewhere. One commentator puts it like this, 'The closer in language [Satan's] religion can be to the truth, while yet being different, the better this wily prince is pleased.' Since you died with Christ, says Paul, you are no longer governed by rules, but by your relationship with him. You are saved not by what you do but by what Christ has done. God has put the church in the world, but we must make sure that the world does not get into the church.

✎ *Father, you have taken me from the world and put me into your church. Help me not only tell others where and to whom I belong but to show them by my every action, my every attitude. Amen.*

The problem of the self

FOR READING AND MEDITATION – COLOSSIANS 2:23

'Such regulations ... have an appearance of wisdom,
with their self-imposed worship, their false humility ...' (v.23: NIV)

I wonder how the small group of people at Colosse who were caught up propagating error responded to Paul's sharp and incisive condemnation of their theories. The advocates of this new doctrine had persuasive arguments, lived lives of self-discipline, and showed great commitment to what they believed, but the motivation behind it all was worldly pride and the appearance of wisdom. Their self-imposed worship, their false humility and their harsh treatment of the body made no impression on the mind of the great apostle. Paul saw these things as just another way of showing off.

J.B. Phillips translates 'self-imposed worship' as 'self-inspired efforts at worship'. They worshipped God not in the way he wants to be worshipped, but in the way they thought he should be worshipped. Referring again to Phillips' translation, he renders the NIV phrases 'false humility' as 'their policy of self-humbling' and 'their harsh treatment of the body' as 'their studied neglect of the body'. These graphic phrases take us to the very heart of their motivation – they were using spiritual thoughts and ideas as a means to pander to their self-centredness and pride. Self-centredness lies at the root of most of our spiritual problems. And self-centredness is never more deadly than when it is dressed up in a spiritual garb.

◁ *Gracious and loving heavenly Father, help me not to use my faith in the service of self-centredness and egotism. Help me to have a faith that works by love, and nothing but love. In Jesus' Name. Amen.*

Our chief business

'Since ... you have been raised with Christ,
set your hearts on things above ...' (v.1: NIV)

Paul's purpose in this letter is to show that Christ is pre-eminent and that the life of every Christian should reflect that priority. Eugene Peterson paraphrases: 'So if you're serious about living this new resurrection life with Christ, act like it. Pursue the things over which Christ presides.' Rooted in him, alive in him, hidden in him and complete in him, we must live for him.

Living for him is delineated in terms of relationships. First, our relationship with Christ, then, relationships in the local church, relationships with the family, relationship to one's daily work and relationships with unbelievers. If our relationship with Christ is not kept intact then it is impossible for other relationships to succeed.

The injunction to set our hearts on things above, where Christ sits, is based on the fact that we have been raised with him. Think what that means: we have been granted a relationship with Christ, who is at God's right hand. We pursue this relationship by holding fast to Christ, the centre and source of all our joy. A Christian is someone who lives in two places at once: in their earthly place of residence and in Christ. The question we have to ask ourselves is this: where are we most at home?

✎ *Father, in coming to Jesus I have come home. Now help me be at home in him – even more at home than I am in my own home. In your Son's Name I pray. Amen.*

At home in the heavenlies

FOR READING AND MEDITATION – COLOSSIANS 3:2–3

'For you died, and your life is now hidden with Christ in God.' (v.3: NIV)

'Look up and see what is going on around Christ. That's where the action is. See things from his perspective' (THE MESSAGE). It has been said that the Christian faith has no geographical centre. Judaism focuses on Jerusalem and Islam on Mecca. The Christian faith, however, focuses on heaven, where Christ is seated at the right hand of God. Without being 'other worldly' and ignoring our responsibilities here on earth, we seek the things that are beyond the earth. We have died in Christ and now we enjoy a new life – a life that is hidden with Christ in God. Why 'hidden'? Well, the union that exists between Christ and his people is hidden from the eyes of the men and women of this world. Though they see us going about our tasks they are unaware that the strength by which we live and the power by which we practise our faith is drawn from another world. But believers can only enjoy and draw upon this life as they daily reach up through the avenue of prayer and avail themselves of the resources that are hidden with Christ in God.

A wise old Christian was once asked, 'Where do you live?' With a twinkle in his eye he passed on his business card to the enquirer and said, 'This is where my residence is, but if you really want to know where I live – I live in Christ.'

✒ O God my Father, forgive me if my energy is drawn more from the resources that are below than those that are above. Help me to be at home in the heavenlies. In Jesus' Name. Amen.

What a day that will be!

FOR READING AND MEDITATION – COLOSSIANS 3:4
'When Christ, who is your life, appears,
then you also will appear with him in glory.' (v.4: NIV)

Here the thought is brought to completion. The day will dawn when the Christ will be revealed to the world in all his glory. If we were to paraphrase this verse it would read something like this: 'When Christ, your real life, shows himself physically and visibly once again in the world, you, who are his people, will be as glorious as he.' What a day that will be! I remember as a boy in Wales going to the local pithead to listen to the miners sing as they came up to the surface after their day's work. They would sing a song that has ineffaceably imprinted itself on my memory:

Oh that will be, glory for me,
glory for me, glory for me,
when by his grace I shall look on his face,
that will be glory, be glory for me.

Although usually just a handful of Christians would start up the chorus, everyone else would join in. Often tears would flow as they sang, leaving white stains on their coal-blackened faces. Whenever I come to this verse, my mind goes back to that song and those childhood memories. When Christ returns it will not just be that his glory is manifested; it will be glory for you and me also.

✎ *Father, the promise that I will be with you in glory is what keeps me going. What a day it will be. Even so, come Lord Jesus. Amen.*

An idol factory

FOR READING AND MEDITATION – COLOSSIANS 3:5–6
'Put to death, therefore, whatever belongs to your earthly nature …' (v.5: NIV)

The thrust of Paul's argument is irresistible: if Christ is your life, then that means putting to death all things connected with the way of death – sexual immorality, impurity, lust, evil desires and greed. Setting our hearts and searching our hearts go together.

Some Christians believe self-examination to be a negative approach to life. Concentrate on Christ, they advise, and sinful things will drop away of their own accord. But the phrase 'put to death' suggests that something has to be done to rid us of the evils that reside in our hearts, and that that something has to be done by us. Utilising the power, of course, that comes from Jesus Christ.

Even though we are Christians and have been saved from sin, that does not mean the roots of sin have been dislodged from our hearts and will never trouble us again. Some believe we can have such an experience of God that sin is completely eradicated and we reach a state of what they describe as 'sinless perfection'. I do not share that view myself. I know that my heart – even after five decades of divine working – has the possibility of becoming an idol factory. That's why, in addition to setting my affections on things above, I must also search my heart. The one follows on from the other.

✒ *Father, ask for your divine illumination as I search my heart. I want no idolatry within me, no worship of other things. And whatever I find there, help me not to put it to sleep but put it to death. Amen.*

I'm in for it now

'Because of these, the wrath of God is coming.' (v.6: NIV)

Paul's imperatives are always supported by incentives. He presents us with the highest of standards and provides incentives to reach them. If the incentive of Christ's appearing is not enough, he attaches to his imperative another kind of inducement, namely that 'the holy anger of God falls upon those who refuse to obey him' (PHILLIPS).

Paul is talking here about those who continue in sin. Those who sin and immediately cry out in repentance are at once forgiven and restored. But for those who continue in sin things are quite different. The NIV Study Bible says in its commentary: 'God is unalterably opposed to sin and will invariably make sure that it is justly punished.' When? This is not talking about the judgment at the end of time, but that which God metes out while we are in this body.

God often does not seem in a hurry to judge. How many times have believers committed sin, not repented, and said to themselves, 'Uh! That was a terrible thing I did. I'm in for it now'? But seemingly nothing has happened. The truth is that God's judgments are often silent – something dies within us when we continue in sin. We become less of a person. Our creativity shrivels up, our zest for life is eroded by guilt, our ability to stand stress is reduced. The worst thing about sin is to be the one who has sinned.

O Father, help me to understand that your judgments are not retributive but remedial. You search me in order to save me. Drive this point deep into my spirit. In Jesus' Name. Amen.

Life is decision

FOR READING AND MEDITATION – COLOSSIANS 3:7–10

'But now you must rid yourselves of … anger, rage, malice, slander …' (v.8: NIV)

Every one of the six sins mentioned here – anger, rage, malice, slander, filthy language and lying – have the potential to destroy relationships. Each one makes harmonious relationships impossible. What an ugly bunch of words they are.

These things are understandable before our conversion, says Paul, but they ought not to be practised by those who belong to Jesus Christ. I know many Christians who react by saying, 'Easier said than done.' So how do we get rid of anger, rage, malice, slander, filthy language and lying? We stop ourselves having anything to do with them.

Let me expand on that last statement because to some it might sound like exhortation without explanation. 'Life,' said one philosopher, 'is decision.' We can decide to be angry or not angry, to lie or not to lie, to use filthy language or not to use it. These things do not just flow out of us of their own accord. Prior to angry or inappropriate words coming from your mouth you have a moment of choice – to stop them or let them come out. If our lives are under the rule of Christ then it follows that our decisions will come under his rule as well. So it is just a question of willpower. You have to decide, 'I will no longer do this.' You supply the willingness – he will supply the power.

✍ *Father, I decide now to have done with the old life. I am going to strip off the filthy set of ill-fitting clothes and put them in the fire. Instead I'm going to have a new wardrobe – custom-made by Christ. Amen.*

A meditation on the cross

FOR READING AND MEDITATION – MATTHEW 27:32–56
'About the ninth hour Jesus cried out ...
"My God, my God, why have you forsaken me?" (v.46: NIV)

Three thoughts on the mystery of the cross and the wonder of the open tomb: (1) Apart from the cross I would never realise the enormity, the wickedness, of my sin. We call our sins 'mistakes' or 'slips'. How terrible my sins must be to a holy God if the only way he could expunge them was to allow his Son to die for me.

(2) Apart from the cross I would have no clear focus for my faith. Oswald Chambers said, 'Life is more tragic than orderly.' Every day thousands of babies are aborted because they are an inconvenience. Can God be Love and allow tragedies to continue? Whenever a doubt arises in my mind concerning God's love, I stand at the foot of the cross where it is quickly laid to rest. A God who loved me enough to die for me has got to be Love.

Apart from the cross I would not have a Saviour. I need a Saviour. I need an Example, too, a Teacher, a Friend. But most of all a Saviour. The cross shows me that God has done everything he can to save me, and all I need do is to fall on my knees in penitence, reach out to receive the gift of salvation, and it is mine. Mine just for the asking. What marvellous mercy. Apart from the cross I would have nothing.

My Father and my God, thank you for the mercy that streams towards me from Calvary. You do not love me because Christ died, but Christ died because you love me. I am loved, lifted and loosed. Amen.

In the spirit he waits

FOR READING AND MEDITATION – LUKE 23:44–56

'The women … followed Joseph and saw the tomb
and how his body was laid in it.' (v.55: NIV)

How calm and private the sepulchre was after all the dreadful and shameful publicity of the crucifixion. It is difficult to work out the exact time between our Lord's arrest and his death on the cross, but it was about eight to nine hours. Eight to nine awful hours!

Could he not have died in quietness in the company of his loved ones? No, the cup of suffering had to be drunk to its dregs and the ghastly publicity was part of the bitterness of the cross. There was the mix of noise, dust, pain, thirst, jeers and sobs as he hung stark naked between earth and heaven. Not long after the cry: 'Father, into your hands I commit my spirit' (v.46) he bowed his head and died.

And then the sepulchre. Do you think of a tomb as being cold and eerie? This one is filled with destiny. Our crucified Saviour lies there on a cool bed of rock. In the Spirit he waits. What is he waiting for? To fulfil prophecy, to reverse the human verdict passed on him, to prove that he really died on the cross and did not just swoon, to validate the victory won on the cross. There are many reasons. He waits and waits and waits. And then, to quote Alice Meynell:

All alone, alone, alone,
he rose again behind the stone.

✒ *O Father, I never tire of hearing the story of my Lord's death and resurrection. It is the most glorious thing that ever happened. My salvation is assured because of it. All honour and glory be to your Name for ever. Amen.*

The New Year's Day

FOR READING AND MEDITATION – JOHN 20:1–18
'Then Simon Peter ... saw the strips of linen lying there,
as well as the burial cloth ...' (vv.6–7, NIV)

Peter burst into the tomb and looks in amazement at the linen clothes lying there. Moments later John followed. They saw the strips of linen as well as the burial cloth that had been around Jesus' head.

Some scholars sense a strange overtone in the Greek word used to describe the headcloth. The word used suggests that it still had an annular shape, that it still showed the outline of his head – 'the sacred head once wounded'. Keep in mind we are listening to the account of eyewitnesses. And that makes you almost feel you are an eyewitness yourself. Look again at the collapsed clothes lying there. What does it all suggest?

When Jesus came back from the dead he did not quietly and laboriously unwind the grave clothes. He came through them. This was not an unwinding, this was a glorious uprising! The very concept of resurrection is supernatural. The natural process of physical decomposition was not arrested or reversed, but superseded. Peter and John were the first to see the evidence of the most sensational thing that has ever happened on this planet. As John Stott puts it, 'We live and die; Christ died and lives.' And because he lives we live also. No wonder A.B. Simpson described Easter as 'The New Year's Day of the soul'.

Lord Jesus Christ, how can I thank you enough that although it was possible for you to die it was not possible for you to be held by death? And now, because you live, I live also. All honour and glory be to your Name. Amen.

The charter of equality

FOR READING AND MEDITATION – COLOSSIANS 3:11

'Here there is no Greek or Jew ... but Christ is all, and is in all.' (v.11: NIV)

The verse before us today is one of the most important in Scripture, depicting our life in Christ, and our relationship to one another in the church. In an age seeking equality of opportunity for all, this is the charter of equality. Nothing today can compare with it. Listen: 'Here [in the new nature of those who form Christ's church] there is no Greek or Jew [no racial distinction], circumcised and uncircumcised [no religious distinction], barbarian, Scythian [people known for their brutality], slave or free [no social, economic or cultural distinction].' Galatians 3:28 adds: 'There is neither ... male nor female [no sexual distinction].' That sweeps the field. There just cannot be any distinctions in Christ. If you hold to distinctions then you cannot be in Christ. You are governed by something else. The equality in Christ's church is not artificial, a statement of rights not worth the paper it is written on – it is real.

Then notice also: 'Christ is all, and is in all.' What it means is this: Christ is all that matters. If Christ becomes all in all to us, we cannot remain the people we were. What is more, everyone else becomes all in all also. Why is the church so slow in showing the world what a classless, raceless society is like?

✎ O Father, you inspired your servant Paul to sweep the decks of all artificiality and snobbery but we, your people, have been so slow to accept this. Forgive us, dear Lord, and help us fulfil your purposes. Amen.

Overalls or evening dress

FOR READING AND MEDITATION – COLOSSIANS 3:12–14
'Therefore, as God's chosen people, holy and dearly loved,
clothe yourselves with compassion …' (v.12: NIV)

Astonishingly Paul here takes the characteristic descriptions of Israel and applies them to the church: 'God's chosen people, holy and dearly loved.' But there's more: the qualities he urges on the Colossian Christians are the very qualities which ancient Israel came to recognise in God's dealing with them: 'compassion, kindness, humility [or lowliness], gentleness and patience'. God chose the people of Israel to be his 'shop window', so to speak, through which the Gentile nations could look in and see the blessings that come to those who serve the Lord.

Israel, as we know, failed miserably in this respect, but it is Paul's hope and prayer that the church at Colosse – part of the new Israel of God – would treat others as God in Christ treated them. How could this happen? First, by being considerate to each other – despite all provocation – and by forgiving each other. 'Forgive as the Lord forgave you' (v.13). This is how the Lord acts towards you, Paul is saying, so it is only right that you follow suit. Verse 14 is one of my favourite texts: 'And over all these virtues put on love, which binds them all together in perfect unity.' 'Love,' it has been said, 'is a colour that can be worn with anything – overalls or evening dress.' Love is the garment the world sees. All other virtues are undergarments.

Father, help me to remember that virtues can become vices when love is not present, and that love makes all other virtues blend in unity. And may I not just remember this but live by it. In Jesus' Name. Amen.

Every church a haven?

FOR READING AND MEDITATION – COLOSSIANS 3:15

'Let the peace of Christ rule in your hearts ... And be thankful.' (v.15: NIV)

Perhaps no other verse in the New Testament has been wrested from its context as much as this one. I have heard it interpreted as: if you don't have a troubled spirit then it indicates that you are walking in the perfect will of God. Others use the verse to teach that when you wish to know the will of God, imagine yourself going through the different options, and the one which gives you the most peace is the one you should choose. That is not what the text is indicating.

Paul tells us here that when we are under the rule of Christ, the inevitable result is peace in our relationships. Listen to these words again: '... since as members of one body you were called to peace'. Every Christian congregation ought to be a haven of peace. Sadly, many are not. One preacher likened the church to Noah's ark, saying 'If it wasn't for the storm on the outside we wouldn't be able to stand the strain on the inside.'

Is it unrealistic to expect Christians with different views, backgrounds and temperaments to live harmoniously? Some might think so. But Paul wouldn't share that view. When Christ rules in the hearts of believers, then peace will rule in that community of believers. Nothing could be more simple, yet nothing, it seems, is more difficult.

⊲ *Gracious Father, our life strategy is all wrong and thus things don't work out right. We become tangled up because we do not take your way. Help us see that for peace to rule we must come under your rule. Amen.*

Gratitude for grace

FOR READING AND MEDITATION – COLOSSIANS 3:16

'Let the word of Christ dwell in you richly as you teach
and admonish one another …' (v.16: NIV)

An interesting spiritual exercise is to examine many of the 3:16s of
the New Testament. Are you familiar with 1 John 3:16? Look it up
and you will see why it is not a verse that Christians like to mem-
orise! The verse before us today is one of the New Testament's most
beautiful 3:16s. The word *dwell* here *(enoikeo)* has the meaning of
permanent residence, of being at home. Eugene Peterson paraphrases: 'Let the word of Christ have the run of the house.'

How wonderful when Christians allow the Word of God to be
at home in their hearts, when they draw their spiritual sustenance
from the Word of God. This is not to say that we cannot enjoy spiritual experiences, but we are not to let them divert us from attention to the Word. The Word of God must control all the ministries
of the local church. It is to dwell in us richly as we teach, admonish
and counsel.

It is the Word of God, also, that must guide us as we sing. Paul
has in mind not so much the different types of praise and worship,
but the content. All the songs we sing in church should be consis-
tent with the Word of God – that's his point. A gospel of good news
must be echoed by songs of gratitude – gratitude for grace.

✑ *O God, save us from being so carried away by the melody of what we sing
that we overlook its meaning and content. You have saved us by grace; help
us reflect that in the worship we offer to you. Amen.*

The Jesus Christ man

FOR READING AND MEDITATION – COLOSSIANS 3:17

'And whatever you do, whether in word or deed,
do it all in the name of the Lord Jesus …' (v.17: NIV)

Paul has emphasised the receptive side of being in Christ, but the receptivity must work itself out in activity. We are to *do* as well as receive and be. Being can only be manifested by doing, and the doing has a definite characteristic: you do everything in the Name of the Lord Jesus. You are to do everything as representing him, you are to do it in his Name, in his stead, and in his Spirit.

Dr E. Stanley Jones told of riding his bicycle along a country road in India and hearing a young cowherd call out to another in the field, 'The Jesus Christ man is going along.' He wanted to get off his bicycle, drop to his knees and pray he might live up to the village boys' estimation of him as a 'Jesus Christ man'.

We are all to be Jesus Christ people – to do everything in his Name. As is said, 'We are the only Bible some people will read.' But do not live out your lives in fear of doing something that misrepresents him. We are to be controlled by a spirit of thankfulness: '… giving thanks to God the Father through him'. The more we focus on how good God is, the more we are set free from fear.

Dear Father, I want to represent you today just as Christ represented you. Grant that my words and my deeds shall be the clear instruments of your glory. When I speak may it be you speaking. In Jesus' Name. Amen.

A word to wives

FOR READING AND MEDITATION – COLOSSIANS 3:18
'Wives, submit to your husbands, as is fitting in the Lord.' (v.18: NIV)

Many Christians, conditioned as they are by a secular society, approach these words of Paul somewhat warily and see them as belonging more to the culture of the first century Christians than to the contemporary Christian church. Let's understand what Paul is teaching here before we attempt to apply it to the present day.

First, he addresses wives, exhorting them to submit to their husbands. What does it mean for a Christian wife to submit? Is it doing everything her husband demands of her? I do not believe so. Submission is a disposition – a disposition to defer in everything that is right. It is not to be seen as servility or obsequiousness – those are negative characteristics. A woman who practises Biblical submission will have a strong positive desire to support her husband as he fulfils his role in the family unit. Some say Paul's teaching here contradicts what he says in Galatians 3:28, where the equality of male and female is celebrated. Equality and submission (they say) cannot co-exist in a relationship. But they can. Christ is equal with God but yet is in submission to him.

Before a woman can submit to her husband she must first be submitted to God. Without submission to God, submission to one's husband does not constitute a spiritual exercise.

O God, we live in a day when culture shouts at us in ways that contradict the teaching of your Word. Help us in the clash between Christ and culture to take your way. For Jesus' sake. Amen.

Love is ...

FOR READING AND MEDITATION – COLOSSIANS 3:19

'Husbands, love your wives and do not be harsh with them.' (v.19: NIV)

A well-known Christian feminist says, 'Many husbands don't deserve a wife who shows a submissive spirit; they mistake it for weakness and exploit it to their advantage.' Well, Paul has a word for such husbands: 'Love your wives and do not be harsh with them.' It's interesting that here Paul knows that one of the easiest things in the world is for a husband to fail to demonstrate that love in a practical way. A woman told me on one occasion, 'My husband's parting words to me when he goes off to work are, "I love you," but then I go to the bathroom, find his shaving kit all over the place, the bathroom sink filthy, and towels strewn all over the floor. If he really loved me then he would clean up after himself.' I agree. Love is not just something you say, love is something you do.

And here's a further test of love. 'Do not be harsh with them.' J. B. Phillips' translates: 'Husbands, be sure you give your wives much love and sympathy; don't let bitterness or resentment spoil your marriage.' Take this scenario: a woman fails to meet her husband's expectations, so he turns on her harshly and says, 'The Word of God says you must submit.' In that action he has violated the law of love. It's not his wife's problem he needs to be concerned about, but his own.

✎ *O God, strengthen my spirit as I follow a way of life that is governed by your Word and not by the moods and whims of culture. May I embrace your way whether others live by it or not. In Jesus' Name. Amen.*

How to serve the Lord

FOR READING AND MEDITATION – COLOSSIANS 3:20

'Children, obey your parents in everything, for this pleases the Lord.' (v.20: NIV)

Many commentators on Colossians have expressed the wish that Paul would have dealt more deeply with the subject of relationships in the home. Dick Lucas says, 'It is daring to summarise complex relations in such short compass.' Paul, however, states basic principles, short but certainly to the point.

On one occasion a family with a somewhat rebellious young son of 12 came to me. He obviously loved the Lord, and he told me he would like to serve Christ in the field of Christian journalism. I asked him if he would be interested in knowing how he could express his desire to serve the Lord Jesus at the present moment – and he nodded his head vigorously. I read him our text in *J.B. Phillips'* translation: 'As for you children, your duty is to obey your parents, for at your age this is one of the best things you can do to show your love for the Lord.' He got the point. We prayed together and his parents told me later that the transformation in him was remarkable. He is now working for the Lord in a distant country, not as a journalist but as a preacher of the gospel.

Disobedience to parents is one of the frightening features of this present age. I see little hope for the families of the future unless they come under the rule of Christ.

✎ *Father, forgive us that we ask for light and guidance in running our families and yet sometimes balk at the directions you give us. Help us see that we either heed the helm or heed the rocks. In Jesus' Name. Amen.*

Problem fathers?

FOR READING AND MEDITATION – COLOSSIANS 3:21

'Fathers, do not embitter your children,
or they will become discouraged.' (v.21: NIV)

There are two sides to every relationship, and Paul, as always, shows that not all the rights are on one side or all the duties on the other. Fathers too have a responsibility to their children – not to 'over-correct [them], or they will grow up feeling inferior and frustrated' (PHILLIPS). Why aren't mothers included in this instruction? It is my conviction, that by and large fathers tend to be harsher with their children than mothers. A Christian psychiatrist says, 'Behind most problem children you will find a problem father.' I think statistics do support the statement that fathers tend to come down more heavily on their children than mothers.

Hear what Paul says once again: 'Fathers, do not embitter your children, or they will become discouraged.' Coming down hard on children crushes their tender and sensitive spirits. It is no good a father lamenting the fact that his child is not as strong and self-reliant as he himself is, if he uses his strength to squash and under-mine the child's fragile ego rather than develop it. Endless criticism, harsh punishments, unrealistic expectations will have their effect in the long run. Many a child who is timid, fearful and plagued with deep feelings of inferiority and guilt has got that way not so much by nature as by nurture.

O Father, our slowness in heeding the principles of your Word is written in the devastation, frustration and breakdown of our family life. Help us to learn the ways of your Word. In Jesus' Name. Amen.

Free – on the inside

FOR READING AND MEDITATION – COLOSSIANS 3:22–24

'Slaves, obey your earthly masters in everything ...
with sincerity of heart and reverence for the Lord.' (v.22: NIV)

Paul's instruction to slaves to obey their earthly masters in everything has brought him in for a great deal of criticism. One critic says, 'I cannot help feel a tinge of disappointment that Paul did not use his influence to call for social change as it related to the distressing subject of slavery.' Another comments, 'His instruction that slaves obey their masters puts them on the level of childhood for ever.'

I tended also to view Paul's instructions here as helping to fasten the yoke of bondage more firmly. However, I came to see that Paul was writing, not to the leaders of society, but to the church. If Paul had told slaves to revolt it would have hindered the gospel rather than helped it. The truths he presented in his letters did eventually lead to the abolition of slavery, albeit many centuries later. Being unable to deal with the situation horizontally, Paul focuses on dealing with it vertically. He exhorts those who find themselves in slavery to concentrate on working for the Lord, and not for men. This change of perspective, Paul believed, would enable them to find inner freedom. Pagan slaves might obey out of fear, but the Christian slave is to obey out of reverence for the Lord. Paul was unable to set the slaves of his day free on the outside, but he certainly showed them how to be free on the inside.

✒ *Father, help me learn the lesson that even when I cannot change the outer climate, I can change the inner climate. I am so thankful. Amen.*

A heated talking point

FOR READING AND MEDITATION – COLOSSIANS 3:25–4:1

'Masters, provide your slaves with what is right and fair, because ...
you also have a Master in heaven.' (4:1, NIV)

The break imposed when the Bible was divided into chapters suggests that Paul's exhortation to the slave masters does not start until the beginning of Chapter 4. But it is difficult to read the last verse of Chapter 3 without feeling that Paul had in mind not only Christian slaves but their Christian masters also.

Once again (4:1) Paul presents the other side of an issue and, having addressed slaves, he has a word for their masters. Who was the greater wrongdoer, the slave who held back part of his efforts, or the master who held back a proper reward and consideration because it was not in keeping with the culture? It must have been a new thought for slave masters that they should show consideration towards slaves, and I can imagine it becoming a heated talking point in the slave markets. Did you notice how often the word *Lord* (or *Master*) is mentioned in the verses to do with slavery? Five times. 'Lift up your eyes and see the Lord as your Master,' he says to the slaves. And to the slave masters he says the same: 'Don't forget for a minute that you too serve a Master – God in heaven' (THE MESSAGE). Just as Christ showed fairness in the way he dealt with the slave masters, so they in turn are to show fairness in the way they deal with their slaves.

Father, I see that to have mastery in life I must bow my knee to the Master. Your ways, and your ways alone, are the ways of mastery. Help me follow them in all of life's difficult situations. In Jesus' Name. Amen.

First talk to God

FOR READING AND MEDITATION – COLOSSIANS 4:2–4

'Devote yourselves to prayer, being watchful and thankful.' (v.2: NIV)

Paul now focuses on the Christian's relationship to outsiders – those not part of the family of God.

He points out that before we talk to others about God, we ought to talk to God about others. Evangelism is best undertaken in a spirit of prayer – by praying for people, before talking to people. Paul asks for the prayers of the Colossians, that even in prison God will grant him many opportunities to preach the gospel. 'Pray that every time I open my mouth,' he says, 'I'll be able to make Christ plain as day to them' (THE MESSAGE). There is a God-dependence here. Paul does not rely on his gift of apostleship or his previous experience of planting new churches; he knows that without prayer his efforts will bear little fruit.

I am sometimes astonished when I read through training courses on evangelism and notice how little emphasis is placed on the need for personal, powerful intercessory prayer. Evangelistic techniques, methods, systems and procedures all have their place. However, they are but the ashes upon a rusty altar if they do not come out of a heart that is given to prayer. When Paul talks about prayer he also adds this: '… being watchful and thankful'. Prayer needs to be coupled with praise, just as praise needs to be coupled with prayer. The one fuels the other.

✎ *Father, drive this truth deep within my spirit – that before I talk to people about you, I must talk to you about people. Help me be more than just a hearer in this issue; help me be a doer. In Jesus' Name. Amen.*

The right to say No

FOR READING AND MEDITATION – COLOSSIANS 4:5–6
'Be wise in the way you act towards outsiders ...' (v.5: NIV)

Eugene Peterson's rugged paraphrase of these verses is well worth considering: 'Use your head as you live and work among outsiders. Don't miss a trick. Make the most of every opportunity. Be gracious in your speech. The goal is to bring out the best in others in a conversation, not to put them down, not cut them out.' Many are not wise in the way they share their faith. They are insensitive and intrusive. A dear old Christian I used to know wrote in the flyleaf of my Bible, 'To win some be winsome.' When the apostle talks about our conversations being 'always full of grace, seasoned with salt, so that you may know how to answer everyone' he is not thinking of memorising systematically prepared theological arguments. No, he is thinking not so much about what we say, but how we say it.

How many times have you bought something just to get rid of a slick salesman? Evangelism should never be a 'hard sell'. We should take advantage of every opportunity to share Christ, but we must always respect the right of the person to whom we are witnessing to say 'No'. There was an occasion when Jesus talked to a rich ruler who turned away from his words (Luke 18:18–25). Did Jesus run after him and try to press him into making a decision? No, he let him go because he respected his right to say 'No'.

✎ Father, forgive me if I put people off by insensitivity and aggressiveness. You respect my right to say 'No'; help me respect that right in others. In Jesus' Name. Amen.

Paul – a people-person

FOR READING AND MEDITATION – COLOSSIANS 4:7–9

'Tychicus … a dear brother, a faithful minister
and fellow-servant in the Lord.' (v.7: NIV)

Paul was a true people-person. Paul was greatly loved because he loved greatly. This final section of his epistle is rich in personal messages and greetings. Paul wants his friends to realise something of his tremendous concern for them. He begins with Tychicus and Onesimus. Onesimus was a runaway slave who had almost certainly robbed his master, escaped, then met Paul and accepted Christ.

Tychicus was a companion of Paul and represented him on a number of different occasions. He is described as 'a dear brother, a faithful minister and fellow-servant in the Lord.' The most significant thing about Tychicus was that he was 'a faithful minister'. He had a call, and was faithful to that call, and that gave him drive and direction. But he did not allow this single-mindedness to prevent him being a dear brother and a fellow servant. Some Christian workers are faithful servants but not very 'dear,' and not good 'fellow-servants' either. This is particularly true of the strong, devoted, driven types. They are extremely busy and absorbed in fulfilling their mission, but no one would ever refer to them as 'dear'. And they are so taken up with their own ministry that they cannot work with others. Tychicus was a well-rounded person, faithful in his ministry, a dear brother and a fellow worker.

✎ *Father, I too would be a well-rounded person. Help me submerge my will and affection in a larger will and affection, for it is only then that I can expect to attain wholeness and roundedness. In Jesus' Name. Amen.*

More names on the list

FOR READING AND MEDITATION – COLOSSIANS 4:10–13

'Epaphras … is always wrestling in prayer for you …' (v.12: NIV)

Paul adds four more names: Aristarchus, Mark, Justus and Epaphras. Aristarchus was a Macedonian accompanying Paul on some of his missionary travels. He was seized during the riot in Ephesus (Acts 19:29) with Paul in prison.

Mark is also mentioned. Remember him? Paul and Barnabas had a violent quarrel over Mark, and Paul had little confidence in the young man who was ready to run at the first hint of trouble (Acts 15:36–40). Now, about 12 years later, the wound had healed. Elsewhere Paul describes him as 'helpful to my ministry' (2 Tim. 4:11). Justus was an unknown friend or colleague of Paul and there is no other record of him.

We met Epaphras earlier. Paul adds one more quality: 'He is always wrestling in prayer for you.' The foundations of this man's character and the secret of his spiritual success were set deep in the soil of prayer. This phrase suggests that his prayers were largely intercessory. What an insight Paul must have gained into the character of Epaphras during their time together in Rome, as he listened to him pray for the church back at Colosse. He was great in soul because he prayed much, and because he prayed with unselfishness. Earnest and persistent prayer was the secret of his sanctity. That secret is available to us all.

Father, I always need a prod to pray. Forgive me if I do not commune regularly with you. Prayer moments are the only real moments. Help me to see prayer as not just a luxury, but a necessity. In Jesus' Name. Amen.

Final greetings

FOR READING AND MEDITATION – COLOSSIANS 4:14–16

'After this letter has been read to you, see that it is also
read in the church of the Laodiceans ...' (v.16: NIV)

Paul ends his greetings with the names of Luke and Demas. Luke
often accompanied Paul on his travels and was with him in Rome
during his imprisonment. Demas was also a companion of Paul
but sadly later deserted him because of his love for this world.

Paul then turns from sending specific greetings to giving more
general greetings – to the brothers at Laodicea, and to Nympha and
the church in her house. For the most part the early church met for
worship, instruction and fellowship in homes, as we can see from
such verses as Romans 16:5, 1 Corinthians 16:19, Philemon 2 and
Acts 12:12. Paul asks that his letter be read in the Laodicean church
as well, and the Colossians in turn were to read the letter from Laodicea. This exchange of letters shows the importance of reading all
we can. The more of Scripture we absorb the stronger our defences
against false teaching will be.

The reference to the letter from Laodicea, however, is somewhat puzzling. It could mean that the Laodiceans were to send the
Colossians a letter that Paul had originally written to them. It was
the practice in the early church to read letters aloud to the assem-
bled congregation. What a thrill it must have been to receive a letter from the apostle Paul. Little did they realise they would be read
by the whole world close on two thousand years later.

*Father, may I be diligent in my reading of Scripture. Help me learn all I
can so that I may be the best I can be. Amen.*

Say 'No' to the marginal

FOR READING AND MEDITATION – COLOSSIANS 4:17

'Tell Archippus: "See to it that you complete
the work you have received in the Lord." ' (v.17: NIV)

Though it is dangerous to read between the lines, I can't help feeling that there is a slight suggestion that Archippus was a man who did not find it easy to follow through on things. Even Paul's description of him as a 'fellow-soldier' in Philemon 2 does not stop me thinking that here he was drawing attention to a matter that Archippus needed to work on. J.B. Phillips was obviously of the same opinion, translating the verse this way: 'God ordained you to your work – see that you don't fail him.'

I wonder, was Archippus the kind of man who allowed himself to be so absorbed in the marginal that he had little drive left for the central issues of his life? Paul said on one occasion, you remember: 'But one thing I do' (Phil. 3:13), not 'These forty things I dabble in.' Those who focus on what they are supposed to be doing leave a mark; those who don't leave a blur.

The temptation to do the easier things and not to follow through plagues us all. Paul's words: 'See to it that you complete the work you have received in the Lord' strike home to every one of us. Everybody in the Lord is in service for the Lord. It means being involved in the Lord's plans for us. Let no unimportant weeds choke the fine wheat of the kingdom. Say *No* to the marginal so that you can say *Yes* to the central.

✎ *Lord Jesus Christ, you fulfilled your Father's purposes in everything that you had to do. Help me too fulfil the ministry you have chosen for me. Amen.*

Closing words

FOR READING AND MEDITATION – COLOSSIANS 4:18

'I, Paul, write this greeting in my own hand.
Remember my chains. Grace be with you.' (v.18: NIV)

Paul's closing words are as rich and as beautiful as any of the others in this highly personal letter: 'Remember my chains. Grace be with you.' This was a plea, of course, to the Colossians to remember him as he remained incarcerated in prison. But what do we remember of Paul's chains? Nothing, because they have rusted away. However, although the chains have gone, his words have not. They leap across the centuries and come home to our hearts with as much force as they did to those to whom they were directly addressed.

I wonder what we would say if we found ourselves in a similar position – locked up in a jail because of our passion for the gospel. Probably this, 'I am in chains. Ask God to give me grace.' But listen again to Paul's words: 'I am in chains. Grace be with you.' I believe one of the greatest evidences of spiritual maturity is the desire, when under deep personal pressure or pain, to reach out and give to others. Paul was such a man. In the midst of overwhelming difficulties, his final thought was for others.

So ends an important letter, in which he encouraged us to see Christ as all-sufficient and all-supreme – 'all' and 'in all' (3:11). We are all in all to Christ. But is he all in all to us?

O Father, I offer myself to you again today and pray that just as your Son is the centre of all things in your universe, so may he be the centre of all things in my universe. In Christ's precious Name I pray. Amen.